Creolized Aurality

CHICAGO STUDIES IN ETHNOMUSICOLOGY

A series edited by Philip V. Bohlman, Ronald Radano, and Timothy Rommen

EDITORIAL BOARD

Margaret J. Kartomi
Bruno Nettl
Anthony Seeger
Kay Kaufman Shelemay
Martin H. Stokes
Bonnie C. Wade

Creolized Aurality

Guadeloupean Gwoka and
Postcolonial Politics

JÉRÔME CAMAL

The University of Chicago Press
Chicago and London

The University of Chicago Press, Chicago 60637
The University of Chicago Press, Ltd., London
© 2019 by The University of Chicago
All rights reserved. No part of this book may be used or reproduced in any
manner whatsoever without written permission, except in the case of brief
quotations in critical articles and reviews. For more information, contact the
University of Chicago Press, 1427 E. 60th St., Chicago, IL 60637.
Published 2019
Printed in the United States of America

28 27 26 25 24 23 22 21 20 19   1 2 3 4 5

ISBN-13: 978-0-226-63163-9 (cloth)
ISBN-13: 978-0-226-63177-6 (paper)
ISBN-13: 978-0-226-63180-6 (e-book)
DOI: https://doi.org/10.7208/chicago/9780226631806.001.0001

Publication of this book has been supported by the AMS 75 PAYS Endowment
of the American Musicological Society, funded in part by the National
Endowment for the Humanities and the Andrew W. Mellon Foundation.

Library of Congress Cataloging-in-Publication Data

Names: Camal, Jérôme, author.
Title: Creolized aurality : Guadeloupean gwoka and postcolonial politics /
    Jérôme Camal.
Other titles: Chicago studies in ethnomusicology.
Description: Chicago : The University of Chicago Press, 2019. |
    Series: Chicago studies in ethnomusicology
Identifiers: LCCN 2018051860 | ISBN 9780226631639 (cloth : alk. paper) |
    ISBN 9780226631776 (pbk. : alk. paper) | ISBN 9780226631806 (e-book)
Subjects: LCSH: Popular music—Guadeloupe—History and criticism. |
    Popular music—Political aspects—Guadeloupe. | Postcolonialism and
    music—Guadeloupe.
Classification: LCC ML3486.G8 C36 2019 | DDC 781.62/96972976—dc23
LC record available at https://lccn.loc.gov/2018051860

♾ This paper meets the requirements of ANSI/NISO Z39.48-1992
(Permanence of Paper).

Each generation must discover its mission, fulfill it or betray it, in relative opacity.

FRANTZ FANON, *The Wretched of the Earth*

CONTENTS

List of Online Resources / ix

INTRODUCTION / Listening for (Post)colonial Entanglements / 1

ONE / The Poetics of Colonial Aurality / 31

TWO / Building an Anticolonial Aurality: *Gwoka modènn* as Counterpoetics / 59

THREE / Discrepant Creolizations: Music and the Limits of Hospitality / 89

FOUR / Diasporic or Creole Aurality? Aesthetics and Politics across the Abyss / 115

FIVE / Postnational Aurality: Institutional Detour and the Creolization of Sovereignty / 143

CODA / *Bigidi* / 175

Acknowledgments / 177
Basic Gwoka Rhythms / 181
Notes / 183
Discography / 211
Bibliography / 213
Index / 225

ONLINE RESOURCES

Words cannot do justice to the vibrancy of gwoka. Supplemental photographs, videos, and recorded examples can be found at the website Tanbou o lwen (https://tanbouolwen.com/creolized-aurality/).

Introduction
Video: Dominik Coco, "Mwen sé gwadloupéyen," from *Lèspri kaskòd* (2008)
Photo: Statue of Solitude
Video: Léwòz, Baillif, July 2017.

Chapter 1
Photo: Indestwas Ka, Sainte-Anne, July 2017

Chapter 2
Photo: Rapport culturel de l'AGEG, 1970 (cover)
Recording: Lockel, "Léwòz, mode no. 4," from *Gwoka modènn en concert* (1997)
Video: "Fò zòt savé," live performance, Baie-Mahault, 24 July 2017.

Chapter 3
Recording: Erick Cosaque and X7 Nouvelle Dimension, "A koz don byé san fwan," from *Musique, voix, percussion* (1984)
Recording: Guy Konket, "Lapli ka tonbé," from *Vélo & Guy Conquête*
Recording: Guy Konket and Emilien Antile, "Faya faya," from *Patrimwan, Volume 1*
Recording Guy Konket, "YouYou," from *Guy Konket et le Group Ka*
Photo: Cover of Tumblack's LP
Recording: Tumblack, "Caraïba," from *Tumblack* (1978)

x / Online Resources

Chapter 4

Photo: Franck Nicolas in concert, Sainte-Anne, July 2017.

Recording: David Murray and the Gwo Ka Masters, featuring Guy Konket, "On jou matin," from *Yonn-dé* (2000)

Recording: David Murray and the Gwo Ka Masters, featuring Guy Konket, "YouYou," from *Yonn-dé* (2000)

Recording: David Murray and the Gwo Ka Masters, "Southern Skies," from *The Devil Tried to Kill Me* (2009)

Video: Jacques Schwarz-Bart, "André," from *Abyss* (2008)

Video: Jacques Schwarz-Bart, "Simone," from *Abyss* (2008)

Photo: Jacques Schwarz-Bart performing with Jazz Racine Haiti in Junas, France, 21 July 2016

Chapter 5

Video: Wozan Monza, "Nasyon," from *RExistans* (2011)

Video: Soft, "Krim kont la Gwadloup," from *Kadans a péyi-la* (2005)

Coda

Photo: Dancer doing a *bigidi*, Sainte-Anne, 10 July 2010

INTRODUCTION

Listening for (Post)colonial Entanglements

In July 2009, I attended a performance by singer-songwriter Dominik Coco during a music festival in Baie-Mahault, Guadeloupe's second-largest city. I was there with a group of friends, chatting and listening inattentively to the performance. One song, though, caught my attention:

> *Mwen sé timoun enkyèt a on lilèt enkyèt*
> *Onti lilèt ki vwè parèt é disparèt syèk dèyè syèk*
> *Disparèt é parèt* . . .
> I am a worried child on a worried island
> A little island that has seen century after century come and go
> Go and come . . .

Coco sang "Mwen sé gwadloupéyen" (I am Guadeloupean), off his then-recent album *Lèspri kaskòd*.[1] The song is based on a text by Guadeloupean separatist poet Sonny Rupaire, and while performing it, Coco held the green, red, and white flag of one of the most prominent separatist political organizations on the island:

> *Fanm é nonm zòt senné kon ban pisyèt*
> *Fan é nonm zòt dékatyé fanmi a yo*
> *Fanm é nonm zòt vann anba laplas a lankan kon bèsyo*
> *Fanm é nonm zòt maké kon bèsyo*
> *Zòt maré kon bèsyo* . . .
> Women and men that you have caught in your net like a school of fish
> Women and men whose families you have destroyed
> Women and men that you have sold on the market like cattle

2 / Introduction

Women and men that you have branded like cattle
That you have tied like cattle . . .

This kind of patriotic display is not unusual from artists who associate their music with the aesthetics and ideologies of *gwoka*, Guadeloupe's secular drum-based music and dance:

> *Apré sa kijan fè ou vlé fè mwen kwè mwen sé vou*
> *Vou sé mwen?*
> *Mwen tala!*
> Now how can you try to make me believe that I am you?
> That you are me?
> Me!

I was somewhat surprised, then, to overhear a man sitting behind me virulently criticizing the performance. He was not ranting against the political message of the song; rather, he denounced the type of harmony that Coco was playing on guitar: "He bugs me with his arpeggios!" To this man, Coco's musical setting of the poem sounded like a betrayal of his national identity, an affront to Rupaire's nationalist message:

> *Vou sé vou akaz aw*
> *Zafè aw bèl!*
> *Mwen vlé mwen menm*
> *Sé kòz an mwen . . . Sé mwen ki an kòz*
> *Di-y fò: mwen sé gwadloupéyen!*
> You are yourself in your home
> Your life is good!
> I want to be myself
> It is my cause, I am the one concerned
> Say it loud: I am Guadeloupean.[2]

Coco's song, like Rupaire's poem, offers a denunciation of French colonialism and its legacy. However, to this disgruntled audience member, the message was compromised because the performance lacked expected musical markers of Guadeloupean identity. Sure, the sound of the gwoka is clearly present—he played an easily recognizable *kaladja* pattern—but some people in Guadeloupe are likely to interpret Coco's rather conventional arpeggiated tonal harmony as indexing not only a "universal pop aesthetic" but also, more precisely, Guadeloupe's former colonial power, France.[3]

Sounding Antillean (Post)Coloniality:
Between Integration and Differentiation

At the center of this example of contested listening lays the political status of Guadeloupe. Describing France as a "former colonial power" would undoubtedly irritate many a cultural activist on the archipelago. Composed of six islands, Guadeloupe is—along with Martinique, Guiana on the South American coast, and Réunion in the Indian Ocean—one of the so-called old colonies of France, a territory claimed by the French crown in 1635. Like many Caribbean colonies, for nearly three centuries, Guadeloupean sugar plantations enriched the French economy, first by using slave labor, then, when slavery was abolished in 1848, by turning to indentured workers from other French colonies in Africa, South Asia, and the Middle East. When the sugar economy collapsed following World War II, Antillean politicians chose a path to decolonization that did not lead to political independence. Instead, Antillean and Réunionais political leaders appropriated the language and ideology of republicanism to demand full political and economic equality within the French state. Largely thanks to the political acumen of Aimé Césaire, this logic of decolonization through political integration was successful, and in 1946, Martinique, Guadeloupe, Guiana, and Réunion became Overseas Departments of France (DOMs, or *départements d'Outre-mer*).[4]

Because they chose to decolonize by incorporating into the French state, Richard Burton has described the French Antilles as "anomalies."[5] It is true that they present a challenge to the usual binary that opposes colonizers and colonized or that thinks of decolonization as a linear progression leading to political independence; but the French Antilles appear anomalous only if one takes the breakup of the former British Empire as a normative model of decolonization. They appear anomalous, moreover, if we keep the sovereign nation-state as the paragon of postcoloniality, understood strictly as a rupture from the colonial past. But as Bonilla and Stoler have argued, these reductive models do not do justice to the complexity and endurance of imperial formations.[6]

Here, I move away from teleologies of independence to take a relational approach to French Caribbean history and focus on the political, economic, and ideological structures that keep France and its so-called old colonies intertwined. As Gary Wilder has so rightly highlighted, the French Republic has never existed without its overseas territories in the Caribbean.[7] Conversely, although the French Antilles have been "decolonized" sensu stricto, they did so by imagining a political future within the republic. It was only a

4 / Introduction

decade after their political integration into the French state that the Antilles saw the emergence of anticolonial, autonomist, then separatist movements. Although these movements have had important impacts, most notably on expressive culture and on the education system, they have not succeeded in breaking the political and economic entanglements that keep France and its old colonies together.

Shalini Puri struggled with this situation in her book on the Caribbean postcolonial, eventually deciding that, rather than being "post"-colonial, Martinique and Guadeloupe remain "classically colonial," a sort of arrested development that seems just as partial and unsatisfying a description as the alternative it tries to replace.[8] In fact, the DOMs' economic relationship to France illustrates a neoliberal entanglement that is very different from the "classic" extractive regime of colonialism (chapter 5). But rather than bemoaning the French Antilles' ambivalent political status or reducing it to a symptom of alienation, we need to seize it as an opportunity to rethink (post)coloniality beyond narratives of resistance and liberation.[9]

The French Antilles' nonsovereign status offers an opportunity to explore what Ann Laura Stoler calls imperial "duress." Indeed, the Antilles illustrate both a "colonial present" and a "colonial presence."[10] As do all territories touched by colonialism, they offer evidence of the continued presence of their colonial past. This past is engraved in the landscape and is made visible most notably by the various forts that circle the coasts of Guadeloupe and Martinique or the plantation windmills that still dot their countryside. It also persists in an enduring socio-racial hierarchy in which the descendants of the planter class (known in Creole as *béké*) still form an economic elite and an economic structure in which Martinican *békés* and metropolitan actors own most of the largest economic assets.[11] At the same time, although political integration was intended as a form of decolonization, it actually resulted in a "colonial present" marked by politics of exemptions and exceptions that Stoler has identified as typical of colonial regimes.[12] This regime of exception is enshrined in article 73 of the French constitution, which, even as it promises complete equality in the application of the law in the DOMs, ends up—for better or for worse—conferring a degree of legislative specificity to the overseas departments.[13] Other exceptions have included the special bonus salary that metropolitan government employees have received to work in the DOMs; the migratory policies of the Bureau pour le développement des migrations dans les départements d'Outre-mer, or BUMIDOM (discussed in chapter 3); and the *octroi de mer*, an import tax imposed on all goods entering the islands that both contributes to the financing of local governments and to the high cost of life in the DOMs.

The *octroi de mer*, which originated as colonial law in 1670, in fact illustrates both colonial presence and colonial present.

For these reasons, I follow the poet Albert Wendt, who defines the prefix *post* in *postcolonial* as meaning not just "after" but also "around, through, out of, alongside, and against."[14] Neither unambiguously colonial nor truly postcolonial, I adopt Stoler's practice and describe the French Antilles as (post)colonial. The parentheses here not only speak to imperial continuance; they are also symbolic of the relative position of France's old colonies within the Republic: neither separate nor totally integrated. Indeed, if it is common to describe the French Antilles as being "on the margins" of the French state, it is also equally productive, if not more so, to understand Guadeloupe, Martinique, Guiana, and Réunion as being "in the hold" (as in the hold of a ship) of the Republic, differentiated but within republican unity.[15] As Césaire quipped, one may wonder whether Antilleans are not "français entièrement à part" (entirely differentiated French) rather than "français à part entière" (entirely French). The DOMs, then, highlight the tension between, on the one hand, the professed indivisibility and universality of jacobinical republicanism and, on the other hand, the (post)colonial experience of differentiated citizenship. In Guadeloupe, the tension between these two poles leaves open a political space in which demands for sovereignty and demands for citizenship coexist in unstable tension. To make sense of this tension, I adopt Michaeline Crichlow's double metaphors of fleeing (the colonial state) and homing (the [post]colonial state and modern economic forces) to discuss the often contradictory yet complementary movements of resistance and accommodation. While demands for sovereignty or citizenship occasionally explode in the open at particular historical flash points (e.g., the 1980s bombing campaign of the Alliance révolutionnaire caraïbe as fleeing, or the economic protests of the Liyannaj kont pwofitasyon, or LKP, Alliance against Profiteering, in 2009 as homing (see later in this introduction and chapter 5), I argue that they are always audible within gwoka's contested aurality.

Choreographer Léna Blou (also known as Lénablou) once commented to me that, "because of its creation, gwoka has always been political." But what does it mean for gwoka to be political? What political program does it sound? What kind of community does it enunciate? And what was its moment of creation? The plantation? Or the moment in the late 1960s when anticolonial activists put the drum at the center of their efforts to redefine the Guadeloupean nation, both culturally and politically? Singer-songwriter Fred Deshayes remarked during a 2015 conference on the aftermath of gwoka's newfound status as Intangible Cultural Heritage of

Humanity (ICH) that the music had become "overdetermined politically and poetically." Indeed, as the episode in Baie-Mahault reveals, gwoka carries an incredible representational weight in Guadeloupe, but its precise meaning remains fluid and, most of all, contested. Since the late 1960s, its sounds have often escaped the strict control of cultural nationalists to participate in the emergence and expression of divergent political imaginaries and sometimes-dissonant poetics of belonging. In short, in spite of all the nationalist rhetoric surrounding it, gwoka has always-already been a creolized aurality shaped by a long—and ongoing—history of imperial entanglements. More than offering an analysis of gwoka as musical practice, the following chapters explore these entanglements—made audible through gwoka—to consider the broader interplay of cultural politics and political culture in the French Antilles, the overlap between "the space of political representation and the space of aesthetic representation."[16] I do so by focusing on the instrumentalization of gwoka, by which I mean both the initiatives to transform its practice and its sounds by adding new instruments (what Thomas Turino describes as "modernist reformism") and its deployment as a symbol and a tool of political action.[17]

I have chosen to discuss what Guadeloupeans refer to as the contemporary expressions of gwoka (*gwoka modènn*, *jazz ka*, or the new Creole *chanson*) because they—more so than other styles of music, including the so-called traditional form of drumming—have generated debates that are symptomatic of the tensions that define French Antillean (post)coloniality. If "traditional" gwoka has become a nationalist symbol since its revival by separatist activists in the late 1960s, then the contemporary expressions of gwoka—fusing traditional drumming with various other genres—challenge strict nationalist readings by inscribing the sounds of gwoka within Afro-diasporic, pan-Caribbean, or more generally transnational sonic networks. Examining musicians' and audiences' responses to musical encounters articulated around transnational connections therefore offers a window onto Guadeloupeans' multiple and occasionally contradictory imaginaries.

In Guadeloupe, politics, history, imagination, and the arts are closely intertwined. A novel transformed the *mulâtresse* Solitude—of whom so little is known, she is little more than a myth—into a national symbol of resistance against slavery and French imperialism.[18] Today, a statue of Solitude stands in all of her pregnant glory, the mother to the black republic that wasn't, in the middle (in the hold) of a roundabout built using French or European funds. Social contestations are as likely to come from cultural organizations as from labor unions. Carnival groups give unions expressive symbols and the culture of the *déboulé* (carnival parade) infuses protest marches. This was clearly in evidence during the Liyannaj kont pwofitasyon in January and February 2009 as protesters replaced carnival revelers and took over the streets to the sounds of "La Gwadloup sé tan nou, la Gwadloup sé pa ta yo" (Guadeloupe is ours, Guadeloupe is not theirs), a protest anthem set to music by the carnival groups Akiyo and Voukoum.[19] Since the late 1960s, gwoka songs have relayed social messages, and the drum has animated picket lines. Guadeloupean gwoka, then, invites an investigation of the relationship not only between aesthetic and political representation but also between imagination and practice, between (post)colonial citizens and the metropolitan state. As Lénablou declared, gwoka—as a specific social field of cultural production—is always-already enmeshed in a larger field of (post)colonial politics.

As I consider these audible (post)colonial entanglements, I am less interested in what the music tells us about anticolonial nationalism than in what it reveals about Antillean engagement with French (post)coloniality. Both before it became a nationalist symbol in the 1970s and 1980s and since, gwoka has always resonated "in the hold" of the French empire. In other words, it has always been specifically Guadeloupean and incorporated into France. For this reason, gwoka doesn't simply serve to perform the Guadeloupean nation; it also sounds the complexity of an Antillean (post)colonial.[20] To get at these (post)colonial relations, my analyses carefully delineate the problem-spaces within which Guadeloupean musicians, dancers, and activists have operated at different historical moments.[21] My study, then, takes Guadeloupean artists and activists' cultural and political projects as a point of departure to move beyond gwoka's symbolic nationalist function. This perspective avoids reducing decolonization to an act of resistance with the sole goal of creating an independent nation-state. It also avoids limiting cultural nationalism to the mobilization of expressive culture in the service of the nation.[22] Instead, this book is animated by two central concerns. First, when considered as a creolized aurality, gwoka allows for an exploration of the ways in which music participates in the emergence, dissemination, and performance of various anticolonial and (post)colonial subjectivities even in the absence of an independent nation-state. This, in turn, allows me to consider the following question: can music help us make sense of a form of (post)colonialism that is defined not by anticolonial rupture, but by an ongoing negotiation of the relationship between (former) colonies and their metropole, not only by a demand for sovereignty but also by claims of citizenship?

8 / Introduction

Creolized Aurality and Politics of the *Détour*

Taking a long historical view to better understand Guadeloupean musical and political developments since the mid-twentieth century, I propose that gwoka participates in what I call *creolized auralities* that allow the music to express a number of both complimentary and contradictory longings, solidarities, and demands. The episode in Baie-Mahault underscores the fact that performing or listening to gwoka takes place within a fraught, historically layered social field that I call an aurality.[23] The concept of aurality has emerged from sound studies' interest in listening practices.[24] Here, I build on Jairo Moreno's work to consider aurality beyond listening. Moreno defines aurality as an "intersensory, affective, cognitive, discursive, material, perceptual, and rhetorical network."[25] While I like Moreno's definition, I chose to move away from the metaphor of the network for two reasons. First, I feel that a network is not as fluid as a field. It involves elements that can, at least in theory, be identified and isolated (the "intermediaries" and "mediators" of Latour's actor-network theory).[26] A network is necessarily bounded, lest it become the all-encompassing Network and loses much hermeneutic potential. In contrast, the field is amorphous; its limits are porous. Second, scholarship influenced by actor-network theory has tended to privilege material connections. However, an overemphasis on materiality tends to overlook the role of the affective and the unconscious in relationships. I therefore prefer to follow Ana María Ochoa Gautier's take on aurality as a less-than-transparent field of sonic relations. In the chapters that follow, sound-producing subjects and objects, actually listening subjects, and intended or imagined listeners come together within "mutually constitutive and transformative relation[s]" that Ochoa Gautier calls "acoustic assemblages."[27] Although the chapters that follow focus primarily on music, music constitutes only one facet of these acoustic assemblages, which also include, among other things, both the structural and micropolitics of language use in this diglossic territory. Such consideration opens up my investigation of music's significance to explore its role in the construction and experience of (post)coloniality. Indeed, gwoka has participated in acoustic assemblages that span the hierarchies of France's perennial imperial nation-state. These assemblages both shape and are symptomatic of always-emergent and protean (post)colonial ontologies and epistemologies. Aurality, then, considers the ways listening is both an exercise and an object of power alongside the ways in which sounds carry knowledge and enable ways-of-being-in-the-world. Fields are, of course, social spaces animated by the production and circulation of various forms of capital. Thus, aurality also encompasses the

Listening for (Post)colonial Entanglements / 9

ways in which sounds are valued, amplified, muted, or ignored. Understood as a field, aurality can have geographically specific manifestations and can overflow any spatial boundaries. For example, gwoka does not carry the same symbolic, epistemological, or ontological weight in Guadeloupe and in metropolitan France, but its practice and significance are informed by developments on both sides of the Atlantic Ocean. Finally, if fields shape the actions of agents, they are also shaped by other fields as well as by the actions of agents within them.

Dominik Coco's performance in Baie-Mahault reveals gwoka to be both an object and a terrain of contestations. Creolized auralities, then, are contested and contesting auralities. Yet they are more than that, more than terrains of resistance.[28] I realize that the appeal to creolization is problematic because the word has itself become overdetermined. When turning to creolization, we need to pay close attention to the difference between the theoretical qualities and function that academics and intellectuals project onto creolization and creoleness (looking back at the past from the present in an exercise of reinterpretation of the colonial past or mining the colonial past for metaphors to describe our globalizing present) and the vernacular use that people have made, at different historical moments and geopolitical locations, when they have claimed their identity as Creole. There are great differences in the deployment of *Creole* and *creolization* in Jamaican nationalism, in the Antillean manifesto *Éloge de la créolité*, and in the late-1980s work of anthropologists Ulf Hannerz and James Clifford. Jamaican Creole nationalism described a political attempt to unify a multiethnic population. The Martinican Creolists, for their part, staged an intervention into French cultural politics and offered a platform for the construction of artistic solidarity spanning the Caribbean and the Indian Ocean. Meanwhile, Hannerz and Clifford used creolization as a metaphor for the creative processes taking place in a globalizing, hybridizing world.[29] These examples highlights a small part of the long history of semantic shifts that *Creole* and *creolization* have undergone since the term *criollo* was first introduced to designate the Spaniards and Portuguese born on American soil. As Stephan Palmié elucidates, in the social sciences, the unexamined borrowing of creolization from history into linguistics and from linguistics into cultural studies has created a problematic conceptual feedback loop that muddles its analytical potential. And when scholars of globalization unmoored the concept from the Caribbean and the plantation societies from which it emerged, and made it more or less synonymous with broader concepts such as syncretization and hybridization, they not only emptied creolization of whatever hermeneutic specificity it still carried but also flirted with a form of epistemic violence by

10 / Introduction

erasing the specific forms of power that shaped cultural encounters in the Caribbean.[30]

To recover creolization for the circum-Caribbean, then, we cannot rest on the kind of straightforward definition of the term such as that offered in a classic ethnomusicological survey of the region: "Creolization . . . connotes the development of a distinctive new culture out of the prolonged encounter of two or more other cultures."[31] This type of definition—which equates creolization with syncretism—leaves open a number of questions. Most important, if we reject the idea that there are any "pure" cultures, untouched by encounters and borrowings, anywhere, are there any cultural practices that are not, in some ways, creolized? It follows that if we want to argue that creolization cannot entirely be reduced to syncretization or hybridization, we need to tease out its specificity. How is the process of creolization in the Caribbean and other plantation societies different from other modes of cultural appropriation and syncretism elsewhere around the world? One solution would be to restrict creolization to a process specific to colonial plantation societies. This, in turn, raises the question of creolization's temporality. Is creolization a colonial event or does it extend past the moment of "early rapid synthesis" that Mintz and Price theorized? What is the difference between the ongoing processes of synthesis in the Caribbean and those that took place in the colonial period? Can we speak of a "post-Creole imagination," as Michaeline Crichlow writes, to describe these contemporary formations?[32]

In this book, I reclaim creolization for the Caribbean by carefully reframing the concept in relation to agency in colonial and (post)colonial contexts. To avoid reducing creolization to resistance, I approach it as a byproduct of colonial conviviality. I borrow the idea of conviviality from Gilroy, and, like him, I do not mean to idealize colonial and (post)colonial relations.[33] Conviviality here does not deny the brutality of the colonial regime; rather, it recognizes that plantation colonialism brought together people who—in violently contrasting ways—were displaced and who had to find ways to live together and adapt to their new environment in order to survive and sustain imperial economies. I define creolization, then, as the process through which ideas and practices are appropriated or affirmed, manipulated, and blended in response to the particular power structure of colonialism in all its forms: so-called classic colonialism and neocolonialism, but also anti- and postcolonialism. I combine the original meaning of the word *Creole*, referring to what has been made local, with the later meaning of *creolization* as syncretization.[34] Therefore, I understand creolization as the act of creative and open-ended incorporation of external elements into the vernacular. Significantly, creolization always involves the antithetical yet complementary pulls or resistance and accommodation to structures of domination. Redefined through the prism of conviviality, creolization enables us to move away from an emphasis on the break, be it the anticolonial break from colonialism or the break of the Middle Passage. Instead, (post)coloniality, no longer understood solely as rupture, is redefined as a relational matrix, a process of mutual transformation.[35]

I must also acknowledge that many of the musicians I have worked with would object to my reliance on the concept of creolization. Undoubtedly influenced by nationalist thinking, many of them reject claims of a Creole identity and regard creolization with suspicion (see chapter 4). Moreover, unlike in New Orleans, *Creole* does not refer to a specific socio-racial category in Guadeloupe, where those of mixed racial ancestry are usually referred to as *mulâtre*.[36] Finally, French Antillean politicians have not relied on tropes of creoleness to unify the nation, as has been the case in Jamaica or Trinidad.[37] Nonetheless, as we'll see in chapter 5, it is becoming increasingly common for some Guadeloupeans to embrace a form of creoleness and to use that mode of identification to activate regional solidarities. I do not, then, necessarily rely on "creolization" as a "native" category. Yet I find the term useful for two reasons. First, it points to the persistence of colonial categories and the strategies put in place to undermine them. Second, it simultaneously foregrounds the undeniable hybridizing practices of contemporary Guadeloupean musicians. Indeed, the musics heard and performed in Guadeloupe are, without question, the products of emergent processes of creolization. Although these processes can be traced back to the plantation, the significance of their by-products (in addition to gwoka, quadrille, and biguine, creolization has produced a Creole language, a cuisine, and a range of supernatural beliefs and practices) is itself emergent and tied to specific sociopolitical contexts that are traversed by an unequal and contested distribution of power.

Creolized auralities, then, include sonic fields of (mis)appropriation, destabilizing performances, and ambiguous listening. Understood as participating in a creolized aurality, the "audible entanglements" of contemporary gwoka offer the sonic traces of an Antillean experience of (post)coloniality that cannot be reduced to tropes of escape and overcoming but instead is characterized by constant engagement and negotiation, by strategic embrace and disavowal, by fleeing and homing. Creolized auralities are animated by processes, strategies, longings, and poetics that have been shaped by the long history of European colonialism and the modern pressures of neoliberal globalization: assimilation and mimesis, but also opacity, *détour*, and *détournements*.

Opacity is actually—and perhaps counterintuitively—central to understanding the importance of creolized auralities for the emergence of (post) colonial epistemologies and ontologies. Without falling into a simplistic opposition between the auditory and the visual, it is undeniable that colonial control relied on the visual.[38] On the plantation, the master's gaze allowed for the control of enslaved bodies: only by inspiring fear through surveillance was the white minority able to maintain its dominance over a black majority. But as Fanon so aptly remarked, to inspire fear, the master had to be constantly visible, to become an exhibitionist.[39] If the imperial gaze and colonial exhibitionism demanded transparency, Glissant surmises, then opacity emerged as a logical form of resistance. For Glissant, opacity— that is to say subalterns' desire to protect themselves in a shroud of opacity— manifests itself first in tactics of concealment and hiding—for example, by retreating to the protection of the forest.[40] But as Britton explains, there are few hiding places in small islands like Martinique and Guadeloupe. Opacity, then, cannot simply be reduced to hiding: it has to "be produced as an *unintelligible* presence from within the *visible* presence of the colonized."[41] It participates in the creation of modes of expression that defy colonial desires to control through the production of knowledge. In other words, if the concurrent expansion of European colonialism and scientistic universalist philosophies established the subaltern Other as an object of knowledge, then opacity and obfuscation became "active strateg[ies] of resistance" by producing a "visible but *unreadable* image."[42]

Or they became so by producing unintelligible sounds: opacity cannot be reduced to a visual metaphor. Edwin C. Hill has theorized the ways in which colonial auralities exposed the limits of the European imperial and humanist epistemological enterprise. Faced with the sounds of the plantation, imperial listening was revealed as "impaired, unreliable, or faulty" (see chapter 1). In this context, the Creole language, music, and dance became opaque media for the construction and expression of a creolized subjectivity that was both constitutive of and resistant to coloniality.[43] Glissant proposes that, on the plantation, the sounds that resisted colonial understanding came to carry meaning: "For Antilleans, the word is first and foremost sound. Noise is speech. Din is discourse."[44] Glissant—and Fred Moten after him—have focused on the scream, but the scream wasn't the only thing that carried meaning. What was true of language was true of other sounds, especially drumming. Glissant writes: "It is not surprising to declare that, for us, music, gesture, and dance are modes of communication, just as important as the art of speech. It is through these practices that we first left the plantation."[45] Because they resisted the understanding and control of colonial authorities, sounds were essential to the construction of creolized epistemologies and ontologies. Opaque to colonial ears, the sounds of Creole and of drumming allowed for strategies of *détournement* and the performance of the *détour*.

Within colonial and (post)colonial contexts, the colonized (who Glissant identifies as the "determining class") was able to transform the colonizer ("the dominant class") through the poetics of the *détour*. Glissant defines the *détour* in opposition to the *retour*, terms that Michael Dash translates as "diversion" and "reversion."[46] The *détour* results from the impossibility of a colonial community to actualize itself in practice, to accept its ruptures from the past, and to heal its internal divisions. Furthermore, the *détour* is symptomatic of a system of domination that is so pervasive that it becomes invisible, forcing the subaltern community to seek the principle of domination elsewhere.[47] The *détour* is both tactical and ambiguous. As Celia Britton explains, "it is essentially an indirect mode of resistance that 'gets around' obstacles rather than confronting them head on." The *détour* is a trick, but as Britton remarks, "it is itself marked with the alienation it is trying to combat." She adds that "it is both an evasion of the real situation and an obstinate effort to find a way around it."[48]

Michel-Rolph Trouillot locates the origins of the *détour* in the everyday acts of *petit marronnage* at the edges of the plantation. Although in theory the plantation was a total system of domination, in its actual instantiations, the system contained many interstices, cracks that slaves could exploit to manipulate the system from within. Trouillot explains: "And as slaves repeated such manipulations—on the one hand acknowledging the system, on the other circumventing its actualization in carefully chosen instances—they solidified the *détour*, the social time and space they controlled on the edges of the plantations." It is through the creative manipulation of these openings that slaves were able to develop Creole languages, music, and religions—cultural practices that would come to shape not only their own environment but also that of their overseers. Trouillot concludes, "This creation was possible because slaves found a fertile ground in the interstices of the system, in the attitude provided by the inherent contradictions between that system and specific plantations."[49] There is a slight difference between Glissant's theorization of the *détour* and Trouillot's. Whereas Glissant's *détour* speaks of a general principle, a poetics symptomatic of a (post)colonial unconscious, Trouillot outlines actual specific acts and practices that I understand as *détournements*.[50] The French *détournement* collapses several English words that are all appropriate—to various degrees and in various forms—to creolizing strategies: misappropriation and hijacking, diversion

14 / Introduction

and perversion. Through its *détournements*, creolization not only localizes but also transforms—domesticates or homes—its source material, claiming not only place but also ideologies and politics. *Détournements*, within an overall poetics of the *détour*, make possible the emergence of subaltern epistemologies and ontologies. *Détour* and *détournement* are central to a (post)colonial "worlding," a "mapping of modernity" that involves both homing and fleeing.[51] Gwoka makes these (post)colonial worlds audible and visible.

Gwoka: What Is Left When We Have Forgotten Everything

In July 2009, I was in Goyave, sitting in the house of radio host Alain Jean, a self-styled "lover of black music." Jean is a complex personality, an embodiment of the impenetrability of (post)colonial entanglements. He has spent his life moving back and forth among mainland France (where he was born), Guadeloupe, and Tahiti, where he was stationed for several years, for Jean was both an anticolonial activist and career military. Being anticolonialist, he explained to me in response to my incredulous look, doesn't mean being anti-France. It means being against France's presence in Guadeloupe. Jean has now retired in Guadeloupe, where he has long hosted a gwoka show on the nationalist radio station Radyo Tanbou. An avid collector of Caribbean music recordings, he has been filming music performances in Guadeloupe for more than twenty years—with a special attention to gwoka—and his private collection of films, recordings, and press clippings constitutes an incredibly rich archive. He had invited me to his house to consult some of these documents and to do an interview. We sat in his study, surrounded by floor-to-ceiling shelves lined with albums, CDs, and videotapes. Jean was digitizing some of his old footage, which appeared simultaneously on a video monitor and on his computer screen. Another TV, set to Réseau France Outre-mer (RFO), showed images of African animals, with the sound muted. A radio softly broadcasted Radyo Tanbou in the background, rounding off the audiovisual collage.[52]

Jean is a man of strong opinions, and I started the interview with a question that was as central as it was likely to trigger an impassioned explanation: "What is gwoka?"

"It's simple," replied Jean. "If you have a *léwòz* in each *commune* [township] in Guadeloupe on the same night, there will be a complete group of musicians, singers, and dancers. There will be an audience. In all thirty-two *communes*. For me, that's what I call gwoka."[53]

Not satisfied with this "simple" answer, I pressed on, pointing to the rich musical tradition that enlivens Guadeloupean wakes on the eve of funerals.

These songs are typically not accompanied by drummers but, rather, by a group of singers who layer onomatopoeias to create the *boulagyèl* (literally mouth-drum), a dense rhythmic foundation to the call-and-response singing. "So the songs of wakes are not gwoka?"

"Yes," countered Jean.

"But they are not part of the *léwòz*."

Jean elaborated: "The *léwòz* is the most direct expression of gwoka. Gwoka, for me, is everything that is part of Guadeloupean culture. There isn't one bit of culture in Guadeloupe that escapes gwoka."

Defining gwoka—perhaps like defining any other musical genre—is a fraught enterprise, made all the more complicated by the fact that the music carries so much political baggage. Efforts vary from the specific to the poetic. Thus, the Guadeloupean ethnomusicologist Frédéric Négrit writes that gwoka is "the ensemble of rhythmic musics, dances, and songs of Guadeloupean origins, based on percussions and orchestrated by a minimum of two drummers, each with a separate function." In contrast, multi-instrumentalist, composer, and educator Christian Dahomay declares that gwoka is "what's left when we have forgotten everything."[54] This is because, in Guadeloupe today, gwoka often designates a range of musical practices associated with a mostly rural, bygone way of life, practices that are reputed to have their roots in the slave populations of the colonial plantation. These practices include the songs and dance of *swaré léwòz*, the songs and games performed during wakes, and the music used during stick fighting known as *mayolè*. Understood broadly as an umbrella term, the category of "gwoka" may also come to include work songs (Creole, *chan travay*) and the *bèlè*, a competitive singing tradition. By extension, some people argue along with Alain Jean that gwoka is the core expression, or *potomitan* (central pillar), of Guadeloupean culture. Jean elaborates his definition in this way: "It is a lifestyle. For me, all of these things are gwoka: the way people drink, the way they walk. It's all gwoka. I don't know how to explain it. But, personally, I don't think that gwoka is limited to music. It is a complete way of life, a style, customs. Yeah. And I think that all of Guadeloupe, whatever it is, lives to the rhythm of the gwoka."

Approaching gwoka as an aurality sidesteps the need for a specific definition. Gwoka is a constellation of musical and social practices that mutually inform one another. Jean is right: gwoka is a lifestyle. Gwoka's aurality englobes the militant use of the Creole language as well as a dedication to resisting assimilation through the consumption of local foods (e.g., roots, breadfruit) and style of dress (e.g., natural hair, head wraps for women, jewelry made from local seeds). In this book, I deal primarily with musics that stretch gwoka's definition, from *gwoka modènn* (chapter 2) to Franck Nicolas's *jazz ka* (chapter 4) and the uncategorizable music of the group Soft (chapter 5). In Guadeloupe, there are endless debates around the boundaries of what constitutes *mizik a tanbou* (drum music). In taking an inclusive approach, I follow the logic of Fred Deshayes, Soft's lead singer. As the group appeared on the stage of the thirtieth gwoka festival in Sainte-Anne in 2017, Deshayes reminisced about the comments they received following their first appearance on that stage, back in 2005: "Moun ka di nou pa jwé gwoka. C'est vrai. Nou pa jwé gwoka kon Kannida, nou pa jwé gwoka kon Bwadi. Mé nou sé pitit a péyi-la. É mizik annou sòti gwoka-la" (People say that we don't play gwoka. That's true. We don't play gwoka like Kannida [a well-respected "traditional" group], we don't play gwoka like Boisdur [Esnard Boisdur, another well-known singer from Sainte-Anne]. But we are the children of this land and our music came out of gwoka.) Within gwoka's contested aurality falls any musical style whose inclusion becomes a terrain of contestation. The debates themselves contribute to the construction of the sonic assemblage.

Nonetheless, in its most common expression, gwoka is a music and dance typically accompanied by an ensemble of at least two barrel-shaped, single-headed drums, themselves called *gwoka*, or simply *ka*. The lowest of the two drums, the *boula*, maintains a steady rhythmic ostinato. Generally, a gwoka group has two *boula* playing in unison, but larger numbers of players are fairly common. *Boula* players, known as *boularyen*, sit astride their instrument, which is laid on its side on the ground. They hit the drumhead with their bare hands and provide the foundational groove of the music by playing a rhythmic ostinato in unison. It is commonly said that there are seven basic rhythms in gwoka—*tumblack, graj, kaladja, padjanbèl, léwòz, woulé,* and *menndé* (see appendix 1)—although, in practice, some of these rhythms are more commonly played than others, some have multiple variants, and some groups introduce new patterns into their music. Gwoka songs call for specific rhythms that are adapted to their melody type and tempo. Each rhythm carries a specific *santiman* (mood), which in turn calls for specific dance steps. A higher-pitched drum, called *makè* (also spelled *mawkè*; the term also designates the musician playing this drum), improvises above the rhythmic groove provided by the *boula* in response to the movements of the dancer in front of him (or occasionally her), sonically inscribing or "marking" their steps. Unlike the *boularyen*, the *makè* sits on a small bench (*tiban*) and plays with the drum in front of him or her. There is little to distinguish the appearance of the *makè* from the *boula* (figure 1.1). Although the *makè* can be slightly smaller than a typical *boula*, this is frequently not the case. The main

0.1. Gwoka drums: *makè* on the left, *boula* on the right

difference between the two drums comes from the thickness of the skin used on the head. *Boula* generally use skin from a male goat, whereas *makè* use thinner skin from female goats. Adjusting the tension of the head allows players to produce the desired tone for either *boula* or *makè*. The tension system used on the gwoka distinguishes the Guadeloupean drum from others found in the Caribbean: the drumhead is maintained in place by a *zoban*, a large metal hoop wrapped in foam and rope. The *zoban* is a critical part of the drum. It not only maintains the tension of the head but also provides a contact surface that the drummer strikes to create certain sounds on the instrument. The tension of the *zoban* is adjusted by twisting small wooden sticks (*klé*) inserted through the tension rope.

Gwoka occupies a peculiar place in Guadeloupe's musical landscape: it is both highly present and sonically muted. When I first arrived in Guadeloupe in December 2007, zouk still dominated the soundscape of the island. It was the soundtrack to the bus ride that took me from the airport to the seaside town of Sainte-Anne, and its beat could be heard flowing from businesses and car windows.[55] Since then, musical tastes have somewhat evolved under the forces of globalization. With the arrival of better internet connections and satellite TV, popular music in Guadeloupe has become much more pan-Caribbean. The beats of zouk have given way to those of *konpa*, dancehall (in English and Creole), and soca that now dominate the island's soundscape.

The contemporary media landscape leaves very little room for gwoka, quadrille, and biguine. The private FM station Radio Caraïbes International (RCI) has a weekly gwoka show on Saturday mornings hosted by the singer Erick Cosaque. The nationalist Radyo Tanbou (see chapter 5) still regularly broadcasts gwoka music. Beyond this, quadrille and biguine are all but absent from the airwaves. Biguine has experienced a bit of a resurgence in the past few years, but, unlike in Martinique, it hasn't recovered from its demise, brought about by nationalist activists who associated it with colonialism. Nevertheless, at the jam sessions I participated in at a restaurant in Le Gosier—which attracted a solidly middle-class clientele—a few biguines added local flavor to the otherwise cosmopolitan mix of jazz standards. Quadrille, for its part, has become a marginal folkloric practice with a few groups of mostly elderly dancers keeping the music alive. Guadeloupe in this respect is very different from Dominica, where the local form of quadrille, *jing ping*, is held up as a national symbol.[56]

Yet even if gwoka struggles to be heard in Guadeloupe, it is an ever-present symbol of place, if not always of the nation. The tables of a popular beachside restaurant in Sainte-Anne are designed to resemble oversized drums. Drawing of the *ka* adorn placemats and vinyl tablecloths sold to tourists and locals alike at all the big supermarkets. Orange Caraïbes—a local cell-phone provider—used a photograph of gwoka drummer Daniel Losio for one of its advertising campaigns in 2012. Using the trope of the drum as an instrument of communication to advertise its 3G network, the advertisement declared, "Let's reinvent our means of communication each day." But if gwoka is more often seen than heard in mainstream media, it does have a significant sonic presence on the island nonetheless. The annual Festival Gwoka, held every July in Sainte-Anne attracts hundreds of visitors each night, the large majority of them Guadeloupeans.[57] As Jean mentioned, there are private gwoka schools around the island. The *rue piétonne* (a pedestrian alley) in Pointe-à-Pitre has become the destination of a weekly pilgrimage of sorts, as everyone who thinks of themselves as defenders of Guadeloupean culture gathers to listen to the drummers of Akiyo Ka, an offshoot of the carnival group. Other informal gatherings, called *kout tanbou*, are also frequent and can often be heard in the distance on weekends. "Tanbou o lwen ni bon son" (the distant drum has a pleasant sound), for example, is one Guadeloupean saying. ("Tanbou o pré ni santiman nou pa vlé tandé," or the nearby drum has feelings we don't want to hear, responds

Fred Deshayes in "Gouté Gwadloup," underscoring the drum's contested semantics). By far, though, the most common way of participating in gwoka is by attending one of the many *swaré léwòz* (often shortened to *léwòz*).

The *léwòz* has its roots in the celebrations that accompanied the *kyènzènn*, the day when workers would get paid on sugarcane estates. Today, not-for-profit organizations, trade unions, and municipal governments organize *léwòz* throughout the archipelago. *Léwòz* can take place year-round, but they are most common from the end of *carême* to the beginning of the Christmas season.[58] They are part of a yearly musical cycle, coming between the *mizik a mas* that accompanies Carnival and the *chanté nwèl* of the Christmas season. *Léwòz* are not only celebrations; they are also good fund-raisers, as participants buy food and drinks throughout the evening. *Léwòz* are most commonly advertised by word of mouth and in large banners hung at major intersections. As cell-phone service and internet connections have improved in Guadeloupe, it has become more common for organizations to use texting and social media to advertise their upcoming events. Now information about *swaré léwòz* circulates on Facebook and WhatsApp. *Léwòz* can be held in a number of outdoor locations—I've attended *léwòz* in schoolyards, open-air markets, and on the beach—and if the new media offer ways to precisely indicate the location of a *léwòz*, it is nonetheless often still the case that directions are rather vague, frequently limited to the name of a district.[59] Thus finding a *léwòz* involves driving with one's windows down, trying to pick up the sound of drums while looking for large numbers of cars parked on the side of the road.

Late on June 30, 2017, I drove to Baillif—on the leeward coast of Basse-Terre—to attend the annual *léwòz* organized by Sòlbòkò, a gwoka school that Bébé Rospart runs. Rospart is one of the most respected figures in traditional gwoka, and his *léwòz* has a reputation for being one of the best and most authentic in the archipelago. While a *swaré léwòz* can start as early as 8 p.m., it is well known that the best singers, *tanbouyé* (drummers), and *dansè* (dancers) will not show up until much later in the evening. And so I arrived around 11 p.m. As soon as I entered Baillif, I started to notice the cars lining up the side of the main boulevard with increasing density. I had been to this *léwòz* before, but I couldn't remember its exact location, so I drove on, foolishly hoping that I could find a parking spot closer to the actual event. Unlucky, I passed the grounds where the *léwòz* had been set up and found myself having to turn around and backtrack. I finally found a place to park and walked back to the grounds. People streaming in and out of a narrow street veering off of the main boulevard toward the small fishing harbor let me know, along with the distant sound of the drums, that I had made it to the right place.

0.2. Dancer at a *swaré léwòz*, Sainte-Anne, July 2017

A *léwòz* is, first and foremost, a social gathering. The area bordering the small harbor was filled with several hundred people. There are typically very few children at a *léwòz*, and teenagers usually prefer to mill around the outskirts of the event. The core audience ranges from young adults to gray heads. The atmosphere that night was joyful as friends met and greeted one another. The community of gwoka performers and aficionados is small enough that most *léwòz* feel a bit like extended family reunions, and this was especially true of this one. Anyone who takes gwoka seriously made it a point to attend: choreographer Lénablou was there, so was Dominik Coco, singer Wozan Monza, and historian Jean-Pierre Sainton. Most members of the most prominent "traditional" groups—Foubap, Indestwas Ka, the women of Fanm Ki Ka, and the young crew of 7son@to—were in attendance. People milled around and bought drinks and food at the *buvette* (beverage stall) that had been set up inside a small, permanent wooden structure. But most of the audience was congealed into a *lawonn* (large ring) around the perimeter of an open tent, the musicians forming a solid raw on one side. The *makè* sat on his *tiban*, flanked by the two *boularyen*. Behind and around the drummers stood the *répondè* (chorus) from which emerged the *chantè* (lead singers), who relayed one another throughout the evening at the microphone. Among the *répondè*, a small cluster played *chacha*, a large shaker made from a hollowed calabash filled with dried seeds. As is usual at

Listening for (Post)colonial Entanglements / 21

a *swaré léwòz*, microphones had been set up behind the drums and among the *répondè*. Several oversized speakers made sure that this event was—in typical Caribbean fashion—properly loud.

A young *chantè* seized the microphone: "Léwòz-o! Léwòz-o, léwòz mwen rivé!" (O *léwòz*, I've arrived at the *léwòz*). The declamation was dramatic, meant to capture the attention of all those present. He repeated his opening gambit, this time with greater rhythmic precision: "Léwòz-o! Léwòz-o, léwòz mewn rivé!" This time he went on: "An ka mandé lé répondè, lévé lavwa ban mwen" (I ask the *répondè*, start singing for me). The chorus joined in with the response: "Léwòz-o! Léwòz-o, léwòz mewn rivé!" The lead singer interjected: "O la sonora! Jwé on ti léwòz ban mwen" (O musicians! Play a small *léwòz* for me). The chorus again jumped in, "Léwòz-o! Léwòz-o, léwòz mwen rivé," as the *makè* cued in the drummers with the heartbeat rhythm typical of the *léwòz* pattern. The musicians and singers quickly settled into a groove that felt both anchored and unstable. The back-and-forth between lead singer and chorus continued. Some people in the audience joined in the singing. Suddenly, a young man entered the ring, dressed all in white: off-white jeans and a matching collarless linen shirt, with a white straw fedora for extra flourish. He walked toward the *makè*, looked him in the eyes, extended his right leg toward the drum, and hit his heel on the ground then quickly brought it back behind his left foot. He then slowly but deliberately spun upon himself. His turn completed, he and the *makè* stared at each other while the drummer played a short rhythmic pattern: the *rèpriz*, the punctuating signal of gwoka performances. Now in sync, the dancer and *makè* marked the end of the *rèpriz* together, the latter with a strong accent, the former by jumping up in the air and hitting his heels together. From there, the dancer introduced a step. Although the *makè* had his head slightly cocked, his eyes remained squarely on the young dancer, his hands echoed the dancer's every move, sonically inscribing his movements. After a few repetitions of the simple step, the dancer intensified his movements. He dramatically moved away from the drum, then back toward it: *déboulé*. The drummer responded in kind, marking all of the dancer's gestures. The music greatly intensified. Finally, the dancer had come almost right up against the drum. His right heel hit the ground, and his body pivoted. The two stared at each other. *Rèpriz*. The dancer once again leaped into the air. Dancer and *makè* would repeat this sequence several times. A dialogue emerged, each using the energy of the other to display his inventiveness. Gwoka acts out a friendly competition. While the dancer tries to surprise both the *makè* and the audience with unusual moves, he needs to make sure that the moves remain legible to the lead drummer, that they respect the tradition's codes.

After several minutes, another dancer entered. He leaped into the *lawonn* right at the end of the *déboulé*, almost falling onto the previous dancer. Amused, they marked the *rèpriz* together, then the first dancer ceded the ground to the new arrival, who would do his best to outperform his friend. His style was different. This particular rhythmic pattern—*léwòz indestwas*, meaning "square" or "according to the rules"—calls for a special quality in the dance, a controlled stumbling that is described in Creole as *bigidi*. *Bigidi* involves being both off-balance and grounded. *Bigidi pa tonbé* goes a Creole saying: stumbling is not falling. This new dancer demonstrated this: he staggered, seemed like he was about to lose balance, but he never did. His movements were both loose and precise. At the *rèpriz*, he stood and stared defiantly at the drummer. He would not jump. Instead, his hands flew back, as if he were about to hit the *makè* in the face. The two stared at each other. The dancer walked back toward the middle of the ring and started a new step. He would go on until someone else claimed the ground.

Swarè léwòz are participatory events, meaning that there is, in theory, little to no distinction between performers and audience members.[60] Anyone is, again in theory, welcome to jump into the *lawonn* to dance or join the singers and drummers. In reality, *léwòz* are highly scripted events, and many gwoka practitioners would frown at anyone entering the *lawonn* who does not understand *les codes du gwoka* (the codes of gwoka). And those who understand the "codes" would know better than assume a role for which they are not ready. In practice, one is seldom welcome to join the *répondè* unless he or she knows some of the people in the group. Those who are learning to play the drum can sometimes play early on in the evening or at the very end of the night if they know one of the musicians. If a *boularyen* struggles to properly match the rhythm and phrasing of the other drummers, though, the lead singer may reprimand him. Occasionally, the *makè* will cut a song short and ask a fledgling drummer to relinquish the instrument. And while anyone can enter the ring and dance, *makè* show their disdain for dancers who do not respect traditional performance structures by turning their heads to avoid eye contact, symbolically excluding inexperienced or unskilled dancers from full involvement in the event.

Gwoka is still a highly gendered practice. Men normally perform all three main functions during a *léwòz*: singer, percussionist, and dancer. Women's roles are much more circumscribed. If women are encouraged to dance, it is rare to see them playing drums, although there are several all-women gwoka ensembles in Guadeloupe (Fanm Ki Ka and Koséika being the best known). Women's role in gwoka is a topic of contestation, too. I have had several conversations with gwoka musicians who suggested that the gendered roles in gwoka have evolved historically. Some hinted that the nationalist movement of the 1960s and 1970s may have actually contributed to hardening gender roles. What is certain is that, starting in the 1980s, women played a determining role in the institutionalization of gwoka. Patricia Braflan-Trobo highlights the contribution of Jacqueline Cachemire-Thole, a physical education teacher who in the early 1980s was the first to introduce gwoka dancing, then gwoka music, into secondary education.[61] Cachemire-Thole went on to create one of the first gwoka schools in Guadeloupe, which she named Akadémiduka (Ka Academy). The school served as a model for many others schools (mostly run by women), such as Raymonde Torin's Kamodjaka and, to some degree, Lénablou's Centre de danse et d'études choreographiques. These schools—all of the them by-products of the nationalist movement described in chapters 2 and 3—have greatly contributed to transforming gwoka from a stigmatized rural and proletarian tradition to an urban and middle-class expression of national pride. Today, gwoka dance classes in such schools are overwhelmingly attended by young women. Parallel to this phenomenon, female gwoka performers are increasingly welcome in Guadeloupe. Most of them are singers—Marie-Héléna Laumuno and Marieline Dahomay are among the best known—but there is also a small number of talented women *makè*. Some male musicians have proved themselves rather intolerant of women's participation in *swaré léwòz*, but their views are gradually becoming marginalized.

Opacity, Theory, and Ethnographic Methods

Some people will debate whether non-Guadeloupeans should be taught how to play the drum or dance in gwoka. I took my first dance lessons with Jacky Jalème in July 2008. Jalème taught a short summer course at the Pays de la canne, a sugarcane museum set up on the grounds of the former Beauport sugar factory in Port Louis. I wasn't the only "foreigner" attending the classes that summer: all in all, we were three white students who had traveled from France, the United States, and Canada. Our workshop took place outdoors, in full view of museum visitors. One of them was unhappy with what he saw and made a point to let Jalème know. Jalème later told me that the man berated him for teaching gwoka to white folks. Jalème had shrugged him off. As this anecdote illustrates, there is more than a bit of discomfort with teaching gwoka to foreigners; the idea is that Guadeloupeans may be at risk of losing their ownership of the music. Such tension also fueled the anxieties surrounding the proposal to have gwoka recognized as intangible cultural heritage by UNESCO (see chapter 5). Given how much of their identity Guadeloupeans have invested in gwoka and given the long history of white appropriation of black music, these concerns are perfectly understandable. They inform a deployment of the poetics of opacity that has constantly affected my engagement with Guadeloupean musicians and activists, affecting both how I am perceived and what information is shared with me.

I was born and raised in metropolitan France but received my academic training in the United States, where I now teach. I write mostly, but not exclusively, in English. In Guadeloupe, I therefore occupy an ambiguous position as both a French citizen and a US scholar, a position that is potentially doubly imperialist. This position is made visible by my skin color and is audible in my ambiguously accented French, which carries the traces of my migrations. When I first visited Guadeloupe in 2007, I was often introduced as *un étudiant américain* (an American student) and praised for the quality of my French. No matter how often I have explained that I was born and raised in France, I remain an American scholar, a position that is, after all, convenient both for myself and many of my interlocutors. As an American scholar, I am less marked by the stigma of French colonialism in the eyes of the musicians, dancers, and activists I meet. The cachet of American academia allows me to dwell in the liminal zone between the conventional socio-racial categories of Guadeloupe: I'm certainly not a *blan péyi* (the descendants of plantocracy), nor do I fit the stereotypes of the *métro* (metropolitan French who have temporarily relocated to the Antilles). And yet my presence at some *léwòz* or nationalist cultural events continues to raise some eyebrows.

"Hey, jazz!"

It was May 2017, and I was participating in what Guadeloupeans call a memory walk, organized by the UGTG (Union générale des travailleurs guadeloupéens), a nationalist union, to commemorate the reestablishment of slavery in 1802 as well as the May 1967 strikes and their violent repression. I did not remember the name of the tall man calling me any more than he remembered mine, but I knew him to be a member of the carnival group Akiyo, and he knew that I had played with the group some nine years earlier. Being a US-trained jazz saxophonist has opened many doors for me in Guadeloupe, and I have played with nearly all the musicians mentioned in the following chapters. Sharing the bandstand, attending rehearsals, and, most important, simply hanging out has allowed me to experience gwoka in all of its density, to participate in its aurality.

When discussing *gwoka*, a certain number of words never fail to come up. On the surface, they seem to capture a sort of consensus: *rèpriz*, seven rhythms, *lokans*, atonal-modal. But hanging out with musicians helped me realize that, in practice, things are never so simple. A term like *lokans*—which describes the affective quality of a singer—borders on being an empty signifier, used to praise some musicians and exclude others from the canon. Other aspects of the "tradition" are constantly debated in rehearsals, performances, and conversations. Gwoka is secular, except for the many musicians who imbue the drum with spiritual qualities and who would not play without performing a number of—often idiosyncratic—rituals. Then again, there are those who reject such practices as superstitious. Gwoka is "atonalmodal," except when it is played using major and minor scales, or pentatonic scales, or a number of other scales compiled in the steady stream of method books published on the topic.[62] Gwoka is based on seven rhythms, except for all the groups that are composing new grooves using traditional instruments, starting with the group Takouta, which in the 1970s increased gwoka's polyrhythmic density by having three drummers play three different patterns. Although not used in *swaré léwòz*, this new rhythm—called *takout*—has entered the canon, as have the *six/huit* and the *sobo*. As a musician, I have experienced gwoka as much more complex than the rhetoric surrounding it would suggest.

My experience as a musician, then, served to "thicken" what I learned through interviews. This research started as a sort of oral history of gwoka and the Guadeloupean separatist movement. Before I embarked on this project, I was lucky to meet the ethnomusicologist Dominique Cyrille. Cyrille put me in touch with Félix Cotellon (see chapter 5), who, as president of the nongovernmental organization Règpriz (CMDT, the Center for Traditional Music and Dance of Guadeloupe) was able to greatly facilitate my meeting a number of musicians and activists.

I have often been surprised by these musicians' willingness to share their story and their music with me. Yet it also is clear that, for everything people have shared with me, something else laid right under the surface but out of reach. Opacity was always in play in my conversations and in my musical encounters. In Guadeloupe, opacity and *détour* are embodied in the *maskò* (literally the body mask): the feint, ruse, or subterfuge. In gwoka, when the dancer is in dialogue with the lead drummer, at times the two make their gestures clear and predictable. But at the *règpriz*, key structural points in the dance, the dancer can also engage in fancy footwork in a game of *vwè-y pa vwè-y* (now you see it, now you don't) that heightens the physical and rhythmic tension. The *maskò* is a strategy that informs discourse as well, the introduction of a statement that suddenly destabilizes any sense of certainty: "I told you this, but I could have told you the opposite," or "Now you know the whole story . . . or almost the whole story."

The same strategies of the *maskò* informed many of my interviews: much was said but much more was only hinted at, or—I am certain—simply obfuscated. As with the interviews that have allowed me to grasp the history of political separatism on the island (see chapters 2 and 3), I was often presented with partial information that became significant only when cross-referenced with other sources. Without an iterative process of repeated dialogues with several interlocutors, the information shared with me remained opaque. Moreover, many interviews I had hoped for never actually happened: phone calls were not returned, appointments were ignored or repeatedly canceled. Gérard Lockel, the central figure in the creation of *gwoka modènn*, persistently refused to talk to me. "It is too soon," he would say echoing Fanon, "or it is too late." Eventually, I gave up, settling for the explanations he would offer informally during those long conversations meant to explain why he could not talk to me. *Vwè-y pa vwè-y.*

The challenge, then, is to bring to light those things that are left unsaid but not unexpressed. Theory plays an important role in this. As has been already made clear, I draw heavily on the work of the Martinican philosopher, novelist, and poet Édouard Glissant. I do so for three reasons. First, although his ideas have long been critiqued or even ignored in Guadeloupe, they are increasingly becoming part of intellectual discourse (see chapter 5). Second, Glissant remains understudied in the US academy, especially outside of literary studies. If ethnomusicologists and anthropologists occasionally borrow some of his terminology, they rarely subject it to critical examination, probably because only a small portion of his output has been translated to English. Even so, and this is my third point, Glissant does provide a conceptual vocabulary that is particularly adapted to understanding French (post)coloniality. Key concepts in his poetics of Relation (e.g., *détour*, opacity, the trace, or the abyss) help us think through the musical practices and listening regimes that animate gwoka's aurality and, beyond that, a French (post)coloniality.

In keeping with the spirit of Glissant's poetics of Relation, my understanding has remained emergent, partial, and relational. It has emerged as much from my many experiences in the field as from my theoretical reflections and my musical practice away from the field. Any analysis is likewise partial, a mere possibility among other analyses. I must here echo Glissant himself: "If the reader has followed these arguments up to this point, I wish that, through the entanglement of my approaches to the Caribbean reality, he may have seized this tone rising from so many unseen places: yes, that he may have *heard* it."[63] Or, as Guadeloupeans often exhort, "Kouté; kouté pour tann; tann pou konprann" (Listen; listen so that you may hear; hear so that you may understand).

Organization

Theory in this book operates bidirectionally: toward the material analyzed and away from it. First, theory serves to analyze what gwoka can teach us about Antillean understanding of diaspora, Caribbeanness, Frenchness, and anti- and (post)colonial nationalism. Second, I want to elucidate what Guadeloupean gwoka can teach us about diaspora, creolization, (post)coloniality, anticolonial nationalism, and postnationalism. Thus, each chapter makes a point not only about Guadeloupe but also about a particularly theoretical concept: creolization and the contested auralities of colonialism (chapter 1), anticolonialism and forced poetics (chapter 2), discrepant creolizations and minor transnationalism (chapter 3), creolization and diaspora (chapter 4), and postnationalism (chapter 5).

Chapter 1 exposes the long history of audible imperial entanglements to show how sounds and their attendant significance have been reshaped as Guadeloupe evolved from a plantation colony to a "Republican" colony and finally to a (post)colonial overseas department, without sovereignty. This history affords an opportunity to develop the twin metaphors of fleeing and homing to describe the dual strategies of resistance and accommodation that are essential to survival on the colonial plantation. In doing so, the chapter explores the social, political, and audible entanglements of the French Empire from a Guadeloupean perspective. Since the seventeenth-century emergence of plantation societies in the French Antilles, plantation owners, overseers, colonial administrators, *petits blancs*, and slaves have partaken in complex relationships of desire, borrowing, assimilation, and resistance. With Continental France and West African nations serving as constant and opposing poles of attraction and repulsion, music and sounds have contributed to strategies of memorialization, institution building, social control, and social advancement. In this context, sounds in general—and music most particularly—form what I call contested auralities, sonic markers to which different and differing meanings and values can be attached.

Chapter 2 explores the role that music played in constructing an anticolonial aurality. Sooner than re-rehearse tales of invented traditions or condemn anticolonial activists for their elitism and essentialism, I seek to better understand the perspective of those actors who shaped anticolonialism after departmentalization by focusing on the work of Gérard Lockel, a guitarist and nationalist ideologue who created *gwoka modènn*, a musical form that lays virtuosic instrumental improvisations on top of the rhythmic foundation of gwoka. I propose that, for separatist activists, gwoka—whether traditional or modern—is more than a sonic symbol of the nation or a musical rallying point. Rather, the music, along with the Creole language, participated in an anticolonial aurality from which a "new culture"—that is to say, radically modern and liberated ways of thinking and being—could emerge. Animated by restorative nostalgia, or a "reversion drive" (*pulsion de retour*) to a romanticized subjectivity freed from colonialist influences, the sounds and ethics of gwoka were supposed to help Guadeloupeans "think and act as Guadeloupeans" (*penser et agir en guadeloupéen*), as the nationalist saying goes. I conclude by arguing that *gwoka modènn* illustrates what Glissant calls "forced poetics," symptoms of a persistent desire for an emancipated language that is faced with a *manque*—a lack or void—that renders impossible the emergence of a collective expression.[64]

Many of the musical innovations that have surrounded gwoka took place in Paris. In chapter 3, to theorize what I call discrepant creolizations, I turn my attention to Guadeloupean musicians who migrated to the French capital in the 1970s. While many musicians working in Paris shared the prevalent nationalist ethos, they did not necessarily follow Lockel's orthodoxy. Gwoka in Paris, then, offers another perspective on the music as contested aurality. Decidedly nationalist (except when it is not), neither truly creolized nor cosmopolitan, and yet both of these things at once, gwoka in Paris became a container for the antinomies that characterized the lives and subject positions of Guadeloupeans exiled in the metropole from which they wished to become independent. To make sense of this complex position, I return to the metaphors of fleeing and homing. Through two case studies, chapter 3 highlights how gwoka domesticated transnational aesthetics just as Guadeloupeans were involved in a double act of fleeing and homing: literally fleeing the economic downturn that accompanied the collapse of the sugar industry in the Antilles and metaphorically fleeing the Republic that had never truly integrated them; homing in the literal sense of creating a home for themselves on the European continent and also in the metaphoric sense of homing their political subjectivity, making a place for themselves, within France's (post)colonial space. In other words, as Guadeloupean artists moved across the Atlantic, their music came to reflect their geographic and political horizons, their "spatial presences and imaginaries": the places they left, those they longed for, and the spaces they endeavored to create for themselves.[65] At a moment when the neocolonial effects of departmentalization became painfully evident and the separatist movement reached its apogee, gwoka became a vehicle through which "minor transnationalism"—transnational connections between minoritized communities in and around contemporary empires—served to expand a Creole imaginary past the confine of the Caribbean, offering an alternative to the orthodoxy of Lockel's music.[66] As a case in point, I turn to the singer Guy Konket, whose music went through two moments of discrepant creolization, once in Guadeloupe and again in Paris, with different musical results that express different political horizons. I also call attention to the fact that creolization cannot be reduced to an expression of creative resistance. Indeed, as the group Tumblack illustrates, homing gwoka within the structure of a globalizing music industry that clung to its colonial exoticist imaginary necessarily involved negotiations and strategic accommodations. These examples point to the irony and the ambiguous ethics that, beyond the anticolonial nationalist project, have accompanied gwoka's performance as a (post)colonial aurality.

While the first three chapters are largely historical, the following two turn to contemporary considerations. By listening to musical encounters spanning the black Atlantic, from Paris to Guadeloupe to New York City, chapter 4 proposes that jazz and gwoka have—at different times and in different hands—combined to form diasporic auralities through which contested imaginaries are performed, longings and belongings are negotiated and produced, and discrepant Antillean ways of being are sounded. The musicians in this chapter illustrate the tension between nationalism, on the one hand, and Creole and diasporic cosmopolitanisms on the other: Lockel's nationalism informs his diasporic refusal. The collaboration between the American saxophonist David Murray and the Guadeloupean percussionist Klod Kiavué offers an equivocal performance of creoleness that suggests a diasporization of creoleness. Meanwhile, Murray and Lockel did record together, but their encounter made audible an incommensurable *décalage* within the practice of diaspora.[67] In contrast, the Guadeloupean saxophonist Jacques Schwarz-Bart sounds a decentered, or creolized, diaspora. Together, these performances allow me to probe what the strategic embrace and rejection of diasporicity and creoleness tells us about Guadeloupean (post)coloniality. I turn to Glissant's concepts of trace and opacity to clarify how fleeing and homing—read metaphorically as disavowal and embrace—translate into musical aesthetics, or, vice versa, how the sound and silence of music reveal complex and open-ended processes of positioning articulated across the abyss of slavery, colonialism, and their aftermath.

Chapter 5 explores the emergence of what I call a Creole postnationalism in the wake of disenchantment with the nationalist project. In the new millennium, gwoka's creolized aurality functions as a creative space from which new artistic and political poetic formations can emerge. Musicians—such the group Soft—dwell in a Creole postnationalist space defined by ambivalence and instability, from which they find new ways to "home" minor transnationalism and to sound relational modes of belonging that enable them to reconcile their positions as both Caribbean and French. This new generation's Creole postnationalist take on gwoka—marked by strategic audible entanglements—found its political expression in the campaign of activists and musicians who worked together within the Lyannaj pou gwoka (Alliance for Gwoka) to have the drumming tradition recognized by UNESCO on its list of Intangible Cultural Heritage of Humanity. Leading this effort was Félix Cotellon, a well-known separatist figure. The campaign was controversial. Because Guadeloupe is not an independent state, the Lyannaj had to work with, and through, the French government to reach the international institution. The campaign was successful, and in November 2014, gwoka—once heralded as a symbol of anticolonial struggle—was recognized as part of France's cultural heritage and diversity. Why did a nationalist militant pursue this outcome given that, on the surface, it seemed to contradict nearly forty years of nationalist activism? I argue that, far from anomalous, the work of the Lyannaj represents a "continuance" of the nationalist struggle. Nearly seventy years after *départementalisation*, the Lyannaj offers another instantiation of the *détour*. By forcing the recognition of Guadeloupe's cultural specificity within the French state on an international stage, both the Lyannaj pou gwoka and the new forms of *gwoka évolutif* cement the emergence of a Creole postnational citizenship: cognizant of its limited economic autonomy, Guadeloupeans are nonetheless ready to capitalize on their limited cultural sovereignty to redefine—or rather, creolize—their relation with France and enter into new modes of regional collaborations.

What emerges from these five chapters are epistemologies and ontologies of movement and instability. In the conclusion I turn to the work of choreographer Lénablou to propose that the *détour* that defines gwoka's aurality becomes embodied in the *bigidi*, the stumbling aesthetic of the *léwòz*. "Bigidi mé pa tonbé," stumbling is not falling. A feint disguised as a stumble, the *bigidi* reclaims the dance space. It is, according to Blou, a gesture of both resistance and resilience. In the *bigidi*, the antinomies of Antillean (post)coloniality are reconciled.

ONE

The Poetics of Colonial Aurality

The Drum of the Maroon?

Règpriz. "Because of its creation, gwoka has always been political," remarked Lénablou. In Guadeloupe, gwoka is often described has having emerged in resistance to, if not outside of, the plantation. For example, Joslen Gabaly, in the first monograph on the Guadeloupean drum, writes that "it is the *'nègmawon'* [sic; maroon slave], that is to say those slaves who succeeded in escaping to conquer their freedom at the price of untold suffering, who, first, elaborated our music."[1] A monument on the main entrance into Sainte-Anne depicts a maroon breaking free from a structure that resembles the base of a windmill. Instruments of his freedom are cast around him: a broken chain, a hoe, a conch shell, and a *ka* (see figure 1.1). Already in 1970, when the Association générale des étudiants guadeloupéens (AGEG; see chapter 2) proposed its cultural platform, it likewise had linked the gwoka and the *nèg mawon*. A few years later, in 1978, Gérard Lockel—a leading musical voice of Guadeloupean cultural nationalism (see chapter 2)—published an article in the separatist newspaper *Ja Ka Ta* in which he proposed that Guadeloupean music could be stratified into three categories: French, colonial, and Guadeloupean. Gwoka, for him, was the only genuine musical expression of a Guadeloupean culture because the drum alone had escaped the corrupting influence of French imperialism. And in many staged gwoka performances today, the drum serves as the common thread running through a history of resistance to colonialism. For example, a show by the politically-minded traditional group Indestwas Ka during the 2017 Festival Gwoka in Sainte-Anne started with a tableau about slavery and *marronnage*, which was then connected to the 1802 battles against the reinstatement of slavery (complete with a defiant *mulâtresse* Solitude), the events of May 1967 (when French troops opened fire on Guadeloupean

1.1. Statue of the *nèg mawon*, Sainte-Anne

protesters), and the Liyannaj kont pwofitasyon. In each tableau, the rhythm of the gwoka helped convey a particular affect: for example, a *woulé* captured the sorrow of slavery, and a *léwòz* expressed the anger of May 1967. Within Guadeloupe's (post)colonial aurality, this historical narrative—reproduced with minor variations in many a gwoka *ballet*—can be told only through the drum.[2] Conversely, the drum can tell only this kind of history. We can hear Blou's statement quite literally, then: in contemporary Guadeloupe, the drum is imagined as standing outside and in opposition to the colonial sphere.

And yet, given the conditions of its emergence, the *ka* was always already integral to the colonial aurality: drumming was immanent to colonial society, not external to it. Gwoka cannot be reduced to a music of resistance. From its beginning, drumming sounded the poetics of colonialism, the ambivalence and negotiation inherent to colonial conviviality. Since the seventeenth-century emergence of plantation societies in the French Antilles, plantation owners, overseers, colonial administrators, *petits blancs*, African slaves, and, later, indentured workers have partaken in complex relationships of desire, borrowing, assimilation, and resistance.[3] Music and sounds participated in these colonial poetics. Exploring colonial auralities reveals how power and agency were enacted through the sonic. Within colonial auralities, music was both a terrain of control and a space of contestations. Creole musics—African-derived drumming practices or European-derived quadrilles—enabled those who were enslaved to affirm their humanity; but in black musics, white witnesses also heard evidence to support their ideology of racial abjection.

I insist that, when writing about the poetics of colonialism, I do not mean to aestheticize or romanticize colonial rule and its effects. More than by Glissant, for whom the poetics of Relation remain connected to poetry, I am inspired here by Michael Herzfeld's concept of social poetics. "Social poetics," writes Herzfeld, "is about the play through which people try to turn transient advantage into a permanent condition. . . . It links the little poetics of everyday interactions with the grand dramas of official pomp and historiography to break down illusions of scale."[4] Poetics, then, speaks to social and semiotic fluidity and ambiguity, even in the face of hegemonic forces.

In this chapter, I show how the sounds of Creole musics and their attendant significance have been reshaped as Guadeloupe evolved from a plantation colony to a "Republican" colony and finally to a (post)colonial, nonsovereign overseas department. In doing so, this chapter explores the social, political, and audible entanglements of the French Empire from a Guadeloupean perspective. At the center of this argument is the idea that colonialism always-already contained the potential for subaltern practices of disruption and *détournement* and for the emergence of what Barnor Hesse calls the "creolization of the political."[5] Listening for the poetics of colonial aurality, then, helps us understand colonialism's duress and make sense of the postwar campaign to decolonize France's "old" colonies by seeking their political integration into the French state. It also clarifies the later anticolonial backlash that fueled the revitalization of gwoka.

Drumming, Agency and Subjection on the Plantation (1635–1848)

In Guadeloupe, drumming resonates with the long history that has enmeshed sound politics into colonial structures. Which imperial entanglements produced the contemporary Guadeloupean drum—the drum that has gained international recognition as the *gwoka*? What has been the place and role of drumming in Guadeloupe's plantation society? When asking these questions, I do not seek to establish a Herskovitsian genealogy of retention. With poor and faulty documentation of the actual ethnic origin of Guadeloupean slaves, the task is rather futile. Neither do I seek to celebrate the creative and resistant ingenuity of enslaved Africans. Both of these modes of inquiry have already produced valuable contributions to the study of African American musics, but, as David Scott argues, these models have been shaped by specific ideological attachments to narratives of continuity from putative stable points of origin, whether in Africa or on the plantation (see chapter 4).[6] Instead, my interest is in the conflicted place of drumming on the plantation. On the one hand, dances facilitated the emergence of new institutions and forms of solidarities among those who were enslaved. Dances also participated in the transmission of knowledge, helping preserve traces of African aesthetics and technologies. Conversely, apologists for slavery pointed to slaves' "innate" musical abilities as evidence of their happiness: for those involved in the slave trade, the sights and sounds of slaves' dances proved simultaneously that black bodies were devoid of any rational ability (and thus less than fully human) and that slavery was a benign institution. In addition, for those enslaved, music and dance served a cathartic role, making the plantation system more bearable but thus indirectly helping sustain it, something that many planters understood well. This contested and ambivalent legacy forms the basis from which contemporary *gwoka* emerged as a historically and socially constituted object and practice.

The Slave Trade and Plantation Colonialism in Guadeloupe

Before diving further into the emergence and politics of drumming practices in early colonial Guadeloupe, it will be helpful to clarify the social structure from which those practices developed and that they, along with other musical forms, contributed to shaping. French colonization of Guadeloupe started in 1635, when France claimed the archipelago from Spain. To populate the new French Caribbean colonies, landowners relied on the services of poor white contract laborers (*engagés*), who were hired to work for thirty-six months on cotton and tobacco plantations. Unable to rival the North American colonies in the production of these crops, French colonists quickly turned to the production of cane sugar, which promised much higher profits. Cultivating and processing sugarcane required a larger workforce than the *engagés* could provide, and planters turned to the massive importation of African slaves. Within roughly thirty years, Martinique and

Guadeloupe experienced a dramatic demographic shift. In Guadeloupe, Europeans made up 80 percent of the total population in 1654, two-thirds of which were contract laborers. By 1664, that ratio dropped to only half of the overall population; twenty years later, it was down to 39 percent. Meanwhile, Europeans made up 67 percent of the servile population of Guadeloupe in 1654. The rise of African slave labor pushed that percentage down to 13 percent by 1671.[7]

Over the course of the colonial period, some 291,000 African slaves were imported to Guadeloupe from an area that stretches from contemporary Senegal to Angola. The ethnic origin of these slaves remains a point of debate. The historian Frédéric Régent has established that, around the time of the French Revolution, most slaves in Guadeloupe came from the Bay of Biafra (present-day Gulf of Bonny, Nigeria), followed by groups coming from an area ranging from Senegambia, through the Gulf of Benin, and all the way to what is now northern Angola. Nicole Vanony-Frisch proposes that most Guadeloupean slaves were Igbo, with Kongo constituting the second-largest group. However, the Afrocentric linguist Marie-Josée Cérol (Ama Mazama) argues that, in the nineteenth century, Kongo actually represented the largest ethnicity, followed by the Bantu, who were among the last contract laborers brought from Africa. Adding to the confusion, in all these descriptions, the term *Congo* or *Kongo* is rather imprecise. Vanony-Frisch and Régent agree that it was used broadly to designate slaves from an area that extended from what is now Cameroon to northern Angola. However, Cérol seems to restrict the term to the Kongo (i.e., Bakongo) ethnicity, an approach that needs to be tempered to acknowledge that ethnic categories are and have always been fluid historical constructs that have served various political interests, European colonialism foremost among them. Yet Cérol's approach seems consistent with what I have observed to be a tendency to highlight the Kongo heritage of Guadeloupean culture.[8]

As with the rest of the circum-Caribbean, the slave trade produced a fairly rigid social hierarchy. It is common to paint Caribbean societies in broad strokes as a three-tiered socio-racial order with whites on top, free people of color (mulattos and freed slaves) in the middle, and black slaves at the bottom, as Lucien Abenon does in the case of Guadeloupe.[9] Dominique Cyrille proposes a slightly more complicated model of eighteenth-century French Antillean colonial society. Reminding us that the Code Noir considered slaves as disposable goods and therefore excluded them from the colonial social order, Cyrille explains: "Officially, and from the Europeans' point of view, there were three classes in the colony. At the top of the social ladder were the planters, rich merchants, and high administrators. The second social class comprised artisans, clerks, soldiers, and clergy people of European origin. All the free people of color—free-born mulattos as well as newly freed blacks—were placed together at the bottom of the social ladder. They had to show deference to all whites at all times as a general rule."[10]

In addition to this official hierarchy, within the enslaved population, important social distinctions were found between newly arrived and Creole (American-born) slaves as well as between field hands, *nègres à talent* (skilled slaves), and house slaves.[11] To further complicate matters, freeborn mulattos were often wealthier and better educated than lower-class whites and therefore saw themselves as closer to the plantocracy than to newly freed slaves.[12] Within this social structure, music—like the selective use of French or Creole—contributed a contested colonial aurality. The socioracial order circumscribed musical practices: it sought to impose who could perform and dance to what music and when. It shaped how the various musics found around the plantation were heard. Undoubtedly, slaves and their overseers did not hear the sounds of the violin or a drum in the same way. Conversely, music and dance facilitated social solidarity and captured the social aspirations of colonial actors at nearly every social level. A close examination of the role of drumming as well as European-derived social dances on the plantation will illustrate these points.

The Colonial Listening Regime

Guadeloupe has not produced slave narratives such as those that have informed African American studies. The only written records available consists of various books written by European travelers to the Caribbean whose testimonies were shaped by their particular imperial positions. In *Black Soundscapes, White Stages*, Edwin C. Hill builds on Mary Louise Pratt's concept of imperial eyes to question the ways in which European encounter with colonial sounds "produced" but also challenged "an imperial order for the valuable and meaningful mapping of the New World."[13] Whereas imperial eyes were able to produce a "type of scientific knowledge that, in Aimé Césaire's words, 'enumerates, measures, classifies, and kills,'" imperial ears met sounds that defied colonial desires to control through the production of taxonomies and cartographies, foremost among them the din of enslaved black bodies: their speech, music, and, most of all, screams. These sounds escaped colonial rationality and remained opaque to colonial listeners. They inspired extreme affective responses, from fascination and awe to fear. From the seventeenth century in the writings of Jean-Baptiste Du Tertre and César de Rochefort to the oft-quoted eighteenth-century chronicles of

Jean-Baptiste Labat to the unabashedly racist descriptions found in Granier de Cassagnac's nineteenth-century vitriol, African-derived musics in the French Caribbean colonies were variously, but unsurprisingly, described as "barbarous," "horrible," "scary," and "hideous." If European chroniclers' writings produced what Radano called a "sonically absent history," they nonetheless reveal Europeans' collective prejudice and ambivalence toward the presence of black bodies in the colonies.[14] They also make it clear that black music and dancing played an important role in the overall life of the plantation, including the work songs that helped coordinate labor in cane fields, the songs of wakes and funerals, and, of course, those of the *calenda* or *bamboula*, the two terms commonly used by European writers to describe black drumming.[15]

Black sounds exposed colonial hearing as "impaired, unreliable, or faulty," a condition that Hill—channeling Barrett—describes as "hearing double."[16] Hearing double implies two things. First, it acknowledges that colonial listening was marked by mishearing and misrecognition. Second, it highlights that colonial listening was informed by previous listening habits, by the myths, desires, and projections that circulated through European travel writings, with each new text echoing those that came before (sometimes literally, as with Rochefort's 1665 reproduction of Du Tertre's earlier writings).

Even if European chroniclers offer only tantalizing glimpses of the actual sounds of the colony, their texts do reveal a great deal about the importance of the sonic in the exercise of power on the plantation. They can help us elucidate colonial *listening regimes*, what I propose as an aural equivalent to "the gaze," a socially constructed way of hearing that structures and is structured by power relations.[17] For one, as Hill explains, colonial soundscapes—the term here encompasses both "natural" and human-made sounds—made audible the *ratés*, or "sonic breakdowns," of the plantation: "a failure in time, a sonic symbol of slippage, excess, waste in the colonial machine."[18] These sonic breakdowns were symptomatic of the fissures in the colonial regime, the epistemological incommensurability that marked the distance between the rational discourse on which colonialism was built and the sensorial experience of its logic of racial abjection within a structure of imposed and strained conviviality. Simply put, the argument that slavery was a benevolent enterprise could hardly be reconciled with the screams, the cracking of whips, the barking of dogs, or the firing of guns that made audible the violence of the plantation.[19]

If the colonial record is marked by hearing double, the archive it produced demands a double take. In Guadeloupe today, the argument that plantation owners and colonial officials prohibited drumming remains pervasive. For example, in its 1970 *Rapport culturel*, the AGEG cites the writing of Jean-Baptiste Labat—a French Dominican priest who traveled extensively throughout the West Indies, owned a plantation in Martinique, and periodically resided in Guadeloupe—to demonstrate that colonial powers tried to muzzle the drum: "We passed many ordinances in the islands to prohibit *calendas*, not only because of the indecent and totally lascivious postures that form this dance, but also so as to avoid large assemblies of negroes who, finding themselves thus gathered in joy . . . could start a revolt, some uprisings, or a stealing party."[20]

Indeed, Epstein identifies several edicts forbidding drumming in the French colonies: first in 1654, then in 1678, and again in the Code Noir of 1685.[21] But even Labat concedes that these ordinances had little effect in restricting slave dancing. It could be, of course, that regardless of the discipline imposed on them, the enslaved always found ways to defy the colonial regime, to engage in *petit marronnage* even without fleeing the plantation. But it could also be that slave owners did not always enforce these edicts. Labat denounces the Spaniards who, far from outlawing the *calenda*, had started to dance it themselves. And even though he was charged with managing an estate, his detailed descriptions suggest that Labat himself likely tolerated such dances and was often witness to them. Writing in the early nineteenth century, in a period (1802–1848) during which slavery was reinstated following its first abolition in 1794, Longin reported that *bamboula* "took place every Sunday night, either in the countryside or on the estates. . . . It is a pleasure that is ordinarily not prohibited to slaves."[22]

In fact, slave owners were likely fascinated by the spectacle of dancing and singing black bodies. Filtered through their colonial listening regime, misheard and misunderstood, these dances inspired fear and titillated. Granier de Cassagnac, in 1842, admits to watching an enslaved woman dance for four hours. Even as he expresses his disgust at this spectacle ("Never in my life have I seen anything quite as frightening," he writes), his prose also reveals his erotic fascination for this dancing body—with her "raspy voice," "flaming eyes," and "half-parsed lips"—who ends lying on the ground, "drenched in the sweat flowing from her limbs, entangled in the madras scarf that had fallen from her head and in her skirts that had come loose from her body."[23]

What the archive suggests, then, is that despite the fear they inspired and the prohibitions they elicited, slave dances may have been tolerated because they entertained not only those enslaved but their owners as well. Dances such as the *calenda* and the *bamboula* undoubtedly offered an oppositional space to those enslaved, but not even such spaces were ever free from colonial encroachment. Even the rings of creolized drumming could be spaces of subjugation.

Colonial Aurality and Subjugation

Through their writing, Labat, Granier de Cassagnac, and other European chroniclers not only bore witness but also staged black singing, drumming, and dancing for white audiences. Saidiya Hartman asks us to consider whether such acts of witnessing represent a "kind of looking no less entangled with the wielding of power and the extraction of enjoyment" than the scenes of terror and physical brutality central to most writing about slavery. She continues: "Does the captive's dance allay grief or articulate the fraught, compromised, and impossible character of agency? Or does it exemplify the use of the body as an instrument against the self?"[24] It is clear from the examples already cited that the spectacle of slaves dancing comforted European witnesses in their ideology of racial alterity and abjection. In addition, in the eyes and ears of European chroniclers, slaves dancing and musicking mollified European guilt over the cruelty of slavery. "By singing and dancing, the negro tolerates everything and console himself of everything," Léonard writes in the late eighteenth century.[25]

Moreover, Martin Munro remarks that even if drumming and dancing offered a form of catharsis that was essential to reestablishing slaves' sense of their own humanity in the face of oppression, this release valve also helped maintain the plantation system that it mitigated. Indeed, however suspicious they may have been of African-derived music and dance, planters soon accepted that "their slaves worked more effectively while they sang" and thus appointed lead singers to work crews.[26] Moreover, some plantation owners encouraged slave gatherings with the idea that giving slaves controlled liberties could actually lessen chances of rebellion.[27] César de Rochefort explained in 1665 that, in Saint Christopher (today known as St. Kitts), slaves were allowed to gather to sing and dance on Sundays after church "to release their bodies . . . without prejudice to their capacity to work for their masters."[28] Especially following the particularly punishing rhythm of the harvest season, when the necessity to harvest and process sugarcane at its peak required slaves to work up to eighteen hours a day, "two days of dancing released slaves from the tyranny of industrial time and returned them fleetingly to their more benign, organic rhythms." Munro concludes, "In a sense, therefore, the slave dances helped perpetuate the plantation system, as they were a means of releasing some of the tensions that forced labor inevitably created."[29]

Slave music, then—even in those forms that have been hailed as most oppositional, such as drumming—never escaped the political economy of the colony. Rather, it participated in its extractive regime, either directly in the case of work songs or indirectly in the case of slave entertainment. As Radano emphasizes in the case of colonial North America, slave music should not be reduced to an unintended and resistant by-product of the colonial political economy but rather should be regarded as integral to it.[30] To put it another way, black music, when considered within a colonial aurality, elucidates the complex articulation and overlap between entertainment and pleasure (of those enslaved as well as their masters), labor, and racial subjugation.

The quadrille illustrates another way in which the music making of those enslaved was subsumed under the colonial economy. Labat comments, "There are some [among his slaves] who play the violin rather well and who earn some money during assemblies and their wedding feasts."[31] Labat notes that slave owners taught several European dances to their slaves in an effort to undermine their desire to participate in their African-derived dances. He does not similarly acknowledge that, in all likelihood, slave owners also encouraged some of their slaves to learn to play European instruments such as the violin so that those slaves could provide entertainment for the plantocracy. It is clear, though, regardless of their slave owners' motivations, that both forms of cultural imposition contributed to the symbolic violence of slavery. As Hartman concludes, even in the "'benign' scenes" of slave music making, "we confront the everyday practice of domination." She asks: "Is the scene of slaves dancing and fiddling for their masters any less inhumane than that of slaves sobbing and dancing on the auction block? If so why? Is the effect of power any less prohibitive? Or coercive? Or does pleasure mitigate coercion? Is the boundary between terror and pleasure clearer in the market than in the quarters or at the 'big house'?"[32] All of this to say that, in a small island like Guadeloupe where the possibility to flee the plantation, to engage in *grand marronnage*, was inherently limited, music making could never truly escape the colonial regime of domination and subjugation. Yet I do not want to suggest that the colonial aurality did not provide openings for oppositional self-making. Indeed, the colonial aurality contained within itself the potential for countercolonial practice.

Colonial Aurality and the Poetics of the Détour

Even as colonial writers used African-derived music and dance practices to justify slavery, their fundamentally unreliable listening regime created

The Poetics of Colonial Aurality / 41

opportunities for sonic *marronnage* steeped in the ethics of opacity and the politics of the *détour*.[33] Indeed, we should not dismiss the fact that music and dance offered privileged spaces for the affirmation of black subjectivity at the edges of the Antillean plantation. Whether covert or tolerated, dancing and drumming participated in the development and performance of an oppositional aurality among those enslaved. While drumming cannot be reduced to an act of resistant fleeing of the plantation (as its association with the *nèg mawon* suggests), music and dancing afforded slaves a *détour*, a way to possibly reshape the plantation society from its margins, inflecting its funeral and religious rites and allowing for the emergence of organized solidarity networks. Faced with the homogenizing and dehumanizing experience of the plantation's protoindustrial rhythm, slaves managed to use the rhythms of the drum to foster solidarity—in other words, to preserve and affirm their humanity. Caught up in the regime of colonial conviviality, those who were enslaved used music to "home" the plantation.

Labat, writing in the early eighteenth century, offers perhaps one of the earliest descriptions of something akin to contemporary gwoka on the plantation. He reports on a dance that he calls *calenda*, which, according to him, was mainly practiced by slaves captured on the coast of Guinea and in the neighboring Realm of Arad. This dance was accompanied by drums carved from tree trunks (a technique now referred to as *bwa fouyé* in Creole). As in contemporary *gwoka*, one drum was used to set the pace of the dance while the other improvised:

> To give the cadence of this dance, they use two drums made of two carved-out tree trunks of uneven size. One of the extremities is open, the other covered with the hairless skin of a sheep or goat, scraped like parchment. The largest of these two drums, which they simply call the big drum, can be three or four feet long and about fifteen to sixteen inches in diameter. The small, which is called baboula, is about the same length but eight to nine inches in diameter. Those who beat the drums to structure the dance put them between their legs or sit on them, touching them with the length of four fingers of each of their hands. The one who touches the big drum beats it with regularity and calm; but the one who touches the baboula beats it as fast as he can, almost without keeping time, and as the sound that he produces is far quieter than that of the big drum and much higher, it only serves to make noise, without marking the cadence of the dance, nor the movements of the dancers.[34]

The dance described by Labat, however, departs from contemporary practice. Similar to contemporary *léwòz*, the audience formed a large circle

42 / Chapter One

and participated in the performance by singing and clapping hands. However, in contrast to contemporary practices, dancers formed two lines facing each other inside the circle, women on one side, men on the other:

> They stand with their arms spread like those who dance while playing castanets. They jump and twirl, come within two or three feet of one another, step back in cadence until the sound of the drum warns them to meet and strike their thighs against one another, that is to say men against women. Seeing them, it may seem like they are striking their bellies, but only their thighs bear the blows. They step back in a moment while twirling and do the same movement again with completely lascivious gestures, as many times as the drum signals them, which they often do several times in a row. Every once in a while, they cross their arms and do two or three turns while still striking their thighs and kissing.[35]

Importantly, Labat suggests that slaves tended to gather along ethnic lines, this in spite of most plantation owners' efforts to systematically break up ethnic and family groups when purchasing new slaves. These meetings served to create or reinforce solidarity networks organized around putative "nations." Moreover, Labat describes with particular detail the differences between those slaves of unspecified ethnic affiliation who learned to dance the *calenda* and those he called "Congo"—who may have arrived in Guadeloupe more recently than other slaves—who had preserved their own dance. Similarly, Léonard paints a picture of a wedding during which slaves gathered according to their respective nations, each nation holding its own flag and performing its own dance.[36] Over time, these networks became the seeds from which mutual-aid societies emerged, societies that, in turn, provided the foundation for social and political activism among Guadeloupe's black working class in the later half of the nineteenth century, as we will see later in this chapter.[37]

Beyond their role in emergent forms of solidarity, music and dance also afforded slaves a way of preserving, transmitting, and adapting practices brought over from Africa. The descriptions found in the writings of Labat and Léonard suggest that slaves' gatherings and their organization into nations somewhat mitigated the process of acculturation by allowing them to re-create ethnic ties across plantations.[38] Labat's description fascinatingly suggests that different ethnicities may have used dancing to preserve their particular practices (aside from the Congo, Labat singles out the "Mines," slaves from Cape Verde, and those from the Gambia), the widespread popularity of the *calenda* may have made it a site of musical synthesis. Whether slaves used music and dance to preserve specific languages, gestures, and religious rituals or simply to transmit a general aesthetic grammar, as is generally argued in writings about music in the African diaspora, we can argue along with Martin Munro that the sounds and rhythms of the drum enabled slaves to begin "to (re)form an idea of themselves, an identity other than, if not entirely different to, that of the deadening machine of the plantation."[39]

Dancing and drumming did not exist, then, in a straightforward opposition to the plantation system; rather, they participated in a complex negotiation of planters' desire to maximize their slaves' productivity and to deny their humanity, on the one hand, and, on the other hand, slaves' capacity to use whatever limited form of freedom they were given or could carve out for themselves to reclaim their bodies and their humanity. Drumming was thus both an expression of the *ratés*, or "sonic breakdowns," of the plantation system and an essential aspect of the *détour* described by Trouillot, "the social time and space [that slaves] controlled on the edges of the plantations."[40] Whether they were allowed or even encouraged to gather and dance by their masters or whether they seized that space through acts of *marronnage*, slaves were able to use music and dance to preserve what Glissant calls "traces" of cultural knowledge and to develop forms of solidarities that would eventually become institutionalized. At the same time, drumming and dancing acted as a catharsis that enabled slaves to endure the brutality of their condition, to remember where they came from, and to confront the source of their suffering.[41] In this sense, dances were themselves traces, that is, an embodied epistemology, an inscription of a history in the body, a way of physically making sense of one's condition and acting out alternative ways of being-in-the-world than those offered by colonial oppression. Conversely, because drumming existed on the "edges" of the plantation system and not entirely outside of it, slave dances could not help but somewhat reinforce that system. This is the tragic aspect of the *détour*: even as slaves were able to use music and dance to reinvent themselves following the trauma of the Middle Passage, drumming cannot be reduced to an act of *marronnage*. It is not entirely resistant in that it cannot escape the system of domination that it opposes.[42] Rather, drumming participated in an overall colonial creolizing aurality. In the ears of the planters, drumming awoke fears of potential revolts and also provided hope of higher profits; to the ears of the slaves, drumming provided a way through which they could reclaim their humanity and inflect the plantation system without escaping it. Stripped of its oversimplified, heroic, and resistant connotations, the drum can be heard anew as a technology of Relation, one of the symptomatic sounds of the economic, cultural, and social entanglements of French colonialism.

The creolization of the quadrille represents another example of a sonic and kinesthetic *détour* made possible within a creolized aurality. Contrary to what Lockel claimed in his 1978 article for *Ja Ka Ta*, the quadrille cannot be reduced to a sonic marker of French culture, although it offers an unmistakable symptom of the assimilationist pull of French colonialism.[43] As Dominique Cyrille explains, once the contradance and the quadrille were introduced to the Lesser Antilles in the eighteenth century, they quickly spread throughout the social fabric of Caribbean colonies.[44] Planters proudly danced the quadrille—which they learned from French dance masters—to reinforce their connection with the French aristocracy and to distance themselves from free people of color and from poor whites who could not afford dance lessons. Poor whites adopted it to reinforce their connection to the plantocracy and to distance themselves from free people of color. Mulattos embraced the quadrille to reinforce their claim to social recognition. Freed blacks saw in it an opportunity to distance themselves from house slaves. Finally, house slaves—some of whom may originally have been coerced into learning it—appropriated it to distance themselves from field slaves who danced the *calenda*. In appropriating the quadrille, slaves transformed it, infusing it with various African-derived elements. Conversely, in some instances, structural elements of the quadrille found their way into drum-based dances. This is most clearly the case of the Martinican *bèlè* but also of the now nearly defunct *léwòz o komandman* tradition of Guadeloupe. In this tradition, once common in the region of Mare Gaillard in Grande-Terre, a caller directs couples who dance to the rhythms of a *boula*. In short, the creolized quadrille should not be reduced to a symptom of the assimilationist pressures of the colonial system—and the mimetic impulse that animated it—as nationalist rhetoric claimed in Guadeloupe.[45] Rather, in the quadrille, we see the working of creolization as an effort to domesticate, or home, the colonial space and its nascent culture. Considered within the complexity of the colonial aurality, the quadrille illustrates the impossibility of colonial powers to control musical practices. Incapable to truly "hear" colonial sounds, not only did they never truly silence the drum; they also created opportunities for the creative misappropriation, and thus creolization, of European music and dance. The persistence of drumming and the creolization of the quadrille, then, are examples of sonic assemblages made possible by the *décalage* between the ideal plantation model and its actual implementation. They reveal the plantation as a positive structure of power within which both drumming and the quadrille participated in the double play of accommodation and resistance, of fleeing and homing, that characterizes the *détour*. As we will see in the following section, the French

The Poetics of Colonial Aurality / 45

Republican political system, though designed to perpetuate France's colonial empire, likewise found itself open to the creative manipulations of the *détour,* strategies that eventually led to the 1946 law of departmentalization.

Republican Colonialism and Assimilation (1848–1946)

Let us make a rather abrupt turn from the sounds of the plantation to consider its outgrowth, more precisely the entanglement of colonialism and nineteenth century French republicanism. I want to do so for several reasons. First, I seek to disturb the common understanding of assimilation that strictly aligns the process with a loss of identity. Rather, I show how the assimilationist policies of the Third Republic were open to creative manipulations from its margins, strategies that eventually enabled French Antillean politicians to decolonize their islands through their political incorporation into the French state. Taking measure of this long history will help us elucidate the context in which, starting in the 1950s, autonomist—and eventually separatist—movements emerged in the Antilles. To a great extent, Guadeloupean nationalism of the 1960s, 1970s, and 1980s is rooted in nineteenth-century black labor activism at the same time that it is an ideologically inflected reaction against the heritage of nineteenth-century assimilationism. Finally, this discussion of nineteenth-century social and political dynamics provides a basis from which to hear anew the contested place of biguine and drumming in the century between the 1848 abolition of slavery and the 1946 law of departmentalization, and thus to better understand the cultural-nationalist turn of the late 1960s. Indeed, assimilationism framed a reinterpretation of the musical legacy of the plantation, thickening its fields of contested connotations within the web of a colonial aurality.

Today, assimilation carries a negative connotation both in scholarship and in politics. Since Fanon, the charge that it leads to alienation has been repeated often and, as I will show here, this assertion certainly proves well founded in the French Antilles.[46] Unsurprisingly, then, in 1970, when the AGEG outlined its cultural-nationalist platform, it sought first and foremost to combat assimilation, an essential prerequisite for the emergence of a Guadeloupean nation. Within the "problem-space" from which anticolonialist activism emerged in Guadeloupe, assimilation could be regarded only as a form of oppression that had to be resisted. Dany Bebel-Gislert captured the zeitgeist when she declared that, in the 1980s, Guadeloupeans faced the challenge of "devenir ce que nous sommes" (becoming who/what we are).[47] In the domain of music, this meant a rejection of those musical forms that could most easily be heard as hybrid such as the quadrille and the biguine, as Lockel so clearly stated. However, without denying the long-term psychological and economic toll of colonialism, I argue that assimilationist policies—emanating from the metropole and manifest in the colonies—created the very institutions and structures that actually enabled the gradual emergence of Antillean nationalisms, paving the way for the more radical demands that blossomed in the postwar period. Following David Scott, I am inspired here to think of assimilation as participating in a "positive structure of power, a historical formation of certain constitutive and productively shaping material and epistemological conditions of life and thought."[48] Conversely, in the words of Glissant, assimilation functions as a *camouflage* that obscures the source of oppression in the French Antilles. As such, it has demanded, but it has also made possible, strategies of the *détour*.[49] Moreover, following emancipation, assimilation offered a prism through which the sounds of Antillean "popular" and "folkloric" musics were refracted and contested.

Assimilation in the Third Republic

As Josette Fallope reminds us, the idea of assimilating the colonies into the Republic was born in the Enlightenments.[50] On the one hand, jacobinical republicanism dictated that the Republic protect its territorial integrity; on the other hand, it gave Antillean politicians a platform from which they could make demands for greater equality. It is important to note that assimilation engaged negotiations among four groups: French metropolitan politicians on one side of the Atlantic and, in the Antilles, the white plantocracy, a fast-rising *mulâtre* middle class, and an emerging black political class.[51] Jacobinical republicanism and its promise of radical egalitarianism swayed the Guadeloupean *mulâtre* and black bourgeoisie to assimilate into a political culture that offered them tools for greater freedom. The white plantocracy, meanwhile, regarded assimilation as a threat to their power and status. Assimilation was thus both the expression of France's will to continue—and even expand—its imperial control and the main axis around which the Antillean middle class articulated its political demands. That is to say that the assimilationist French nation-state created a structure of power that, on the one hand, protected its own integrity and, on the other hand, allowed for Antillean politicians to negotiate their political and social positions. As Gary Wilder concludes with regard to French imperial policies in West Africa, "A new colonial rationality placed subject peoples in a politically effective double-bind that racialized them as minor members of the French nation. But it was also self-undermining and created possibilities for critical political intervention." This made possible a "creolization of the political" within the French state.[52]

If assimilation emerged during the French Revolution, it only really blossomed during the Third Republic (1870–1940), around the same time as the biguine and drumming congealed into something resembling their contemporary forms. Following its 1870 defeat against Prussia and the loss of Alsace and Lorraine, France sought to further integrate the nation-state, including its old colonies, by extending and consolidating its institutions. As a result, the colonies gained access to national representation, universal suffrage was extended to all male citizens, and educational reforms also reached the Caribbean corners of the empire (though putting them into practice proved problematic). Importantly for our purposes, the Third Republic also saw the conscription of radio broadcasting to the colonial project. In 1931, the French government launched the Poste Colonial, a shortwave radio station aimed at making the French state audible throughout the empire. In parallel, local radio stations were introduced to the "old colonies." The trend was inaugurated in Réunion in 1929. Martinique and Guadeloupe got their respective stations in 1937. If colonialism had arguably been primarily a scopic regime until then, Republican colonialism marks the importance of the aural in the colonial regime.

The effects of assimilationist policies on the French Antilles were complex, but they mainly benefited the bourgeoisie of color. Thanks to universal suffrage, they were able to gain access to local and national political appointments. Moreover, the multiplication of governmental institutions in the colonies engendered a new class of civil servants (*fonctionnaires*), among whom the *mulâtres* thrived, thus allowing them to position themselves as liaison between the Republic and the Antillean masses.[53]

Educational reform played an important role in the Third Republic nation-building program that posited that free, secular, and mandatory education would boost Republican consciousness and form citizens. Although its economy did not allow Guadeloupe to fully support free education, the availability of scholarships meant that *mulâtre* children again benefited the most from these limited reforms. Through public education, these children were socialized in the French Republican habitus. In time, they formed a new intellectual elite who had fully absorbed assimilationist ideology and were therefore more likely to keep pushing for its realization and inflect its outcomes.[54]

But the expansion of colonial education did not simply affect the *mulâtre* middle class. It also contributed to the rise of a nationalist consciousness in a *négriste* political class. As both Turino and Boehmer highlight for the Anglophone colonial world, the education system played an important role in diffusing the ideology of nationalism throughout the empire, making it available for recuperation by anticolonial intellectuals. Although French administrators failed to fully gauge the appeal that nationalism could have for colonized elites, they recognized the subversive potential of education. We should also note that other factors facilitated the circulation of political ideologies and the birth of a pan-colonial consciousness: these included military conscription as well as administrative "pilgrimages" that sent civil servants from the Antilles to both the metropole and other corners of the empire.[55]

In turn-of-the-century Guadeloupe, a rising black political class emerged from labor organizing efforts to promote a new form of nationalism. The black Guadeloupean elite joined the assimilationist wave for different reasons from those of the *mulâtres*, and their political activism was closely linked to the development of trade unions around the turn of the twentieth century. While the *mulâtres* favored a moderate form of republicanism, black leaders embraced socialism and thus remained close to the proletariat. For them, assimilation offered the promise of French social protection, higher wages, and access to education.[56]

Because of their dependence on popular support, the black leadership could not shed vernacular cultural expressions as easily as the *mulâtres* could. On the contrary, by the early twentieth century, black leadership strategically embraced Creole and, taking advantage of the new freedom of the press, published newspapers in that language. While Creole popular culture had previously been perceived as impeding assimilation, around the turn of the twentieth century, black leaders adopted the seemingly paradoxical position of making assimilationist social demands while also simultaneously expressing racial pride by foregrounding their cultural specificity.[57]

I see the emergence of this black leadership and its awareness of its cultural specificity as the first manifestation of Antillean nationalism, its point of departure, to borrow Partha Chatterjee's phrase. The rise of *négriste* politicians anticipates the more radical cultural nationalism of *négritude*. However, the birth of Guadeloupean nationalism does not match Chatterjee's Indian model. Chatterjee explains that "anticolonial nationalism creates its own domain of sovereignty within colonial society well before it begins its political battle with the imperial power." He situates the origin of Indian nationalism within a "spiritual sphere" independent of the control that the British exerted on the material sphere. Thus, Chatterjee places the emergence of anticolonial nationalism within the superstructure or, rather, within the part of civil society most separated from the colonial base.[58] In Guadeloupe, however, *négriste* nationalism emerged within a very different problem-space from anticolonial nationalism in India. In fact, it is precisely from labor relations that anticolonial and nationalist activism grew in the French Caribbean. And it is labor activism that has historically most galvanized Guadeloupeans and drawn some of the most violent repressions from the French state, as we will see in the next chapter. Therefore, Guadeloupean nationalism did not emerge from a sphere distant from European modernity, as was the case in India, but instead proceeded from the same modernist transformations—republicanism and industrialization—that were affecting the metropolitan state. Guadeloupean nationalisms, in their successive historical incarnations, then, have never operated from a place of partial sovereignty; rather, they have participated in efforts to home modern power, to paraphrase Crichlow.[59]

From the late nineteenth century to the 1946 law of departmentalization, political demands for greater autonomy from the French Antilles have coexisted with demands for greater equity within the Republic and have found their expression in a productive tension with France's own assimilationist policies. Unlike more straightforward anticolonial nationalisms, sovereignty has not always been the explicit goal of Antillean nationalisms. It is in this context that we must approach the rise of more radical political movements in the second half of the twentieth century.

The Contested Aurality of the Third Republic

Assimilation created the conditions from which both *mulâtre* and *négriste* politicians could strive to transform the Republican colonial system from within. Yet we should not ignore assimilation's alienating effects. In fact, assimilationist policies reinforced the sociocultural stratification inherited from the plantation colonial system, normalizing European and European-derived customs over those practices that continued to bear African traces. Faced with the political ascendancy of a *mulâtre* and, to a lesser extent, black middle class, the white oligarchy attempted to preserve their power and privilege through a racializing and divisive discourse, with the effect of further reinforcing the perceived inferiority of Creole cultural expressions, even among the masses. It should come as no surprise, then, that the *mulâtre* bourgeoisie's assimilationist claims were expressed both politically and culturally. The *mulâtres* adopted a general Francophile habitus—expressed through dress code, religion, and nuclear families—to distance themselves from the masses and facilitate their social ascendency.[60]

Within this logic, acquiring mastery over the French language became the outmost sign of having assimilated into French civilization.[61] The education

50 / Chapter One

system played a central role in amplifying the alienating effects of assimilation and in defining the role of language within late-colonial aurality. Republican education reform contributed greatly to language becoming an especially potent indicator of social status:

> The expansion of education . . . led to profound cultural changes as well, not the least of which was the further penetration of the French language and culture. French—as the agent of French assimilation and its ideology—was the acceptable language of discourse in formal or public institutional settings, such as the government, school, church, court system, and the media. Creole remained the local vernacular for daily communication in the informal or private sector, particularly among the lower strata who did not have access to French or had received little schooling and thus spoke French poorly. Nonetheless, Creole was the primary vehicle of local culture and an indicator of local sentiment, values, and norms that were generally held in low esteem. Frequently Creole was also the language used in situations of unequal relations: for example, a boss to a worker, a proprietor to a servant, grandparents to children. . . . Whereas Creole had negative evaluation, French received positive reinforcement.[62]

Assimilation, though, did not simply produce diglossia and a stratification of the cultural capital of French and Creole within the Republican colonial aurality. It also had long-term psychological and epistemic consequences. Fanon presents the problem of assimilation thus: "Because it is a systematized negation of the other, a frenzied determination to deny the other any attribute of humanity, colonialism forces the colonized to constantly ask the question: 'Who am I in reality?'"[63] Glissant builds on Fanon's work in his exploration of what he calls the *pulsion mimétique* (mimetic drive). "The mimetic drive," writes Glissant, "is a kind of insidious violence," not only because the imitation will never be successful, but also because the mimetic drive itself is unbearable.[64] The resulting trauma is somewhat akin to what DuBois describes as double consciousness, an inability to see oneself but through the eyes of the colonizer. Glissant goes further, arguing that Martinicans' lack of self-subjectivity extends to their inability to apprehend themselves in the world they inhabit. They are "real" but "frustrated" Americans and "impossible" but "satisfied" Europeans. Most of all, they are "Antilleans blind to their own *antillanité* [Antilleanness]." He concludes that "the Martinican sees with eyes other than his own."[65]

For Glissant, then, Antilleans find themselves unable to construct a collective and emancipated attitude about their own culture. Instead, there exists a constant tension between a denigrated Creole culture and an idealized French culture, the values of the latter always mediating the relation to the former. But this situation affords Antilleans a form of epistemological privilege. Indeed, for Glissant, this situation informs the emergence of an unconscious (post)colonial way of knowing expressed through what he calls "forced" or "constrained"—rather than "natural"—poetics. Forced poetics result from a desire to find a collective expression that is frustrated by the impossibility to develop a collective *langage,* that is to say, a shared attitude toward a *langue* (language).[66] Extending the idea to expressive culture as a whole, forced poetics help us understand the complex social dynamics that shaped the Antillean colonial aurality: both language and musical practices—although, or perhaps because, they were always-already caught in the processes of creolization—emerged as both contested objects and tools of contestation that continue to animate cultural and political nationalisms to this day.

To be certain, under Republican colonialism, the cultural capital of the diverse musics heard in the Antilles continued to be contested, each style resonating with its own history and symbolic entanglements—each style informing different relationships to Guadeloupe's past, and each style performing different social and political imaginings of its future. Practices associated with slavery—or rural lifestyles in general—were overall devalued. The rising *mulâtre* middle class especially stigmatized drumming traditions. By the time separatist activism took shape in the 1960s, it was common in families with bourgeois aspirations to describe drumming as "biten a vyè nèg" (literally, the "stuff of old negroes"), an expression that ties drumming to slavery, poverty, and delinquency and other forms of social deviancy. Nonetheless, drumming perdured during this period among agricultural workers and in faubourgs (working-class suburbs). A 1918 article in the newspaper *Le Colonial* even offers the earliest depiction we have of a *bamboula* in a faubourg of Pointe-à-Pitre that more closely resembles contemporary gwoka performances than any prior historical document.[67] Meanwhile, as the quadrille's popularity faded, it lost its importance as a terrain for contesting social hierarchies, yet it remained an important practice, especially among the rural population. Importantly, quadrille, *koud tanbou* or *swaré léwòz* (the overarching category of gwoka was not yet in common usage) were not perceived as opposite.[68] Rather, as the life of the celebrated percussionist Carnot illustrates, these musical practices existed side by side: it was not exceptional for a *balakari* (quadrille ball) and a *swaré léwòz* to take place at the same *habitation,* and musicians such as Carnot were skilled at performing in both styles.[69]

If by the early twentieth century European salon dances had lost their cachet as markers of social boundaries, a classical music education remained the guarded privilege of the white elite.[70] Subsequently, following the common assimilationist pattern, the ability to perform in one of the many wind orchestras and brass bands that flourished in the colony during the Third Republic became an important tool for the middle class to accrue both social and cultural capital. Finally, this overview of the Antillean musical landscape during the Third Republic would not be complete without mentioning the biguine. Biguine emerged as a by-product of the urbanization of Antillean societies in the second half of the nineteenth century. By the 1930s, it had blossomed as the first genre of Antillean music to be commercialized in the form of sheet music and recordings. Through the circulation of these recordings and the migration of Antillean musicians, its popularity quickly grew in the metropole. And from Parisian nightclubs where Antillean and African American musicians performed side by side, the biguine started to circulate through Afro-diasporic networks to the United States.

During the Third Republic, then, language and music were enlisted anew in constructing a number of colonial dichotomies that opposed the written and the oral, the modern and the traditional, the commercial and the folkloric, the urban and the rural. These dichotomies were largely artificial, as Marie-Céline Lafontaine reminds us.[71] Following emancipation in 1848, circulation between urban centers and rural areas increased. Meanwhile, even as assimilation remained the dominant ideology, local elites continued to borrow from subaltern culture, making it impossible to divorce French, elite Antillean, and rural Guadeloupean cultures. Nonetheless, within this imagined spectrum, *koud tanbou* and *swaré léwòz*—during which drums accompany singing in Creole—came to stand at one end, devalued in the eyes and ears of most of the population. Biguine aspired to the other end, although its position was contested. But even as it acquired value as a cultural export, many musicians continued to regard it with some contempt. For example, the trombonist, bandleader, and composer Al Lirvat—one of Guadeloupe's most celebrated biguine performers—recalls Antillean dance orchestras' casual treatment of the biguine: even after World War II, these orchestras used written arrangements or memorized popular performances from recordings for most of their music (whether Cuban or North American). Yet they relied on improvised head arrangements for their biguine numbers.[72] Moreover, the commercialization of biguine meant that its practitioners strived to incorporate elements of competing styles, such as Cuban boleros and *sones* or North American Dixieland jazz. This opened the genre to criticism of inauthenticity coming from both its detractors and its practitioners.[73] Although widely enjoyed across most segments of the Antillean society, biguine quickly became associated with the folklorization of Antillean culture and thus ideologically suspicious in the eyes of those intellectual figures who, in the 1930s, started to push back against assimilation, as we will see.

Négritude and Departmentalization

As the biguine's success spread through colonial and diasporic networks in the interwar period, the intellectuals of the emerging *négritude* movement were transforming the cultural politics of the black Francophone colonial world on their way to reforming its political culture. Biguine found itself at the convergence of two opposite ideological fields: one paternalistically celebrating French colonialism, and the other conversely reacting through a rejection of assimilation and its attendant exoticizing folklorization of Antillean culture. Metropolitan ears quickly inscribed their imperial fantasies on the biguine, just as they had turned the *doudou*—the tragic Antillean woman who has fallen in love with a French officer who leaves her to return "home," as illustrated in the (in)famous *valse créole* "Adieu foulards, adieu madras"—into a paternalist symbol of Antillean longing for French oversight. Within French colonial aurality, the biguine stood as the sonic equivalent of tropical landscapes, warm weather, and *doudous* clad in madras dresses at the same time that it contributed to reinscribing the Antilles within a nostalgic narrative of imperial belonging.[74]

For this reason, male intellectuals of the *négritude* movement such as Léon-Gontran Damas and Guy Tirolien shun the biguine. For them, the biguine's *métisse* (from *métissage*, "mixed," "biracial") aesthetics rendered it suspicious, inherently inauthentic. As Edwin Hill so powerfully demonstrates, within *négritude*'s selective and masculinist aurality, the biguine—still carrying its association with the trope of the *doudou*—became a symbol of miscegenation and colonial violence. Simply put, the biguine's hybridity contradicted the logic of return to a mythical African past. It did not fit within romantic anticolonial narratives that favored "heroic poetic figures who engage in epic struggles with History and make absolute choices." Hill successfully complicates this analysis, showing that female voices developed a form of "*négritude* in the minor" in which biguine's liminality opened the potential of negotiations across racial and colonial lines and expressed "transnational relations of continuity." For our purposes, though, it is important to note the extent to which the *négritude* poets' critique of the biguine announces similar arguments made by Guadeloupean cultural nationalists some thirty years later, Lockel foremost among them.[75]

Like the biguine, the drum came to play a contested role in late-colonial auralities. To imperial ears, the tam-tam—as the drum was commonly referred to—continued to function as the primary sonic symbol of black othering: its sounds and rhythms still signified blackness, Africanness, primitiveness, and danger, including the danger of "infectious" miscegenation.[76] This did not prevent the poets of *négritude* from reappropriating the drum "as a cutting sign of a racial authenticity and anti-imperial resistance."[77] For Senghor, rhythm offers "a source of nourishment for the exile black man in France" who finds himself cut off from the tam-tam and from Africa, to which he must return. As Munro explains, rhythm, for Senghor, was central to an Afro-diasporic epistemology that opposed European rationality and—through its embrace of repetition—teleology. The Senegalese poet encouraged his French Caribbean colleagues to think along with the drum and its rhythms.[78] As a result, both became central elements of their poetry, both through literal evocation (see, for example, Damas's "Ils sont venus ce soir" in *Pigments*) and the structural use of repetition. The poets of *négritude* responded to the alienating and self-exoticizing sounds of the biguine by grounding the Francophone black experience in the rhythms of the drum. As the drum echoed with the history of imperial fears and desires within metropolitan aurality, it resonated with the longing for a *retour* for the *négritude* poets. More important, their drum-centered aurality opened the door for a creative manipulation of the French language. Critically, this creative appropriation of the French language paralleled a radical imagining of an alternative political future within a transformed French imperial nation-state.[79]

There is an apparent contradiction between *négritude*'s Pan-Africanist cultural nationalism and a decolonization project articulated around political integration into the French state. This antinomy is best understood when it is considered as symptomatic, even constitutive, of the contradictory nature of the French imperial nation-state. As Barnor Hesse points out, the internal tension between metropolitan enfranchisement and colonial exclusions inherent to the post-Enlightenment imperial state meant that European liberal democracies always-already contained within them the potential for the eruption of black politics of disruption.[80] Within this logic, it becomes clear that the colonial politics of the Third Republic—and the Fourth—encouraged both the rise of *négriste* militancy and its later blossoming in the cultural and political projects of *négritude*. Within a French imperial nation-state that was always-already modern and colonial, *négritude* intellectuals seized France's Republican ideals as they articulated their efforts to redefine the imperial state. Theirs was not a "derivative discourse" but rather a *détournement* (hijacking) of modernity that combined manipulating France's political rationalism, communist internationalism, and aesthetic modernism (especially surrealism)—all within a practical political program that led, for the Antilles, to the 1946 law of departmentalization.[81] In other words, departmentalization was neither a capitulation to the forces of assimilation nor a straightforward opposition to it, but rather an inevitable postcolonial (not anticolonial) overcoming of assimilationism.

Following World War II, conditions were ripe for Césaire and his allies to take the logic of assimilation to its radical conclusion and make their demand for political integration. In Continental France, the historically right-wing parties had paid a political price for their alliance with the Vichy regime, giving their opponents on the left—including the Communist Party—and the Gaullists complete control of the Assemblée nationale.[82] When, in the context of great economic difficulties, Antillean representatives—headed by Césaire and the Guadeloupean Paul Valentino—introduced a bill to the French parliament to transform the *vieilles colonies* into full-fledged *départements*, the proposal faced opposition only from the *békés*, who feared a further loss of local control. It was adopted by a unanimous vote in March 1946.

Bonilla points out Césaire's ambivalent yet cunning assessment of departmentalization: "By 1956, just ten years after departmentalization, Césaire conceded that the project of departmentalization had perhaps been naive in attempting to abolish inequality without eradicating the colonial regime itself. One could, he argued, read departmentalization as a 'ruse' on the part of the colonizer: an offer of abstract and ultimately unattainable equality meant to quell separatist sentiment. But, Césaire speculated, perhaps in the end '*la ruse de l'histoire*' would reveal the naiveté of the colonized as ruse, and the ruse of the colonizer as naiveté." In fact, the law of departmentalization (a neologism that Césaire crafted to avoid a problematic reference to assimilation) institutionalized and magnified an Antillean entangled colonial citizenship. The law was practical and tactical, both for the postwar French government and for Antillean politicians.

For metropolitan Gaullists, the full incorporation of the French Antilles into the Republic preserved the integrity of France's territory and participated in a broader effort to reconfigure the empire after a war that had weakened France's own sovereignty. It also asserted French presence in the Western Hemisphere, an especially salient issue given growing American influence in the region during the Cold War and, more directly, the United States' direct input in French economic and political matters following World War II. More important, it preserved the French Antilles as a source of cheap labor and as a protected consumer market. Indeed, Antillean immigrants, funneled through the Bureau pour le développement des migrations dans les départements d'Outre-mer (BUMIDOM), contributed significantly to the metropolitan economic growth during the Trente Glorieuses (see chapter 3). Finally, for the French state, departmentalization had the potential to mollify anticolonial demands for greater autonomy or even independence. Conversely, for socialist and communist Antillean politicians such as Césaire, the 1946 law of departmentalization not only represented a victory against the white plantocracy but, at a time when the Antillean economy was crumbling, also promised to bring greater social protection and higher wages to the islands. Finally, socialist politicians hoped that the French government—then dominated by socialist and communist forces—would move to save the ailing sugar industry by nationalizing it.[83] Departmentalization was a ruse, then, but as Césaire so pithily summarized, who tricked whom is difficult to ascertain.

In defending the proposed departmentalization legislation, Césaire appealed to French political traditions and to the legacy of the Revolution.[84] In other words, he worked within the French political structure, exposed its inconsistencies, and managed to transform it: a classic example of the poetics and politics of the *détour*. Conceptualized as a *détour*, the law of departmentalization overcomes its apparent contradictions. Rather than a politics of assimilation, it is revealed as a practical demand for "unconditional legal equality" within the French state. Tied to this demand was a radical, if utopian, effort to home the French state and redefine France as a postnational state.[85] The *détour* also helps us understand what Jean-Claude William sees as the two contradictory impulses within Antillean "desire for *reconnaissance*," or recognition: a "mimetic impulse" on the one hand and an "affirmation of difference" on the other.[86] As we will see in chapter 5, the same play of the *détour* in a push for recognition also animated the postnationalist campaign to have gwoka recognized by UNESCO as intangible cultural heritage. For now, it is important to note that Césaire's political project—to redefine the French Republic and Antilleans' position within it—is unfinished.

Departmentalization initiated a period of rapid transformation for Antillean societies, though not necessarily in the direction that Césaire and his allies had hoped. Massive investments in infrastructure and the service economy were accompanied by equally massive migration to the metropole. Even as the agricultural sector continued its decline and unemployment soared, the newly created Départements d'Outre-mer (DOM) were transformed from societies that produced raw commodities to societies that consumed imported finished goods. A new landing strip was added to the airport in Pointe-à-Pitre to allow jet planes to land; the industrial port was modernized to accommodate cargo ships and their modern containers. Glissant and many others have argued that instead of putting an end to colonialism, departmentalization has created a neocolonial society in which government subsidies are converted into private capital through mass consumption.[87] This radically transformed political and economic landscape created a new problem-space that called for radical political solutions. In his 1956 assessment of departmentalization, Césaire—who was in the process of resigning from the Parti communiste français and creating his Parti populaire martiniquais—denounced the cunning of the colonizing power who promised "abstract equality." "But," warns Césaire, "equality does not suffer to remain abstract. And what a turn when the colonized reclaims the word and demands that it does not remain solely a word."[88] Indeed, starting in the mid-1950s, assimilation and political integration gave way to resentment. And as this resentment fueled autonomist and eventually separatist aspirations, the sounds of Antillean musics were once more recontextualized, reinterpreted, and instrumentalized to serve new political projects. Drumming would be reclaimed and reinvented as the foundation of an anticolonial aurality.

TWO

Building an Anticolonial Aurality:
Gwoka modènn as Counterpoetics

Real revolutionary music is not that which describes the revolution but that which speaks of it as a lack.

–Jacques Attali

It isn't enough to agree on the slogan; we also have to agree on the feeling.

–Gérard Lockel[1]

In July 2017, I participated in a weeklong workshop organized to introduce musicians to *gwoka modènn*, the revolutionary musical genre created by guitarist Gérard Lockel in the late 1960s. The workshop was in itself an event. A gifted musician as well as a staunch ideologist, Lockel is a legend in Guadeloupe, especially among gwoka and nationalist circles. His music is likewise respected, even if it is actually poorly known: most of his recordings are out of print, and those that remain are available only at special events or through a small network of people that the guitarist has entrusted to distribute them. Lockel had stopped performing a few years earlier, but I was lucky enough to have heard him in July 2008. Already then he played only once a year, at his home in Baie-Mahault, which he had originally intended as a *foyer de resistance culturelle*, a center of cultural resistance. That night in 2008, as the city celebrated its *fête patronale*, Lockel had performed with his regular group, some of the only musicians who have truly grasped his musical language: two of his sons—Franck on piano and Jean-Marie on traps—along with a *boula* player whose name escaped me at the time. Even if every musician I had already spoken with had stressed Lockel's historical and ideological import, this was my first opportunity to hear his music. It struck me as particularly abstract: although Lockel's improvisations were anchored in the familiar patterns of the *boula*, they—and those of his pianist—were angular, virtuosic, and lengthy. The piano was perhaps the most impressive: the left hand didn't support the right with chords but rather both hands wove a complex, chopped counterpoint. On guitar, Lockel's melodic lines defeated easy analysis: they sounded "free" to my ears, yet they also seemed to follow a system. I could not grasp that system aurally: it had a pentatonic flavor but it never rested on any easily identifiable scale. Rather, it seemed to move from one pentatonic array to another. This was not a musical language I was familiar with: even though it privileged virtuosic improvisation, it lacked the harmonic framework typical of modern jazz. It seemed to share an attitude and overall aesthetics with the avant-garde jazz I had grown up with. Upon first hearing *gwoka modènn*, one thing was clear: this was music that was both technically and intellectually demanding. That night years ago, the small audience of only nine people listened reverently, participating in what I had been told had become a yearly patriotic pilgrimage. Today, Lockel lives more or less isolated, surrounded by close friends, family, and a few devoted supporters. While many Guadeloupean musicians have struggled to learn Lockel's music on their own, the guitarist himself has had few students, handpicked for their allegiance to the struggle for national liberation as much as their commitment to musical excellence. Nonetheless, his place of honor among the pantheon of Guadeloupean musicians and political activists is ensured.

The 2017 workshop, then, was a historical event. This was the first time since Lockel had come back to Guadeloupe to introduce *gwoka modènn* in 1969 that any Guadeloupean musician—regardless of musical abilities or political conviction—had a chance to crack the codes of this most demanding and patriotic music. Of course, Lockel did not teach that week. Instead, the percussionist Jean-Pierre Phipps and the guitarist Christian Laviso introduced a group of about twenty students to Lockel's compositions and musical vision. Phipps—who is also a renowned *makè* in the traditional style—played in one of Lockel's groups in the 1980s. Laviso, for his part, is himself a virtuosic guitarist with an international career, and he has emerged—alongside Franck Lockel—as heir to Lockel's music.

For a week, the workshop participants gathered in the Foyer Culturel Gérard Lockel in Baie-Mahault and dedicated themselves to learning the practice of *gwoka modènn*. We formed a heterogeneous bunch, men and women, some students still in high school, others already enjoying retirement. Some of us were experienced musicians: besides myself, there were former members of the group Horizon who, since the 1990s, have been developing their own version of *gwoka modènn*. But many were amateurs and beginners who brought their drums, guitars, saxophones, trumpets, and traditional wooden flutes in the hopes of connecting with their musical heritage. Some, such as a teenage pianist living in Bordeaux, were already well versed in Lockel's music; others had only a passing acquaintance with it. Regardless of proficiency, we all practiced for about four hours each day, pushing ourselves to learn a new musical language and to gain the technical proficiency needed to perform this music.

On the first day, for a bit over an hour, we listened to Phipps and Laviso sketch the context in which *gwoka modènn* emerged, from Lockel's beginning as a guitar player in Guadeloupe to his successful career in Paris and his return to the Caribbean to make a revolutionary musical contribution to the then-nascent separatist movement. We were told that, while in Paris, Lockel met and played with many musicians from Africa and its diaspora. These encounters led him to seek to define Guadeloupe's musical essence. The answer took form as *gwoka modènn*, a musical system that, according to Laviso and Phipps, captures all of Guadeloupe's traditional auralities—the singing during *swaré léwòz* and wakes, work songs, the cries of street vendors— and adapts them for instrumental performances. Lockel has insisted that all these practices share a common scale, which he calls the gwoka scale. The scale is a nine-note subset of a longer cycle of alternating major seconds and minor thirds. The goal of the workshop, then, was to familiarize ourselves with this scale and to master a method of improvisation in which the gwoka scale and its transpositions force musicians to operate within a system that Lockel describes as "atonal modal."

The challenge was rather daunting. For one, singers struggled to sing the basic scale, which exceeded their normal range. What were they to do? I had already studied the scale out of Lockel's 1981 *Traité de gro ka modên*—an imposing method book and musical manifesto—and understood that one of its key characteristics was that it denied the octave equivalence. I was therefore surprised when Laviso instructed singers to drop the last two or three notes of the scale down an octave. I questioned Laviso: wouldn't this undermine the logic of the scale? A flautist who also had some familiarity with *gwoka modènn* seemed equally puzzled. In response, Laviso urged us to listen and assured us that the spirit of the scale was preserved this way. I think I understood what he meant: regardless of the octave at which they are played, the last notes of the scale destabilize any perceived tonal center. To confirm, at the end of the session, I asked the guitarist if he knew why Lockel had chosen to stop his gwoka scale after nine notes rather than shorten or extend the cycle. He acknowledged, somewhat mockingly, that he had read and heard many explanations for this, many analyses, and they all got it wrong. (I couldn't help but think that his derision was at least partially aimed at my own analysis, which I had published on my blog a couple of years earlier). The reason, he affirmed, was quite simple: if you play the scale, if you listen to it, you realize that the ninth note gives the feeling of moving outside a tonal center: a set of nine notes is the minimum requirement to create a sense of "atonal modality." Although I hear the effect, I have struggled to understand it. The ninth scale degree effectively creates an interval of a minor ninth with the fourth scale degree (A-flat/G, if starting the scale on C); but the introduction of the seventh scale degree, which creates a minor ninth with the second (E-flat/D), triggers the same effect. Perhaps reading my skepticism, Laviso told me something that he would repeat several times during the week: to understand *gwoka modènn*, "you must abandon all of your tools; you must cast them aside."

With this advice, a key feature of *gwoka modènn* was revealed: more than a strictly musical endeavor, it is an epistemological project. This is music designed to challenge you to think about music differently, to abandon already well-entrenched musical reflexes. This was confirmed when, following my first attempt at soloing on one of Lockel's compositions, Laviso praised me for dancing while I played but critiqued me for falling back on my post-bop jazz idiom. The challenge, for me and other participants, became reinventing our musical vocabulary by limiting ourselves to using the gwoka scale and developing a rhythmic language adapted to each of the *boula* of so-called traditional gwoka, while still finding ways to express ourselves freely. By the end of the week, even as I had successfully controlled my urges to stray from Lockel's harmonic language, Laviso continued to describe my improvisations as *twa maré* (too anchored, too constricted). Fluency and freedom continued to evade me.

But perhaps I was never meant to truly get it. Olivier Vamur, now an accomplished *modènn* flautist, had shared with me several years earlier that he practiced exercises from Lockel's book for years before a friend who played with Lockel finally let him know that he was practicing the exercises incorrectly. Commenting on his contacts with Lockel, Vamur declared: "No musical information filtered through. . . . That is to say, everything that Lockel did was secret, or like a secret, you know."[2] Throughout the week-long workshop, there was a sense that *gwoka modènn* was indeed designed to remain somewhat esoteric. When Laviso circulated exercises copied from Lockel's method book, many musicians stared with puzzlement at the unusual system of notation. Even after the guitarist had explained how to read the numbered grid, some took to "translating" the exercises using Western staff notation. And at the end of the workshop, once we had played our

Building an Anticolonial Aurality / 63

final concert, one of the participants looked at me and said, with a sly smile on his face: "Perhaps it's no wonder that almost no one plays this stuff. It's way too difficult." In this chapter, I try to make sense of *gwoka modènn*, the soundtrack to a yet-unfulfilled revolution. I tease out the links between its politics and its aesthetics and explore the tension between its democratic ideals and its opacity.

Rèpriz. "Because of its creation, gwoka has always been political." This is perhaps most true if we consider that gwoka was "invented" in the late 1960s.[3] Indeed, the creation of *gwoka modènn* cannot be separated from the rise of separatist activism in Guadeloupe. As I detail in this chapter, *gwoka modènn* was part of a revolutionary effort to reinvent Guadeloupean culture and remake its society. Fueled by disenchantment with the 1946 law of departmentalization and its unfulfilled promises of greater social protection and economic parity between the metropole and its overseas territories, separatist activists fought for a complete break with France, working actively to define what they themselves called a "new culture" free of the influence of colonialism and capitalism.

This chapter explores the role that music played in the construction of an anticolonial aurality. Sooner than re-rehearse tales of invented traditions, I critically engage the perspective of those actors who shaped anticolonialist campaigns post-departmentalization. Which ideological forces and material conditions defined the problem-space within which gwoka emerged as a central anticolonial sound? What political future did anticolonial activists imagine? How did Gérard Lockel's music help define, express, and disseminate this political vision? I propose that, for separatist activists, gwoka—whether traditional or modern—was more than a sonic symbol of the nation or a musical rallying point. Rather, the music, along with the Creole language, participated in an anticolonial aurality from which a "new culture"—that is to say, radically modern and liberated ways of thinking and being—could emerge. Animated by a *pulsion de retour* (reversion drive) to a romanticized subjectivity freed from colonialist influences, the sounds and ethics of gwoka were supposed to help Guadeloupeans "think and act as Guadeloupeans," as the nationalist saying went.

In many ways, *gwoka modènn* illustrates what Thomas Turino has identified as a process of "modernist reformism" characteristic of anticolonial nationalisms.[4] Yet I address the situation differently here. Rather than consider colonized and colonizers as two opposing entities caught in a struggle for independence, a narrative that does not fit the French Antillean situation, I take a relational approach that endeavors to move beyond the rhetoric of anticolonial nationalism. Thinking relationally reveals that French coloniality always-already included the conditions and tools that allowed for anticolonialism to flourish, as our analysis of departmentalization has already illustrated. Conversely, enduring French republican entanglements have made it impossible for Guadeloupean anticolonialism to blossom into outright independence. Thus, I am less interested in what the Guadeloupean struggle for national liberation tells us about anticolonial nationalism than in what it says about French coloniality. I propose that *gwoka modènn* illustrates what Édouard Glissant calls "forced," "constrained," or "counterpoetics," symptoms of a persistent desire for emancipated language that is faced with a *manque*—lack or absence—that renders impossible the emergence of a collective expression.[5]

A New Problem-Space

Postdepartmental Disenchantment

It would be hard to overstate the speed and depth of the social and economic changes in the newly integrated French *départements d'Outre mer* (DOM, overseas departments). Far from bringing social and economic parity between the DOMs and the metropole, the 1946 law had the unintended consequence of reaffirming the uneven relationship between core and periphery. Many of the decisions that had been made locally by colonial authorities were now subjected to direct rule from Paris, resulting in a loss of local power. In addition, against Antillean hopes, the French state never moved to nationalize the sugar industry, which continued its steady decline to near annihilation by the mid-1970s. Even with unemployment rising to nearly 25 percent by the early 1960s, an influx of subsidies from France—and later the European Union—artificially maintained economic growth while also accentuating dependency.[6] Meanwhile, the new institutional status meant that the metropolitan standard of living became the norm in the DOMs, generating new expectations for better social protection, higher wages, and greater access to material goods. As consumer goods flooded Martinique and Guadeloupe, local and national governments encouraged consumption as a way to generate revenue through tariffs and sales tax. In short, since 1946, economic development policies that have prioritized the service sector over agricultural or industrial production have transformed the DOMs into societies of consumption. By the 1960s, the Antilles were entering a new neocolonial regime in which they became protected markets as well as a source of affordable labor for the French state.[7]

Even as the rural colonial culture of Guadeloupe vanished, to be replaced by new urban lifestyles, the abuses of cultural assimilation could still be felt.[8] In fact, in spite of Césaire's effort to distance departmentalization from assimilation, following the 1946 law, the domination of French culture in the Antilles only intensified. During the late-colonial period, a rigid socio-racial order had maintained strong barriers between the proletarian Creole-speaking and elite Francophone spheres, effectively preserving Creole culture from further infiltration from French influence. Between the 1960s and the 1980s, these barriers broke down when the collapse of the agricultural sector cut off Creole practices—such as the Creole language and drumming traditions—from the economic structures that had nourished them. Meanwhile, the disparagement of vernacular cultural practices that had started during the Third Republic perdured well into the second half of the twentieth century. For example, choreographer Max Diakok, who was born in the 1960s, recalls how his father, a school principal affiliated with the Communist Party, forced his children to address him and his wife in French even though he himself would talk to them in Creole.[9] Likewise, many of my interlocutors reported that their parents discouraged them from attending gwoka performances in the 1950s and 1960s.

Postwar Guadeloupean nationalist activists—many of them issued from the bourgeoisie—worked in a context, then, in which rural dances were not only stigmatized but also disappearing, victims of the new socioeconomic imperial entanglements. Folkloric troupes who danced for tourists—such as Man Adeline's La Briscante in Pointe-à-Pitre—offered some of the most easily accessible gwoka performances, albeit tainted by more than a whiff of *doudouisme*.[10] At the same time, the *koud tanbou* of the faubourgs and the rural *swaré léwòz* remained off limits for many with middle-class aspirations. Likewise, the Creole language was increasingly subjected to a "kind of infiltration by the structures and vocabulary of standard French."[11] These conditions made it difficult for the militants of nationalist organizations— like the Guadeloupean population at large—to develop a common attitude toward Creole culture that would be unmediated by dominant French culture and values. More so than during the late Republican colonial period, the conditions were ripe for the emergence of forced poetics.

Two other factors contributed to the disenchantment with departmentalization and thus helped define a new, increasingly volatile, problem-space. First, migration to the French metropole exploded in the decade following departmentalization, further interweaving French and Antillean societies. This situation was the product of deliberate political choices. In 1963, at the onset of the Fifth Republic and as the collapse of the sugar industry accelerated, the French government inaugurated the Bureau pour le développement des migrations dans les départements d'Outre-mer (BUMIDOM) under the pretense of combatting the recent demographic boom and high unemployment in the Antilles.[12] BUMIDOM was designed to facilitate the migration of five thousand Antilleans a year to fill low-paying positions in the metropole, primarily in the service industry, a tremendous contribution to the economic growth of the Trente Glorieuses. We further explore the effects of this policy in the following chapter. For now, let's note that this outbound migration was accompanied by the massive relocation of metropolitan French government workers to the DOMs. This influx of *métros*—as Antilleans call metropolitan immigrant workers—prompted Aimé Césaire to speak of a threat of "genocide by substitution" in the late 1970s.[13] These transatlantic migratory movements and labor patterns fueled tensions between *métros* and the local populations in Guadeloupe and Martinique, especially as relocated government workers benefited from a bonus intended to compensate the high cost of living on the islands and to encourage consumption. This bonus effectively reinscribed colonial stratifications between European and indigenous workers.[14] Resentment increasingly led to violent, racially charged confrontations, as happened in Fort-de-France, Martinique, in December 1959.[15]

Second, if departmentalization brought a rapid modernization of the Antilles, it did little to ease the economic woes of Antillean populations. In fact, it contributed much to a growing discontent with the French state. As the economy transformed, leaving many facing a difficult future, strikes and demonstrations multiplied. These strikes were sometimes violently repressed. In Guadeloupe, in February 1952, the French Compagnie républicaine de sécurité (CRS, a branch of the national police specializing in crowd and riot control) killed four protesters from the Gardel sugar factory. By the 1960s, growing economic uncertainty, neocolonial social stratification, and violent repression all made it increasingly difficult to consider the French state as benevolent. If political integration had not resolved Guadeloupe's colonial problems, new solutions were yet to be found.

The Rise of Separatist Activism

A new generation of Guadeloupean students in metropolitan France analyzed the post-departmentalization problem-space to propose new radical solutions. Until a full-fledged university campus was created in the Antilles in 1982, Guadeloupeans who wanted to pursue a college education did so in metropolitan France.[16] In 1928, these students established the Association générale des étudiants guadeloupéens (AGEG) with the goal of facilitating the transition to life in continental France. Originally limited to the French capital, the AGEG spread to every university town in 1958, with Bordeaux quickly emerging as one of the largest and most politically active section.

The late 1950s also saw the AGEG expand its mission beyond its initial social function. As the Algerian War raged and Non-Aligned nations gathered in Bandung, Guadeloupean students in Paris engaged in political discussions with students who came from other parts of the French Empire, especially Africa and Southeast Asia. With its anticolonial commitment spurred by these exchanges, the AGEG organized a seminar in 1956 to formally challenge assimilation policies.[17] When I met the nationalist leader Louis Théodore—or Camarade Jean, a pseudonym taken later on, while in *marronnage* from the French authorities—who was part of this movement, he explained: "There was a growing awareness amongst Guadeloupean students that assimilation . . . was not a system that could solve the problems that faced us. Because, not only were there economic problems but there were also social problems, there was an identity problem, there was a cultural problem. [During the 1956 meeting in Paris,] they came to radically question the entire system, on all levels: on the economic level, on the social level, etcetera. But most of all, they questioned the system as oppressive on the cultural and identity level."[18] Four years after this initial seminar, in August 1960, the AGEG officially took a position against assimilation with a formal declaration during the Conférence de la jeunesse guadeloupéenne in Pointe-à-Pitre.[19]

The AGEG's politics were rooted in Marxism; nonetheless, the organization had a complicated relationship with existing communist organizations. By the late 1950s, many in the DOMs resented the French communist party's apparent lack of understanding of the specificity of the colonial situation.[20] Eventually this discontent led Aimé Césaire to leave the Parti communiste français, or PCF, to launch the Parti progressiste martiniquais in 1958. The communist parties of both Martinique and Guadeloupe also broke from the PCF that year. The students of the AGEG—many of whom had ties to the communist party at home—followed suit without rejecting communism altogether. To the contrary, even as a rift grew between them and those whom Théodore called "orthodox communists," the AGEG formed strong ties with two international communist student organizations: the Union internationale des étudiants and the Fédération mondiale de la jeunesse démocratique.

In addition to its transnational communist connections, the AGEG's emerging political consciousness was also shaped by current anticolonial struggles. As many students faced being drafted to fight in Algeria, the AGEG

68 / Chapter Two

accentuated its support for the Algerian Front de libération nationale (FLN). Guadeloupean students read Fanon and, perhaps inspired by his engagement, some of them organized in support of the Algerian cause.[21] The stakes extended beyond North Africa. Not only did Algeria become an important model for Guadeloupean anticolonialist militants but, having been a French department since the Third Republic, its independence became—in the words of cultural activist and former AGEG member Félix Cotellon—highly "symbolic." Indeed, an Algeria that could disentangle itself from the French empire undermined the jacobinical principle that held the republic to be indivisible and thus offered a precedent to push for statutory change in Guadeloupe.[22]

Located at the center of the fraying French imperial nation-state at a historical moment defined by the Cold War, the Cuban Revolution, growing tensions between the Soviet Union and China, and the emergence of the Non-Aligned Movement, the AGEG was able to frame its emergent political platform informed by the transnational circulation of communist and anticolonialist ideologies and strategies. Students who chose to join in the organization's political activism received a rigorous ideological training, studying Marx, Lenin, Stalin, and Mao under what some have described to me as a stringent disciplinary regime. By the mid-1960s, as anticolonial movements were dismantling the French Empire in Africa and Asia, AGEG members moved to implement their own anticolonial strategies in Guadeloupe.

By 1963, the AGEG had further radicalized its position and started advocating for complete independence from France. The AGEG was then emerging as the central training ground of the Guadeloupean anticolonial movement. Having completed their studies in France, some of the group's former members moved on to lead other anticolonialist organizations back on the island. Several joined the Groupe d'organisation nationale de Guadeloupe (GONG), a then recently created separatist organization.[23] GONG was not the first such organization to emerge from the French overseas departments: the Front antillo-guyanais pour l'autonomie (FAGA)—of which Glissant was one of the founding members—may have provided a model.[24] Regardless, ties between GONG and the AGEG were particularly strong. "GONG was born out of the AGEG," explained Théodore who, having presided over the politicization of the AGEG in the mid-1950s, was one of the group's original members. "Anyway, we shouldn't fool ourselves. That is to say, GONG comprised three groups: intellectuals trained within the AGEG; young people who had links with the Algerian War, veterans; and the third, very important group, were workers issued from the migration [to

France]."[25] By the mid-1960s, the leadership of the *camp patriotique*—as the ensemble of pro-independence organizations would come to be called—was shifting from Bordeaux and Paris back to Guadeloupe.

In Guadeloupe, these militants found a deteriorating social climate. As the 1959 incident in Martinique had already illustrated, tensions ran high between *métros* and the local population. In March 1967, in Basse-Terre, a confrontation between a white shoe-store owner with close ties to the *béké* community (descendants of the white plantocracy) and a black cobbler exploded into outright rioting. By the next day, protesters started to target white residents, especially the *métro*. These events, like those in Fort-de-France, highlight the racial dimension of social struggles in the DOMs at the time. They also illustrate a shift, such that the anger that had historically been directed as the *békés* was redirected toward white residents of metropolitan origins.[26]

The real flash point came a few months later. In May 1967, in a context marked by both decolonization and the Cold War, by the independence of Algeria and the Cuban Revolution, Guadeloupean construction workers went on strike to demand higher pay. On May 26, a large group of protesters gathered in front the Chamber of Commerce in Pointe-à-Pitre, where they faced a contingent of French police newly arrived from the metropole via Martinique. According to sources, some of the protesters may have thrown stones at the police, who responded by opening fire on the crowd, officially killing seven people, a number that has since been widely contested.[27] Several days of rioting ensued as students from the Baimbridge high school joined protesters on the streets of Pointe-à-Pitre.[28] French authorities used the event to strike against GONG. They deliberately targeted Jacques Nestor, one of GONG's founding members, who was shot by a sniper, the first person to die that day. Once the riots ended, the French government prosecuted most of GONG's known leaders for crimes against the integrity of the territory, charges that were later overturned in court. Nonetheless, on June 13, 1967, *France-Antilles*—a newspaper created at the instigation of Charles de Gaulle with the specific intent of drowning out autonomist and separatist voices in the DOMs—announced triumphantly, "GONG has been beheaded."[29] Those left within the organization were divided. A small group resigned and rallied around Camarade Jean, who had gone into hiding to avoid arrest. May 1967 marked a turning point in anticolonial activism. The French government's response to these events, both in its physical and its structural violence, helped further radicalized the Guadeloupean youths. Some members of the AGEG who had shied away from political activism promptly joined the anticolonialist cause. The breakup of GONG eventually spurred the creation of new labor organizations, expanding the reach of separatist ideology through various segments of the Guadeloupean population.

From 1967 to 1970, the *démissionnaires du GONG* (GONG resigners)—as the group who had rallied around Camarade Jean called itself—engaged in a period of reflection and came to the conclusion that Guadeloupe's lack of a sizable industrial proletariat made it better suited to a "democratic and popular national revolution" on a Maoist rather than a Soviet model. Following the example of black socialist organizers of the late nineteenth century, such as Hégésippe Légitimus, and capitalizing on the unremitting crisis of the sugar industry, the militants tied their political demand for independence to social activism rooted in the experience of agricultural workers. They focused their activities on the area around Sainte-Rose and Lamentin in the north of Basse-Terre, where they engaged the local rural community, listening to workers' concerns and slowly promoting an anticolonialist social and political agenda.[30]

There were several reasons why the GONG resigners chose to start their organizing work in northern Basse-Terre. The area around Sainte-Rose was an important center of sugarcane production but also housed a few sugar factories. Louis Théodore explained that this provided the militants with an opportunity to study the relationship between the main segments of Guadeloupean society: agricultural and factory workers on the one hand, and landowners and industrial companies based in France on the other. He further insisted that the Creole culture was still vibrant in the community.[31] This gave the largely middle-class anticolonialist militants a chance to (re)discover aspects of Guadeloupean rural culture that they had had few opportunities to experience firsthand.

As did their nineteenth-century predecessors, these militants embraced rural expressive culture—especially language and music—as the basis for the construction of an anticolonial aurality. The word *anticolonial* here emphasizes that this was not simply a matter of "nationalizing" proletarian culture. In fact, Cotellon pointed to anticolonialism as an umbrella term, a broad-range aspiration under which different movements with different strategies—and potentially different political outcomes—could be unified.[32] Although affirming Guadeloupean cultural specificity quickly became a central argument in justifying the need for an independent nation-state, and although, as we will see in a moment, music played a central role in this endeavor, embracing the oral and musical universe of agricultural workers was also strategic. More than simply providing symbols around which "cultural intimacy" could develop, the Creole language, the moral messages of Creole tales, and the codes of the *swaré léwòz* formed an oral constellation that remained relatively opaque—that is to say, inaccessible to the French and to those whose class aspirations of upward mobility had pushed in the direction of assimilation.[33] Moreover, the oral culture of the agricultural proletariat offered powerful tools to recruit and organize workers. In Sainte-Rose, militants were able to recruit well-respected gwoka musicians, such as the percussionist Kristen Aigle, to their cause. Gwoka became a medium of choice to disseminate the new anticolonial message.

Since the end of World War II, Guadeloupean unions had been branches of French organizations and strictly conducted their business in French, even if many of their members had a limited command of that language. In 1970, the GONG resigners exploited the strategic advantage that their knowledge of Creole provided them and launched the Union des travailleurs agricoles (UTA), the first union organized from Guadeloupe and the first to conduct meetings in the Guadeloupean vernacular. This initial organizing effort proved successful, and several similar unions soon emerged, such as the Union des paysans pauvres de Guadeloupe (UPG, or Union des paysans pauvres de la Guadeloupe) in 1972 and the Union générale des travailleurs guadeloupéens (UGTG) in 1973. Today, the UGTG has become the biggest and most influential union in Guadeloupe.[34]

Traditional musical forms were still very much alive among rural communities in northern Basse-Terre, where people enjoyed listening to *biguine* as well as attending *balakadri* (quadrille balls) or *swaré léwòz*, gatherings that took place on Friday or Saturday nights when agricultural workers—having just received their biweekly pay—sang, danced, and socialized to the sound of the drum. In spite of the popularity of this range of Creole musics, anticolonialist militants chose to reject quadrille and developed a discourse that glorified gwoka as the only true form of national music. Why this focus on gwoka? If the answers to this question lay partially with the fortuitous encounter of specific individuals, they nonetheless highlight that the construction of an anticolonial aurality not only responded to strategic needs—as with the foregrounding of Creole in labor organizing—but also involved ideological debates and selections.

A New Culture: Constructing an Anticolonial Aurality

In 1970, after the AGEG's ninth congress, a group of students met in the South of France to outline the association's cultural platform. The resulting *Rapport culturel* offers great insight into the AGEG's project for cultural and political decolonization. Through discussions of what constitutes Guadeloupean culture and what should be excluded from it, the members of the

AGEG imagined a blueprint for an independent Guadeloupean nation and, by extension, an emancipated Guadeloupean subject.

The report is, on the surface, a classic illustration of cultural nationalism, but with a communist twist. Having embraced Stalin's definition of the nation, the report moves on to a Marxist analysis that understands culture as a "social phenomenon" emanating from the economic base—that is to say, as dependent on the means of production—and considers the dominant class's control of "cultural instruments" as central to its hegemony.[35] In a colonial situation such as Guadeloupe's, the report concludes, "culture" has been co-opted by the bourgeoisie to become an instrument of assimilation. In reaction, the AGEG argues for the creation of a "communal culture in the service of all" and, in typical communist fashion, insists that this "new culture" be simultaneously "national, popular, and scientific."

The report was the result of a fairly recent recognition that the militants of the AGEG themselves had been cut off from what they considered Guadeloupe's roots: the rural communities who were perceived as the repositories of a folk culture untainted by French imperialism. In response to this, and following the injunction of older activists such as Théodore, members of the AGEG began conducting what they called *enquêtes de terrain* (fieldwork) in an effort to capture the essential character of the nation. The new culture was to be "national," then, because it was understood as "preserving and enriching the Guadeloupean cultural heritage." Moreover, as an anticolonialist weapon, a new national culture would "praise national virtues of Guadeloupe" and be used to educate the masses, spread revolutionary ideas, and mobilize the population. It is important to note that the new culture was not simply meant to provide new means of indexing the nation, such as a national language and music; it was also intended to contribute to recruiting, organizing, and educating new anticolonialist activists. It follows that the new culture had to be "popular" because artists were called on to serve the masses and create new works based on their lives and experiences. Nonetheless, the Maoist model that the AGEG followed maintained a critical distance from popular culture. As Roland Anduse—who served as president of the AGEG's section in Bordeaux and was a coauthor of the report—explained to me, "Every just idea comes from the people but not all popular ideas are just."[36] For this reason, the new culture ought to be "scientific." Artists were called on to critically study popular culture in order to identify those expressions that would best serve the revolution. Among other things, they were instructed to criticize reactionary popular expressions and combat popular beliefs and superstitions.[37] In its program of moral regeneration, the AGEG proposed studying the oral culture of Guadeloupe's rural communities, but to reform its practices so that they could be used to both modernize the uneducated masses and decolonize the educated elites.

The AGEG's cultural nationalist project should be understood not solely as an effort to foster a national sentiment among Guadeloupe's population but rather as part of an overall strategic response to a specific political and economic situation. At the local level, this problem-space was defined by the collapse of the agricultural economy, the rise of a consumerist economy in its place, rampant unemployment, and a weakening of local political control—all associated with the long-term cultural and psychological effects of assimilation. But this problem-space, as a historically specific discursive field, was also defined by the transnational circulation of political ideologies, including Marxism and communism in both its Leninist and Maoist incarnations, and in a dialectic with French republicanism. Indeed, the report selectively drew from both the discourse of international communism and Guadeloupean rural expressive culture to combat the effects of assimilation throughout Guadeloupe's stratified society and thus undermine the power of the local bourgeoisie. Expressive culture, then, was mobilized to disseminate anti-imperialist ideas and to assist in organizing the local proletariat into new unions, such as the UTA or UGTG, and eventually into new separatist parties—all of this in the service of an eventual popular revolution. In short, cultural nationalism in Guadeloupe was an essential component of a Marxist praxis: a campaign to change the political and social order.

My interviews with Guadeloupean separatist activists make evident how clearly they understood the synergy of expressive culture, economy, and political status. Their efforts to revitalize certain expressive practices were intended to fuel national consciousness as well as social movements that, together, would lead to a transformation of the economy and, eventually, to separatist demands. In turn, a liberated Guadeloupe in control of its own economy—free to develop its agriculture and industry—could help sustain the cultural expressions of a new, and truly, postcolonial people. In the separatist newspaper *Ja Ka Ta*, the UPLG reprised the language of the AGEG and perfectly summarized the situation as it laid out its cultural program: "To build a national, popular, and scientific culture in the service of a revolutionary transformation of the social relations on political, ideological, and economic grounds."[38] These three facets—culture, economy, and politics— taken together formed the basis on which an anticolonial way of being could emerge, a base that would let Guadeloupean "become what they are," as the anthropologist and nationalist supporter Dany Bebel-Gislert wrote, finally liberated from the cultural shadow cast by French imperialism.[39] At least, that was the idea. As we will see, this ideal was never fully realized.

In some ways, the AGEG's program of modernist reformism offers an anticolonial take on John Hutchinson's analysis of cultural nationalism as "moral regeneration." Like the Gaelic revival movement described by Hutchinson, the AGEG's project focused on reconnecting Guadeloupeans with "the essence of the nation," perceived as the "product of its unique history and geographical profile."[40] And like Irish cultural nationalists, Guadeloupean anticolonial activists moved to "reunite the different aspects of the nation—traditional and modern, agriculture and industry, science and religion—by returning to the creation life-principles of the nation."[41] In fact, and contrary to the often repeated assumption that Caribbean nationalisms necessarily embrace the inherent creolization of their societies, the report seems to be driven by atavistic longings or, to borrow from Glissant, by a *pulsion de retour* (return or reversion path) to an idealized Guadeloupean culture free of imperialist corruptions.[42] Caught in a Stalinist nationalist logic, Guadeloupean activists did not embrace the intrinsic hybridity of Caribbean culture. As such, they rejected the quadrille as a French imposition and regarded the biguine with great suspicion. Rather, they sought a self-referential authenticity embodied in the *nèg mawon* (Maroon slave), who, through escaping from the plantation, had shielded himself from the cultural influence of European imperialism and the logic of capitalism.[43]

The figure of the *nèg mawon* points to the complicated racial politics of Guadeloupean anticolonialism. Indeed, we should not read the Maroon slave solely as a racial symbol. In fact, the AGEG's report interprets black chattel slavery as an extreme manifestation of capitalist exploitation. By downplaying his race, then, the AGEG recasts the *nèg mawon* as a sort of proletarian hero who, by resisting colonial oppression, resists capitalist exploitation. This conflicted symbolic embrace of the maroon illustrates the tension between race and class solidarity within the Marxist-oriented anticolonial movement of both Martinique and Guadeloupe. In Martinique, Aimé Césaire's *négritude*—an ideology based on diasporic unity—directly challenged the communist party's class solidarity. However, Césaire never had the same kind of influence in Guadeloupe as in Martinique. In contrast, in Guadeloupe, the Parti communiste guadeloupéen, or PCG, and the unions associated with it functioned on the premise of class solidarity between Guadeloupean and metropolitan workers. The AGEG, then, found itself in the difficult situation of seeking to distance itself from both Césaire's *négritude* and the PCG without straying too far from the communist discourse of class struggle. Therefore, as it proposed a blueprint for cultural and moral regeneration, the 1970 cultural report promoted a class-based national revolution and even criticized *négritude* for privileging racial over class solidarity. Yet because the AGEG's report all but ignores the cultural contributions of indentured laborers (be they French in the early seventeenth century or Indian in the nineteenth century) and focuses instead on African slave labor, its analysis of Guadeloupean culture tacitly privileges Afro-Creole elements.[44]

In their fieldwork, Guadeloupean nationalist activists sought the weapons to combat assimilation by listening to the oral culture of the rural proletariat, and because most agricultural and factory workers were illiterate, aurality became the privilege mean for anticolonial action. As it moved to define an anticolonial aurality, the AGEG focused its ears on oral and musical elements that, on the one hand, could be construed as entirely Guadeloupean—that is to say, untouched by cultural assimilation, primordial rather than creolized—and, on the other hand, rooted in the experience of the proletariat, going back to enslaved workers and those who resisted the colonial plantation's system of exploitation. These elements included the Creole language, folktales, the games and songs of wakes, and some—but not all—Guadeloupean folk music. Indeed, the AGEG concluded that only one music fit these descriptions and could allow for the unification of the Guadeloupean population behind a common politico-economic project: gwoka.

The focus on gwoka was an odd choice. As Anduse confessed, few members of the AGEG knew much about Guadeloupean drumming.[45] An assimilationist logic of propriety had kept many of these middle-class intellectuals away from the quarters of agricultural workers or the working-class *faubourgs* where the music could still be heard in the mid-twentieth century. By the 1970s, gwoka was also no longer a truly popular music. It survived, in various forms, alongside quadrille mostly in rural communities, but it did not have the wide appeal of biguine or the widely popular and pan-Caribbean sounds of Cuban *son*, Haitian *konpa*, and, later, Dominican *cadence-lypso*.

The choice of gwoka was strategic, then, if not entirely affective. Although it shares many aesthetics with other Afro-diasporic musical traditions—such as Martinican *bèlè* and Puerto Rican *bomba*—the drumming tradition of Guadeloupe has developed a particular set of performance principles that distinguish it from its cousins. In addition to its (relative) local specificity, gwoka's history, specifically its roots in slavery, enabled separatist activists to paint it as a music of resistance, regardless of the complex position of drumming within colonial auralities. Indeed, the AGEG's report specifically links gwoka to the *nèg mawon*. In its anticolonial nationalist logic, the AGEG praised gwoka as the "purest" and "most original" musical form in Guadeloupe: of African origin, it had resisted French imperialism and flourished among the island's rural proletarian populations.[46] For Théodore, gwoka was "a music in itself," meaning that—unlike biguine, whose audible hybridity and often exoticist lyrics made it ideologically suspicious—gwoka could sound unspoiled by outside influences. Rather than a product of creolization, gwoka was understood as having preserved its melodic and rhythmic integrity. It offered a connection to an imagined past, untouched by assimilation: a musical path of return or reversion.

To prove the music's anticolonial specificity, the AGEG insisted that gwoka had escaped the corrupting influence of tonality. Its members wrote that the vernacular music "did not follow the laws of European forms composed from a succession of 8 notes: C-D-E-F-G-A-B-C. It is atonal music, that is to say that it does not have a tonal center of gravity."[47] My analyses of gwoka melodies—generally constructed from a range of scales, including pentatonic and natural minor scales, and generally evidencing some sort of "center of gravity"—suggest that this conclusion reflects the impact of anticolonial ideology on the ways activists listened to and interpreted gwoka performances, with their occasional idiosyncratic microtonal intervals.[48] Who, then, helped shape the students' listening of this music?

Gérard Lockel and *Gwoka modènn*

Before they met to work on the cultural report, Théodore organized a meeting to introduce members of the AGEG to Gérard Lockel.[49] Lockel grew up in Northern Grande-Terre, where his father worked as a supervisor on a sugarcane estate. Having dropped out of school, Lockel became a musician then followed many other Guadeloupeans to France in the 1950s. There, he had a successful career as a jazz guitarist before moving back to Guadeloupe in 1969. While in Paris, Lockel connected with members of GONG and, upon his return to Guadeloupe, got in touch with Théodore and other activists. He also quickly gathered around him some of the island's best musicians and started to work on a new musical concept that he had developed in Paris, which he called *gwoka modènn*, or modern gwoka.[50] Based on the premise of interpreting the melodies, rhythms, and *santiman* (feeling) of gwoka on melodic instruments, *gwoka modènn* mixed long improvisations with the rhythmic foundation of traditional gwoka. All evidence indicates that Lockel was, and to some extent continues to be, a major influence on Guadeloupean anticolonialist thinking about music.

I insist on Lockel's importance as a major ideologue even if his precise role within the overall separatist movement is elusive. Rosan Mounien— former secretary-general of the UGTG—explained to me that Lockel brought his expertise to discussions in the early 1970s. However, he qualified his remarks by insisting that Lockel remained very discreet: he would rarely intervene during meetings, preferring to talk to people individually, behind the scenes.[51] Indeed, several musicians have told me about Lockel paying them a visit to convince them, more or less forcefully, to stop performing in dance orchestras and to stop playing *konpa*. According to Cotellon, Lockel played an important role in defining cultural policies within the UPLG.[52] Anduse, for his part, had this wonderful formulation, a typical illustration of a *maskò*, or faint: "Lockel was nowhere and Lockel was everywhere. He is a free electron. *Il est une autorité du mouvement*," which suggests that Lockel is both an authority of the separatist movement and, as a free electron, an authority on movement itself, ungraspable. Pressed on Lockel's exact impact on the AGEG's cultural report, Anduse became defensive. "We did not let him influence us," he insisted. The biguine became a topic of debate: Lockel had built a theory of three cultures—French, colonial, and Guadeloupean—in which biguine was presented as the symbol of bourgeois assimilationism.[53] In its report, however, the AGEG adopted a slightly different position. For the AGEG, biguine was a "bastard music," mixing French musical phrasing and the *boula* of gwoka. But the students also recognized that biguine was enjoyed by all social classes on the island and thus belonged in "the Guadeloupean cultural field," even if it had been co-opted by French colonialism. In a way, the AGEG reprised the *négritude* writers' take on the biguine as the musical representation of the tragic *mulatta* or, rather, *doudou*. Nonetheless, Anduse did recall how Lockel convinced the UTA and the UPLG to substitute gwoka recordings for the recordings of Soviet, Cuban, or French communist songs they had been playing during their rallies.[54] Moreover, as we will see, the AGEG's attack on tonality is a nearly verbatim formulation of Lockel's ideas, or vice versa.

I should also make clear that *gwoka modènn* was not the only way in which gwoka became part of an anticolonial aurality. As mentioned earlier, so-called traditional forms of the music, especially the *swaré léwòz*, played a central role in diffusing anticolonial ideology and, through their participatory ethics, building a sense of community.[55] But I want to focus on Lockel's music because, within the *camp patriotique*, it presents perhaps the most accomplished and sustained effort to merge form and message and to use music to foster an anticolonial subjectivity. Lockel is very clear on this. In his autobiography, he repeatedly returns to statements such as this one: "I thus commented to a *cadre* [of the *camp patriotique*] that if a worker could see him dance a *toumblak* or a *léwòz* once, this would appeal to his emotions and would do more to help his awakening than all the Marxist masters'

78 / Chapter Two

discourses. Culture is the domain of the soul . . . whereas political philosophy belongs to the domain of knowledge. The two are complementary but, in our situation as a colonized people, I speak to the soul first."[56] Or, later: "This is why I say that traditional gwoka heralded the end of slavery and that *gwoka modènn* may herald something [else]. It will happen, whether we want it or not. Gwoka is the cultural seed from which liberty will grow, feeding the economy and politics."[57]

Gwoka modènn *as Anticolonial Aurality*

Nearly everything in Lockel's *gwoka modènn* serves to establish its cultural specificity, to distance it from other forms of music—mostly jazz and European musics—and to protect it from outside influences or appropriation. From its choice of scale to its written presentation to Lockel's own insistence that no one should learn the music without first committing to the political project of national liberation, the music is meant to remain opaque to all but Guadeloupean patriots who have absorbed its codes or the proletarian masses who, in theory, should understand them naturally.

While opacity is primarily a visual metaphor, I propose that something akin to it plays a central role in an anticolonial aurality. Recall that for Glissant opacity extends from a mode of resistance, with roots in the colonial plantation, to a key element in a (post)colonial unconscious and, finally, an ethical demand for the right not to be understood. Opacity is a practice of epistemological resistance and, both for Glissant and for Lockel, this epistemological resistance includes a form of ethnographic refusal.[58] Opacity foils those—whether colonial officials or ethnographers—who seek to *prendre* (take) as they endeavor to *comprendre* (understand).[59] As discussed earlier, opacity works within an anticolonial aurality by producing sounds that challenge colonial listening techniques, that is, sounds that remain unintelligible to colonial ears and offer an alternative epistemology. Opacity, in short, is an integral quality of counterpoetics. It is from this perspective that I want to briefly examine *gwoka modènn*'s musical characteristics.

Anticipating what is rather recent scholarship on this topic, Lockel seemed to have understood tonality as a tool of empire. Writing some forty-six years after the creation of *gwoka modènn*, Kofi Agawu mounts what amounts to a double attack on both European tonality and African composers' alleged failure to free themselves from its pull. Describing tonality's inherent hierarchical management of desire, its ties to the movement of global capital, and its imposition on the colonized world through the work of military bands and missionaries, Agawu concludes, "All of this amounts to musical violence of a very high order, a violence whose psychic and psychological impacts remain to be properly explored."[60] For Agawu, the lure of tonality fed a colonial desire for assimilation and its inherent experience of alienation.

Lockel would likely agree. Indeed, the guitarist argued that tonality in Guadeloupean music was a product of French imperialism. This allowed him to maintain that biguine was only "half Guadeloupean" and colonial, the result of a mix of Guadeloupean rhythm and European melodies.[61] To mark the Guadeloupean specificity of *gwoka modènn*, he designed his own scale, which he claimed was based on traditional gwoka singing. The guitarist outlined his musical-ideological theory in the liner notes to his first LP, released in 1976: "Like traditional gro ka from which it evolved, gro ka modên [*sic*] is an atonal modal music that utilizes one scale: the gro ka scale. That is to say that this music has no connection with the fundamental laws of Western classical music. Rather, its characteristics are reminiscent of Afro-Asian musical forms. It is an improvised music that is developed from a mode. The mode gives birth to a kind of melody that expresses the musical feeling of the Guadeloupean people." The gwoka scale, then, captures the soul of the Guadeloupean people, its *santiman* (feeling). Within an anticolonial aurality, it functions as a musical equivalent to the Creole language, a musical "dialect of the mother tongue," to quote from Radano's evocative description of black nationalist musical aesthetics.[62]

As mentioned earlier, Lockel's gwoka scale is based on an alternation of whole steps and minor thirds, and it takes no fewer than five octaves to loop upon itself. In practice, however, the guitarist instructs musicians to limit themselves to the first nine notes of the cycle. Again, Laviso offered that the ninth degree gave the scale its particular flavor, and it is entirely possible that Lockel settled on nine notes because that was the minimum range to produce the aesthetic he was seeking. But this explanation does little to help understand the connection between Lockel's gwoka scale and the pentatonic sonorities heard in so-called traditional gwoka (especially melodies associated with the *léwòz* rhythm) and that, incidentally, many of the exercises in Lockel's method emphasize. For this, we need to further analyze the structure of the scale.

A closer inspection of the nine notes forming Lockel's scale reveal that they actually comprised three overlapping pentatonic scales, each starting a fourth apart (fig. 2.1). When I talked with the trombonist Alza Bordin about its participation in Lockel's group, he explained that he first understood Lockel's music as being pentatonic: "First, before it was written down, I was introduced to the method using pentatonic scales." When I pressed Bordin

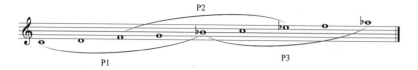

2.1. Gwoka scale with three overlapping pentatonics

on this, he elaborated: "No one introduced the structure of the scale to me. I listened to the music and I developed my own methodology based on the tablature [sic] of my musical knowledge.... I heard [pentatonic scales.] And when you look into this—because there are lots of methods on this—you see a basis in the pentatonic scale."[63] Yet Lockel has rejected this idea on several occasions, including in a phone conversation with me. In his book, he insists, in bold print, that the gwoka scale is not a pentatonic scale.[64] This stance implies three things. First, it signals Lockel's troubled engagement with diasporicity. In particular, Lockel repeatedly stresses the difference between his music and jazz, pointing to gwoka's atonality as proof. Consistent with the AGEG's quest to identify a primordial Guadeloupean culture, Lockel's gwoka scale may be reminiscent of "Afro-Asian" modes, but it remains purely national rather than diasporic. Second, the gwoka scale serves as a repudiation of creolization. Instead of an assemblage of previously existing scales—which might be heard as a formalization of musical hybridity—the gwoka scale exists as a thing in itself, an intellectual formulation intended to sound an undiluted Guadeloupean identity. Finally, Lockel's regular admonitions suggest that those who hear pentatonic scales in gwoka are actually mishearing the music. Thus, Lockel's continued efforts to distance gwoka from both tonality and pentatonicism act as a sort of performance of opacity, an affirmation that the music cannot be understood by those who are lacking the appropriate cultural key. And indeed, after practicing Lockel's methods for nearly a year, I have stopped hearing his gwoka scale as conjoined pentatonics while my ears have learned to recognize its own intervallic structure and play with it.

Gwoka modènn, then, sounds the nationalist rejection of colonialism, diasporicity, and hybridity. In parallel to a mode intended to render what he called a national "melodic sentiment," Lockel also purposed to establish the boundaries of a national music by defining seven rhythmic ostinati that allegedly form the basis for the expression of the Guadeloupean "rhythmic sentiment:" *toumblak, léwòz, gwanjanbel, menndé, graj, woulé*, and *kaladja*. As with the origins of the gwoka scale, there is little ethnographic evidence to justify focusing on these particular seven rhythms. The earliest known gwoka recordings—documented in Grande-Terre by Alan Lomax in 1962—feature only two drum patterns: *toumblak* and *woulé*.[65] For his part, Lockel's first album and his early writings make no mention of the seven rhythms. This seven-rhythm taxonomy appears only in the 1980s, with the publication of Lockel's method book. In contrast, contemporary practice in Guadeloupe reveals a greater complexity. Although the idea that gwoka is defined by its seven rhythms has become nearly universally accepted, most people also knowingly overlook variations—such as between the *granjanbèl* and the *padjanbèl*—that undermine the taxonomy. In practice, some rhythms are much more common than others, and many groups, even those in the so-called traditional vein, continue to invent new rhythmic patterns. The choice of seven rhythms—like the affects that are attributed to each—appears, then, largely symbolic, if not arbitrary. Nonetheless, for Lockel, taken together, "melody and rhythm develop in the Guadeloupean an intellectual, spiritual, and physical strength that has always threatened gwoka's enemies."[66] In other words, the gwoka scale and the seven rhythms form the basis of an anticolonial aurality, an epistemology fed by a primordial energy capable of combatting assimilation and pushing Guadeloupeans to "think and act as Guadeloupeans; to organize themselves politically and empower themselves to liberate their country."[67]

Besides the choice of scale, Lockel also abandoned standard Western musical notation, further complicating the efforts of Western-trained musicians who might have velleities to learn from his *Traité de gro ka modên*—a massive method book published in 1981. All the exercises in this book are notated using square tables of three columns and three rows, with each cell representing a scale degree.[68] Surprisingly, given the guitarist's proclaimed efforts to decolonize his music, pitches are written using conventional French solfège names. Black and red numbers indicate the order in which the pitches are to be played (players go through the black sequence first, then the red). Thus, Lockel's notation only prescribes the relative position of each pitch and its proper sequence; without rhythmic notation, musicians must decide for themselves how to properly phrase each exercise to fit the rhythms of the *boula*. According to Lockel, the system was intended to help people learn music without having to learn to read staff notation. During a phone conversation, the guitarist acknowledged that he purposely avoided using standard European staff notation, preferring a system that he argued better captured gwoka's African elements and therefore was better suited to improvised music.[69] In practice, as several Guadeloupean musicians have shared with me and as was plainly evident during the July 2017 workshop, this notational choice makes his method book rather difficult to use for musicians trained in European solfège. Conversely, each exercise in the *Traité* includes all twelve transpositions of the melodic cell, in contrast to most jazz improvisation methods, which instruct musicians to transpose a basic pattern themselves. The ear, in Lockel's method, is put to work to figure out rhythms rather than pitch. As I have found out through my own practice, playing *gwoka modènn* is an intensive intellectual exercise.

In her book on aurality, Ana María Ochoa Gautier highlights the political and ideological stakes involved in the act of transcribing the acoustic to the written page.[70] Following her example, I understand Lockel's choice of scale and music notation not only as efforts to maintain *gwoka modènn's* opacity but also as a disciplining impulse central to the construction of an anticolonial aurality. Because his notation is not a mediation of technique in writing (as the guitar tabs that it resembles) and only a partial mediation of sound in writing (even compared to staff notation, itself a partial transcription of sound), it requires that players fully invest themselves in learning the new notation, absorb the missing rhythmic element through listening and practice, and, because many of the exercises are technically very challenging, work to master their instruments, molding their technique to the musical language of *gwoka modènn*.[71]

The disciplining of musicians' bodies not only accompanied an effort to redraw musical aesthetics along nationalist lines but also went along with the policing of their political opinions and of their professional activities. There never was quite as clear a demonstration of gwoka's contested aurality. Recall that Lockel and his followers often intervened directly with musicians who played salsa or *konpa* in popular dance groups. For example, Bordin reminisced about how Lucien Martial, who played trumpet in Lockel's group, recruited him: "Lucien seduced me. He helped me realize that the [popular ball] had a *doudouiste* dimension, especially since we played big balls for the *gendarmerie* [a French military police force], things like that. And I told myself: 'Shit, what am I doing here, amusing the police with my music and tomorrow they're on the street ticketing me, beating me?' And it clicked and I was able to quit."[72] Other musicians have described more forceful encounters with Lockel's men. Flautist Vamur remembers the climate he found upon returning to Guadeloupe from Paris in the 1980s: "When I arrived, it was kind of funny because there was a cut-throat attitude between groups. If you played with so and so, you couldn't talk to so and so."[73] Others still reported receiving physical threats for playing the "wrong" kind of music or for performing in groups that did not sound patriotic enough. Those convinced to stop playing "foreign" music still had to pass a political litmus test before they could start studying with Lockel. The multi-instrumentalist and composer Christian Dahomay is fond of recalling his interview with Lockel. Dahomay was interested in *gwoka modènn* and met the guitarist who, apparently, told him, "OK, but first, we have to talk about politics." Dahomay refused to align himself with any one party or slogan and walked away. Dahomay has often joked with me that the separatist slogan shouldn't have just been *on sèl chimen* (only one way) but also *on sèl mizik* (only one music).

Put simply, *gwoka modènn* was a disciplining project that demanded total musical, technical, and political dedication. In this, Lockel went much further than other musicians—such as Georges Troupé, Jean-Fred Castry, and, more recently, Franck Nicolas—who subsequently offered their own "modern," "instrumental," "progressive," or "jazz" form of gwoka and who fell back on Western staff notation in their various methods.

The Vexed Question of Anticolonial Modernity

I cannot conclude this chapter without addressing the *modern* in *gwoka modènn*. We could, along with the Comaroffs, decry Lockel's and Guadeloupean anticolonial activists' reproduction of European evolutionary teleology in their embrace of the traditional-modern dichotomy. Or we could content ourselves with describing *gwoka modènn* as the product of modernist reformism that Turino has outlined. But both approaches risk masking the ambivalent meaning of modernity in racialized (post)colonial contexts, as well as the ways in which musical modernism comes to sound political modernity. It is more productive to follow David Scott and understand modernity as a condition of conscription, that is to say, as a positive field of power that shaped anticolonial political and aesthetic horizons.[74] The AGEG's drive to create a "new culture"—and Lockel's *gwoka modènn* within it—are best understood as efforts to appropriate the rhetoric of modernity and modernism, including the distinction between tradition and modernity, in order to assert their anticolonial political project. The AGEG and the patriotic camp may have foregrounded the figure of the *nèg mawon*, but their anticolonial strategy comprised both an act of rupture, of fleeing, and a drive to home modernity.[75] While the AGEG's rhetoric opposed tradition and modernity, it is important to note that, as far as gwoka was concerned, its so-called traditional and modern forms were in fact the direct products of the nationalist movement and emerged in dialectic with each other. Following the AGEG's initial cultural platform, the new patriotic unions drove the gwoka revival and, taking the *swaré léwòz* of northern Basse-Terre as a model, instigated a homogenization of gwoka practices around the island.

Lockel also played an important role in this process: as we have seen, he was the first to codify the seven rhythms of gwoka in his treatise. Together, Lockel, the new unions, and the musicians—such as Kristen Aigle—who joined them authorized one particular take on what had been a variegated set of musical practices, with numerous regional variants. Union-sponsored *léwòz* and Lockel's own series of "concert-debates" have both contributed to establish gwoka as *the* traditional and authentic music of Guadeloupe. Since the late 1980s, the annual Festival Gwoka in Sainte-Anne—instigated and organized by Félix Cotellon and other nationalist activists—has further contributed to authenticating and asserting gwoka's place within the Guadeloupean cultural field.[76] For the anticolonial movement, then, establishing gwoka as "traditional" was part of a rhetorical strategy that affirmed a narrative of resistance. Gwoka came to sound what Gilroy describes as an anticolonial "victory of survival."[77] "Tradition," then, was an essential component to the AGEG's *pulsion de retour* to a precolonial or, at least, decolonized subjectivity. The patriotic camp needed the legitimacy of tradition to assert their "new" culture. The assertion of tradition made it possible to imagine the Guadeloupean nation-to-be.

Another way of thinking about the "invention" of tradition in this case is to view it as a necessary component of Guadeloupean anticolonial nationalists' efforts to "tame" or domesticate Western modernity, both an extension of and a reaction against *négritude*'s *détournement* of modernity discussed in the previous chapter. Here, I borrow the idea of taming modernity from Tejumola Olaniyan, and I play with the meaning of taming as *domestiquer* in French, which reveals the taming of modernity as "homing modern power."[78] Indeed, the ideology of colonial assimilation established European modernity as a "supernorm"—to borrow Glissant's formulation—that needed to be tamed so that it could be transcended and a decolonized subjectivity could emerge.[79] The musical taming of modernity demanded an appropriation, or vernacularization, of modernist aesthetic values. It would be misguided to critique Lockel's music for its embrace of a modernist avant-gardism. In fact, I believe gwoka *modènn* was always imagined as more than an act of *marronnage*, an effort to escape or flee European modernity. Nor can it be heard simply as a transposition or reproduction of cosmopolitan modernism, a symbolic demand for international recognition. Rather, gwoka *modènn* is best understood as an illustration of the kind of anticolonial overcoming that it sought to produce. Traditional gwoka and gwoka *modènn* form two sides of the same performative endeavor that aimed to transform the Guadeloupean masses into revolutionary decolonialized subjects.[80]

Gwoka modènn as Counterpoetics

The *camp patriotique* may not have achieved its political goals, and Lockel never managed to either recruit a large contingent of musicians or to attract a sizable popular audience, yet we shouldn't look at these effort as simply the "unachieved visions and interrupted imaginaries" of a failed anticolonial movement.[81] Lockel's *gwoka modènn* inspired numerous musicians to embrace the Guadeloupean drum, and, as Vamur mentioned, by the 1980s, there was a profusion of modern or progressive groups on the island: Gwakasoné, Galta, Horizon, Simènn Kontra, and Kafé, to name but a few. Today, gwoka is widely recognized as the *potomitan a mizik Gwadloup*, the central pillar of Guadeloupean music. Beyond Guadeloupe, Lockel also inspired the Martinican group Bèlè Nou to similarly "modernize" *bèlè*. And of course, the gwoka revival and its attendant cultural nationalism built the foundation from which zouk would emerge. But perhaps the separatist movement's anticolonial aural campaign was most successful in its effort to reestablish Creole as the national language of Guadeloupe. By the 1980s, the socialist government of François Mitterrand acquiesced that the cultural demands of Guadeloupean nationalists aligned with its decentralization and regionalist policies, and it agreed to actively support the use of Creole in school and in public media. Today, Creole can be heard not only on the streets of Guadeloupe but also on TV and radio and in classrooms.

And so what is left of *gwoka modènn*'s performative energy fifty years later, in an era when neoliberal policies and the forces of globalization have tighten the weave of Guadeloupe's (post)colonial entanglements? There was something strange, somewhat anachronistic, about playing *gwoka modènn* in Baie-Mahault in 2017, in a period when discussions of Guadeloupe's independence receded from the mainstream of political discourse and gwoka itself had been thoroughly institutionalized. I couldn't help but wonder whether this was a music whose time had finally come, or whether it had become "safer," still acting as a strong identity marker but divorced from the specific political demands once attached to it.[82] And yet, on the last day of our workshop, as we gathered for our closing concert, there was a tangible energy among the participants that went beyond the expected stage fright. Most of us arrived early and spent our time warming up and chatting outside the Foyer Culturel. On the outside wall as we walked in, a mural with a portrait of Gérard Lockel stared at us sternly, imbuing the evening with a certain gravity and a palpable sense of historical continuity and responsibility.

The small concert hall had been rearranged in the afternoon. Modeled on the ring of the *swaré léwòz*, the chairs were set up in a circle: musicians would form the inner ring, with spectators sitting all around them. A lone microphone stand was in front of the drum set, our modern *makè*. When the musicians finally entered the room, following a few obligatory speeches, we found a hushed atmosphere. Silence. We sat down then the group of *boula* started their unison pattern, both hands hitting the center of the drumhead, all together, quiet, deep, and dirgelike. A few repetitions, then the singers came in: "Gwadloupéyen, gwadloupéyenn, Gwadloup an danjé. Nou pé pa rété kon sa. Fou nou mèt tout fòs an nou adan on sèl konba pou nou ré-zisté" (Guadeloupean men and women, Guadeloupe is in danger. We cannot stay like this. We have to put all of our strength into the same fight to resist). Three time, we sang through "Lindépendans" (Independence), Lockel's Guadeloupean anthem. Sitting next to me, a saxophone player held his head high, silent and focused. The only white face in the group, I found myself mouthing the lyrics that, through ten years of scholarly interest in Guadeloupean nationalism, had become very familiar.

For about two hours we went through the small repertoire of Lockel compositions that we had rehearsed, each song stretching into longer performances as soloists became more confident. These songs had been written for another era. Like "Lindépendans," they enjoined Guadeloupeans to wake up, free themselves from cultural and political assimilation, and join the national revolution. The concert ended with "Fò zòt savé," a song specifically meant to counteract assimilation: "Fò zòt savé, nou ni on mizik. Nou ni on mizik ki tan nou. Sé gwoka mizik a pèp-la" (You have to know, we have a music. We have a music that is ours. Gwoka is the music of the people).[83] Three years after a successful campaign to have gwoka recognized as UNESCO Intangible Cultural Heritage of Humanity (see chapter 5), the song had, surprisingly, not lost any of its urgency. So, when Laviso motioned for me to start soloing, I walked over to the microphone and finally felt free. I channeled this energy and my long love for late Coltrane and let it flow through Lockel's "atonal modal" language. The singers, now standing up, chanted "Fò zòt savé!" and one by one Laviso called all the soloists to join me. The volume increased. I reached for both extremes of my instruments, playing overtones and eventually extending the bottom range by putting my knee in front of my bell to gain an extra half step. There was urgency and joy in our playing, and in the midst of all of this, the collective scream of counterpoetics could not be ignored.

As songs like "Fò zòt savé" illustrate, Lockel's work has played a central role in determining *gwoka*'s significance along a very narrow line, not only confining the music to the role of national symbol but also delegitimizing every other vernacular style of music. Turning to forced poetics, or counterpoetics, I hope, offers a step toward restoring a level of fluidity and polysemy. It also reminds us that music cannot be limited to its semiotic function and that we, rather, should engage with it at an epistemological level. This leads us to consider the Guadeloupean nationalist movement as a process unfolding within shifting problem-spaces, a process that cannot be reduced to its political outcomes. *Gwoka modènn* suggests that Guadeloupean nationalism has been most effective as a project of cultural decolonization, an unfinished program to help people "think and act as Guadeloupeans."

Hearing *gwoka modènn* as forced poetics also suggests an alternative to Glissant's definition of the concept. As already discussed in chapter 1, for Glissant, forced poetics form the expression of an unconscious (post)colonial way of knowing. Forced poetics are symptomatic of a colonial aurality: they capture both the persistent desire for an emancipated expressive practice and the impossibility to access it. Within a colonial aurality, meaning is therefore always ambivalent, contextual, and performative (i.e., attached to oral and embodied performances). Faced with the lack of a *langage* that would adequately articulate a (post)colonial collective subjectivity, dominated—but determining—collectivities seek means of expression that escape the logic of the dominant language. Thus, forced poetics give rise to practices of the *détour*, forcing their own logic through a dominant language that resists them or, on the contrary, resisting the logic of the colonial language without being able to quite escape it. *Gwoka modènn*, I argue, is illustrative of forced poetics: at once the sonic marker of a lack (*manque*), a recognition of an insufficiently autonomous social body, and the expression of the fierce dedication to correct this lack through radical musical aesthetics paired with a radical political vision.

But if Glissant conceived of forced poetics as the expression of a collective unconscious, *gwoka modènn* functions on a different level: it is a deliberate, calculated response to a specific problem-space. *Gwoka modènn* encourages us to think the difference between forced poetics and counterpoetics (terms that Glissant used interchangeably), revealing the latter to be the constrained but productive outcome of being conscripted into modernity. As such, I hear the counterpoetics of *gwoka modènn* as the expression of the antithetical drives to flee and to home. *Gwoka modènn* expresses the double bind of anticolonial cultural nationalism in a postplantation context: it is the forced resultant of an operation of synthesis, taming, or homing of external sources that—nationalism obliged—it simultaneously cannot but disavow. This double bind means that, although *gwoka modènn* was intended as a deliberate effort to control meaning, its performance cannot be restrained and its signification overflows its nationalist boundaries. Regardless of the political convictions of the participants in the 2017 workshop, our performance sounded the ambivalent black Atlantic entanglements of the post-departmentalization Antilles. It transcended our partial mastery of Lockel's musical language (our performance was itself a performance of forced poetics) and affirmed through the sheer density of our collective improvisation, through the tumult of our abstract voices. "You have to know," we proclaimed obsessively at the end of our last song. But what needed to be known? What was the political message of *gwoka modènn* in 2017? Following the concert, the young and gifted piano player from Bordeaux who had so impressively mastered Lockel's musical language offered an evasive answer: perhaps this was best left for each individual to consider. Stripped of its strict nationalist anchoring, *gwoka modènn* sounds the ambivalence of forced poetics. The next chapters explore this ambivalence further, discussing the complicated place of gwoka in metropolitan France, its complex diasporic entanglements, and its contemporary significance within a post-national problem-space.

THREE

Discrepant Creolizations:
Music and the Limits of Hospitality

In his effort to both "tame" modernity and capture a Guadeloupean national specificity, Gérard Lockel refused to consider that Guadeloupean musics had always existed not only in dialogue with one another but also in a dialectic relation with French musical values and conventions. Wozan Mounien, the former secretary-general of the Union populaire pour la libération de la Guadeloupe (UPLG), summed up the dilemma created by Lockel's radical, inward-looking, nationalist line:

> The problem is [to decide] where to make a break and what to synthesize. It was this problematic that [Lockel] didn't pose. Because of this, he has remained stuck on a very closed ideological position. However, cultural identity is always shared. There is no culture, even if it is original, that can exist without outside contributions, without outside influences. We are not [with *gwoka modènn*] in a logic of cultural *métissage* (hybridity, cross-fertilization), we are in a logic of creation of a new culture based on our traditions, historical roots, anything you want. But at the same time, we are, somewhat, francophiles. We had, therefore, to find the juncture between the two [French and Guadeloupean cultures] to create something that was different. That may be what was missing from [Lockel's] approach.[1]

What Mounien expresses is the fundamental tension of forced poetics, of the drive to birth a bounded identity from the colonial crucible. Any attempt to restrict the circle of inclusiveness, of belonging, any denial of the dialectics involved, necessarily creates an arbitrary foreclosure. Renouncing hybridity or Francophilia—rather than dwelling in creolization, in a constant state of fleeing and homing—amounts to a degree of symbolic violence. Such violence might be a necessary component of an anticolonial

90 / Chapter Three

effort to break assimilationist cultural shackles, but it is bound, as we saw in the previous chapter, to create a *manque*. Something is left lacking.

Mounien's comment brings up the complex problematic of (post)colonial cultural citizenship. Aihwa Ong defines cultural citizenship as "the cultural practices and beliefs produced out of negotiating the often ambivalent and contested relations with the state and its hegemonic forms that establish the criteria of belonging within a national population and territory. Cultural citizenship is a dual process of self-making and being-made within webs of power linked to the nation-state and civil society."[2] What does cultural citizenship look like and sound like for Guadeloupean (post) colonial subjects? To answer this question, we follow the migrations of Guadeloupean musicians across the Atlantic in the 1970s and 1980s. These (post)colonial migrations amplified and remixed questions of belonging and political subjectivity. *Rèpriz*. "Because of its creation, gwoka has always been political." What are the politics of gwoka when it crosses the Atlantic and let its drums be heard "in the hold" of the metropole? How do its aesthetics reflect its politics?

Listen. Listen so that you can hear. The sound is most definitely of its time: an electric guitar run through a distortion pedal provides the aggressive opening hook, mellow synth pads contrasting with shimmering arpeggio runs offer a gentle background, and the whole thing is anchored by a steady bass drum at a very discotheque-friendly 108 beats per minute. Soon the chorus enters, sung in Creole, and the rhythmic texture gets more complex: the guitarist turns off the distortion to play syncopated arpeggios, a bell and a closed hi-hat add a *tresillo* to the unrelenting bass drum. The result is already very familiar to those who danced to Caribbean musics of the 1970s and 1980s—from Haitian *konpa* to Dominican *cadence-lypso*— and yet it also announces things to come.[3] We are in the early 1980s, zouk is emerging as the new Caribbean dance sensation, and Erick Cosaque has released what would become his best-known song, "A koz don biyé san fwan" (Because of a hundred-franc bill).[4]

The song's aesthetics may be transnational, illustrating a particular kind of pan-Caribbean sound informed by the latest technological developments in global pop, but its subject matter speaks directly to the specific experiences of Guadeloupeans and Martinicans who had migrated to Paris under the auspices of BUMIDOM, a program instituted by the French government in the aftermath of the Algerian War to facilitate the migration of unskilled Antillean workers. Singing in the first person, Cosaque uses his personal experience to describe the struggles of those who have bought into the French government's promises of employment, only to find themselves cut off from their community and unable to make ends meet. The song offers a cautionary tale. "Drugs, theft, and prostitution, that's what you'll find in Paris," it warns Guadeloupeans who might be considering seeking a better future *an lòt koté* (on the other side). And Cosaque adds that men will invite you to parties, take you to night clubs, promise to help you, but they only do so in order to prostitute you.[5] The line is a double entendre. Literally, it alludes to the fact that BUMIDOM primarily sought out young women who, as a result of their relative isolation and economic precariousness in Paris, became targets of procurers. But, as we will see, the line also functions as a veiled comment on artists who, seduced by rich patrons, had sold out.

Cosaque knew the reality of BUMIDOM firsthand. He had grown up in Pointe-à-Pitre, where his father worked on the docks, before his family relocated to Capesterre, a municipality on the windward coast of Basse-Terre. In both places, Cosaque was surrounded by people who played the drums and from whom he could learn the tradition. The singer migrated to France in the 1970s to take on a job with the national telecommunication agency. Upon his arrival in the French capital, he connected with other Guadeloupean musicians and with cultural activists of the AGEG and the Union des travailleurs issus de l'emigration guadeloupéenne (UTEG). These encounters reshaped his music. He explains, "The AGEG and UTEG made me realize that I couldn't sing about just anything."[6] Like many gwoka singers of his generation, Cosaque had an affinity for frivolous, if not risqué, songs. Upon his contact with nationalist activists, though, he decided to focus his lyrics on social issues.

In Paris, Cosaque also ended up altering his musical aesthetics, moving away from "traditional" conventions. There were few musicians with direct knowledge of gwoka in metropolitan France at the time, and Cosaque quickly found himself in demand, playing with a variety of groups, including the folkloric group Karibana. Soon, he was sufficiently active to become a full-time musician. In 1980, he created the group X7 Nouvelle Dimension. The band's name combines the letter X to indicate that it consisted of ten musicians and the number 7 in reference to the seven rhythms of the *swaré léwòz*. However, in spite of this appeal to tradition, many of the musicians did not come with much practical knowledge of Guadeloupean drumming: most of them were active in *konpa*, biguine, and cadence-lypso bands, "all the music of the Caribbean," as Cosaque summarized in 2009. Some of them also played music in church, and two of them—Frédéric Caracas and Harold Abraham—brought in a particularly "jazzy" sensibility. They may not have played gwoka in the past, but "they knew gwoka. They didn't play the drum, but their heart beat when they heard the drum. And gwoka is in us. Gwoka is the soul of the Guadeloupean people," explained Cosaque.[7] Together, the band developed a repertoire that mixed these different influences. Some instrumental tracks (e.g., "Kominiké") made room for extensive improvisations atop a traditional drum ostinato. Others build contemporary arrangements—complete with a prominent electric bass, Fender Rhodes keyboard, and electric guitar—of traditional songs anchored by the polyrhythms of the *boula*, *chacha*, and *makè* (e.g., "Jwé zizipan," a song commonly heard during wakes). But "A koz don biyé san fwan" may be the band's most forward-sounding song.

Cosaque and X7 Nouvelle Dimension illustrate the kind of innovative music making that took place among Guadeloupean migrants in the French capital, a music that kept its ears open to the latest trends while foregrounding a nationalist spirit: the group's arrangements typify the aesthetic transition taking place at the time as musicians combined Haitian *konpa* and Dominican *cadence-lypso* with gwoka's sounds and *santiman* (feeling), each style enriching the others. Importantly, this blend of transnational aesthetics and nationalist ideology makes audible the ambivalent and ambiguous position of (post)colonial migrants caught in the complex process of self-making and being-made within the French nation-state. They make audible the negotiations of (post)colonial cultural citizenship.

It is noteworthy that—from Lockel's *gwoka modènn* to the *zouk* of Kassav'—many of the innovations that have transformed gwoka from the late 1960s through the 1980s originated in Paris. Illustrating Mounien's point, these innovations were all nourished by transnationally circulating musical styles—especially black Atlantic sounds such as jazz, Afrobeat, soul, and funk, to name just a few—and their interactions with both Guadeloupean and French musical references.[8] These musical innovations accompanied and involved deliberations over cultural and political belonging, and these negotiations functioned on two horizons: a cosmopolitan universal and a national vernacular. As cosmopolitan sounding as these musics could be, many of them looked inward, to the nation, rather than outward, to forms of transnational solidarity. This is most clearly illustrated by Lockel, whose contact with Afro-diasporic musicians in the French capital led to a quest to define a nationally-specific Guadeloupean music. His decision to return to Guadeloupe in 1969 made manifest his musical journey from the diasporic cosmopolitanism found in the French capital to a Guadeloupean national specificity.

These hybrid musical styles also reveal the limits of (post)colonial hospitality, understood here as a facet of the ambiguous relationship between former colonial state and (post)colonial migrants.[9] Indeed, in the metropole,

Guadeloupeans experienced the limits of their citizenship. They were "welcome," even encouraged to come, but their presence had to remain circumscribed to specific geographical, economical, and racial positions. (Post)colonial migrants in France experienced the entanglement of hospitality and hostility that Jacques Derrida alludes to in *Le monolinguisme de l'autre*. Conversely, Guadeloupean musicians faced their own ambivalent desire for recognition from, and participation in, the French state, demands that accompanied their simultaneous contestation of the sovereignty of that state over their lives. In other words, for gwoka musicians in Paris, cultural citizenship was simultaneously a claim to have rights within the French state and a demand to have rights elsewhere. (Post)colonial citizenship, then, emerged in Paris as fragmented and multileveled, involving processes of identification or disidentification with political communities of various scales, from the supranational to the national to the supernational. In short, it prompted poetics of the *détour* and entailed both homing and fleeing.

In this chapter, I propose that creolization enables us to bridge the tension between cosmopolitanism and nationalism at the heart of the negotiations of cultural citizenship for (post)colonial migrants. I explore Guadeloupean migrants' cultural citizenship within a theoretical space grounded in what Lionnet and Shih have called "minor transnationalism," not because I seek to emphasize transversal over vertical relations—indeed, I am primarily concerned with the relation between the margins and the center of the French (post)colonial state—but because minor transnationalism creates a space that destabilizes the normative role of the center.[10] Moreover, contrary to cosmopolitanism, minor transnationalism does not deny the continued importance of the nation as both a structuring principle and an object of desire or longing; rather, it is attentive to the aesthetic, political, and imaginary productions of those who move through and dwell in the liminal spaces of the (post)colonial French republic. Furthermore, minor transnationalism opens our understanding of creolization beyond the colonial encounter without losing sight of the power dynamics that have historically animated this process. It allows for a consideration of creolization in the metropolitan center not as a cultural "counterflow" from the colonial margins that somehow enriches the metropole, but as the wholesome (post)colonial displacement of colonial dynamics, as a "continuance" of colonialism.[11] Finally, minor transnationalism allows for a critical distance through which we can consider how the national, economic, and artistic aspirations of those who find themselves minoritized within a (post)colonial world order are circumscribed by the geopolitics and political economy of that order. Taking into consideration the criteria imposed by the state and the music industry for political and economic participation pushes us to examine what I call discrepant creolizations.

Through two case studies, this chapter highlights how gwoka "homed" transnational aesthetics just as Guadeloupeans were involved in a double act of fleeing and homing. Guadeloupean immigrants were literally fleeing the economic downturn that accompanied the collapse of the sugar industry in the Antilles and metaphorically fleeing the republic that had never truly integrated them. They were homing in the literal sense of creating a home for themselves on the European continent but also in the metaphorical sense of homing their political subjectivity, making a place for themselves, within France's (post)colonial space. In other words, as Guadeloupean artists moved across the Atlantic, their music came to reflect their geographic and political horizons, their "spatial presences and imaginaries":[12] the places they left, those they longed for, and the spaces they endeavored to create for themselves.

I turn first to the music of Guy Konket to reveal two different creolization moments: one in Guadeloupe and another in metropolitan France. In this latter creolization moment, at a time when the neocolonial effects of departmentalization became painfully evident and the separatist movement reached its apogee, Konket's gwoka became a vehicle through which minor transnationalism served to expand a Creole imaginary past the confine of the Caribbean, offering an alternative to the orthodoxy of Lockel's music. The concept of discrepant creolization also calls attention to the fact that creolization cannot be reduced to an expression of creative resistance. Indeed, as the example of the group Tumblack—my second case study— illustrates, homing meant that gwoka became a site for the negotiation of strategic accommodations within the structure of a globalizing music industry that clung to its colonial, exoticist, imaginary. Gwoka in Paris, then, offers another perspective on the music as contested (post)colonial aurality. Decidedly nationalist (except when it is not), neither truly creolized nor cosmopolitan, and yet both of these things at once, gwoka in Paris became a container for the antinomies that characterized the lives of Guadeloupeans exiled in the metropole from which they wished to become independent.

Historical Context: Economic Collapse during the Trente Glorieuses

Chapter 5 reengages the questions of cosmopolitanism and creolization in the contemporary moment, but here I focus more specifically on the 1970s and 1980s. At the time, both the migratory and the imaginary movements of Guadeloupean musicians reflected and were constrained by the profound social, political, and economic transformations on both sides of the French Atlantic world. As mentioned in the previous chapter, Antillean societies underwent a rapid transformation in the decades following departmentalization. Because at the time gwoka remained closely associated with agricultural and industrial workers, especially those involved in the production of sugar, the collapse of that industry is perhaps the most significant economic factor for us to consider at this point. A few numbers will give a sense of the rapidity and extent of the transformation. In the second half of the twentieth century, the Guadeloupean sugar industry faced a number of structural challenges: for one, the competition of sugar-beet producers led to declining prices. Second, a pricing scheme that determined the value of raw cane based on saccharin content made it difficult for cane growers to recover their production costs.[13] As a result, sugar production—the historical backbone of Antillean economies—collapsed from a high of 180,000 tons in 1965 to a low of 20,000 tons in 1990. In 1950, there were fourteen sugar factory in the archipelago.[14] Three of those factories had closed by 1960. Then the pace accelerated: while there were still nine factories in 1970, only four remained in 1980.[15] Importantly, that year saw the closing of the Darboussier factory, which, in the late nineteenth century, had been the biggest employer in Pointe-à-Pitre and had remained one of its economic engines. Each factory closing sent ripples through entire communities and neighborhoods, particularly as the businesses that factory workers had once patronized found themselves without customers.

It is not surprising, then, that the organizing activities of the *camp patriotique* picked up significantly during this period. The Union des travailleurs agricoles (UTA) was the first of the "new unions" organized by the GONG resigners in 1970, followed by the Union des paysans pauvres de la Guadeloupe (UPG) in 1972. The UGTG was born a year later, in December 1973. These new unions were quickly augmented by a number of political parties. First came the Parti des travailleurs guadeloupéens, an underground organization that gathered former GONG members and served as the political engine room of the patriotic camp until its role was formalized within the Mouvement pour l'unification des Forces de libération nationale guadeloupéennes in 1981. But the main political arm of the separatist movement emerged in 1978 with the creation of the UPLG. The same year, disagreements over strategies would lead to the creation of the Groupe de la libération armée (GLA), a radical movement founded in 1982 that favored violent actions and had its own political arm, the Mouvement populaire pour une Guadeloupe indépendante.[16]

Through the 1970s and 1980s, the social situation in Guadeloupe was extremely tense: as the economy deteriorated, strikes multiplied, often leading to violent confrontations and arrests. The strike of 1975 opposing sugarcane workers, landowners, and factory management was perhaps the most significant. Organized by the UTA and the UPG, agricultural and factory workers went on a general strike in February 1975. They demanded two things: first, that the price of raw cane be aligned on the cost of production (rather than saccharin content) and, second, that the minimum wage of agricultural workers be brought up to the level of factory workers, ending the 20 percent differential between the two. Rather than agreeing to negotiate with the new unions, though, factory owners attempted to break the strike by hiring undocumented Haitian workers. For a month and half, the French police not only harassed the strikers; in a display of coercion that echoed across centuries, the police also became temporary overseers of a new plantation regime, actively monitoring the work and daily life of the Haitian workers, denying them freedom of movement so that they would not come in contact with the Guadeloupean population.

The strategy almost succeeded in breaking the strike. But in March, when the owners of the Simonet estate in Grosse Montagne, in Northern Basse-Terre, threatened to evict striking workers from their land, Father Chérubin Céleste, the priest of the nearby town of Lamentin, was moved to begin a hunger strike in hopes of forcing representatives of the French government and factory owners back to the negotiating table. The priest took up temporary residence in the small concrete chapel of Grosse Montagne, which then became a meeting point for members of the UTA, UPG, and UGTG, along with members of nationalist Christian organizations such as the Mouvement rural de jeunesse chrétienne. Although the lack of progress to that point had left many sugarcane workers discouraged and contemplating returning to work, Céleste's hunger strike reenergized the unions' grass roots, who dedicated themselves anew to the strike. As the general strike spread throughout the island, the local government-controlled media circulated fake reports of widespread violence to discredit the strikers. In an attempt to behead the movement, the prefect ordered the Compagnie républicaine de sécurité, France's antiriot police, to storm the chapel in Grosse Montagne and arrest Céleste. The priest barely managed to escape by hiding in an ambulance. Faced with growing popular anger, the prefect quickly reversed his position and convened factory and landowners, union representatives, and government officials to the table. Father Céleste ended his hunger strike, and most of the unions' demands were met.[17]

Police repression was just one aspect of the French government's neocolonial response to the economic woes of the DOMs (the structural problems in Guadeloupe were matched by similar issues in Martinique, Guiana, and Réunion). Indeed, the first government of the newly instituted Fifth Republic continued to ignore the need to put in place economic policies that would enable the Antilles to compensate for the steady decline of the sugar industry with different types of agricultural or industrial production. Instead, under the leadership of the prime minister Michel Debré, the French government used the economic difficulties and social unrest in the DOMs to enact a number of neocolonial policies that would benefit the metropolitan economy. Continuing the long-standing entanglement of population control within a logic of racialized capitalist development, metropolitan politicians justified these policies by recycling colonial fantasies and Malthusian anxieties. The problems with Antillean economies, they argued, were not the result of centuries of colonial exploitation topped by postwar neglect; rather, they could be attributed to rising natality rates. And to alleviate the weight of high fertility rates on economic development, the Debré administration imposed a two-pronged approach. First, although the French government pursued aggressively natalist policies in the Hexagon, it advocated for greater family planning in its overseas territories, going as far as turning a blind eye to illegal abortions and forced sterilizations performed in Réunion. Second, it sought to literally displace Antillean natality from the Caribbean to the metropole through aggressive state-controlled migration.[18]

At the center of this migration effort was the Bureau pour le développement des migrations dans les départements d'Outre-mer (BUMIDOM, or Bureau for Migration from Overseas Departments). Created in 1963, BUMIDOM was Debré's brainchild. Officially, the bureau was intended to facilitate the annual migration of five thousand Antilleans, split evenly between Martinicans and Guadeloupeans.[19] But beyond the facade of combating demographic pressures and growing unemployment in the DOM, the BUMIDOM was actually designed to respond to the economic needs of France during the Trente Glorieuses (1945–1975), a period that saw the rapid transformation and expansion of the French economy. (Post)colonial migrations played a large part in fueling this period of remarkable economic growth, providing a steady flow of affordable industrial and service workers. Two factors are especially important to understand France's need for unskilled Antillean workers at this critical historical juncture. As the private service sector expanded and wages grew, French workers who had held positions as low-level state employees relocated toward more lucrative employment in the private sector, thus creating a need for low-level postal, railways, and airport employees, to name just a few state-run industries who benefited from the BUMIDOM. However, following the independence of Algeria in

1962, Algerian postcolonial migrants could not fill these positions, which were reserved for French citizens. Even if the quickly growing French private industries could continue to rely on Algerian migrants as a source of affordable labor, the state had to look for another source of (post)colonial workers, and it naturally turned its eyes on its former colonies in the Atlantic and Indian oceans. Of course, we should not forget that, following the Algerian War, organizing the mass migration of young Antilleans held the promise of also mollifying the nascent separatist movements in the old colonies.

The French government promoted its migration policies in the DOMs through massive media campaigns that touted the slogan *l'avenir est ailleurs* (the future is elsewhere) and by facilitating the recruiting efforts of private companies. Conversely, the state used censorship and repression to quell voices critical of the policy.[20] And yet it quickly became apparent that the program did not have at its heart the best interest of Antillean populations, or Antillean economies. Rather, BUMIDOM—at least in its first decade— functioned as a state-run placement agency responding to the needs and demands of potential employers. Very few of those displaced by BUMIDOM ended up having access to any sort of professional training. As Alain Anselin insists, the goal was first and foremost to place Antillean workers directly in low-paying jobs that required no specialized skills—such as baggage handlers or domestic workers—and to hold them there. In fact, over time, foreign workers (including those who migrated from Algeria following its independence) ended up with greater upward social and economic mobility than did dislocated Antilleans, moving more quickly into better-paid and less precarious jobs. And when the 1975 economic downturn struck France, many Antilleans found themselves laid off, with no transferable skills that could provide the starting point for professional reconversion.[21]

The BUMIDOM, then, created a racialized underclass of French citizens. Displaced Antilleans were forced to home their presence from the liminal zones of the (post)colonial state. Geographically, they came to occupy the outskirts of the French capital, especially its northeastern quadrant.[22] They faced overwhelming obstacles as they sought to home their political subjectivity within the French state. It quickly became obvious that rather than being *français à part entière* (fully French), they were treated as *français entièrement à part* (fully separated French), to riff on Césaire's powerful formula.[23] For all practical purposes, they were migrants and denied full cultural citizenship in the French metropole. But Debré refused to acknowledge that status, preferring the euphemism "work in the metropole" to economic migration. From the perspective of the French state, to recognize Antilleans as migrants rather than citizens amounted to admitting their cultural difference and therefore ran the risk of stoking separatist fires. In other words, upon their arrival in Paris, Antilleans took in the full measure of the "mirage reality" of their citizenship. Anny Curtius explains: "Paris and its suburbs become the locus of an ambiguous exile since one leaves to seek work in a space that is geopolitically defined as one's own homeland; but at the same time, these are places where one comes to experience their difference from both a community of Franco-French and from immigrants from diverse cultural and geographic horizons."[24]

Glissant likewise highlights, "It is in France that Antillean migrants discover themselves to be different and take full measure of their Antilleanness." Not only do Martinicans and Guadeloupeans become "Antillean" in the metropole; more critically for Glissant, it is through migration to France that Antilleans become aware their own alienation, which had in the Caribbean remained occluded. This harshly illustrates one of the tragic facets of the *détour*: French domination and its effects can be apprehended only through travel from the (post)colonial margins to the metropolitan center, but then, Antillean migrants risk finding themselves so transformed by the experience that a return home is impossible. "The *détour*," concludes Glissant, "leads nowhere."[25]

Antilleans' massive economic migration set off a two-pronged process of racialization and ethnicization. On the one hand, the systematic funneling of Afro-descendants into low-leveled jobs in state administrations or the service industry resulted in a racialization of labor relations, with a white managerial class overseeing black employees.

Conversely—perhaps fueled as much by this exacerbated experience of racialization as by the growth of cultural nationalism "at home"—Guadeloupeans in France used "culture," especially music, to affirm their ethnic specificity and belonging. Just as the new unions in Guadeloupe used the *swaré léwòz* to spread their message and recruit members, in Paris around 1970, the AGEG turned to gwoka to raise political awareness among newly arrived students. But the efforts soon spread beyond the AGEG, as cultural events increasingly allowed for the integration of a population that, contrary to many other migrant communities, found itself scattered across different arrondissements and suburbs. More important, "culture" offered cathartic moments of community affirmation that could mitigate experiences of ostracization within a society whose Jacobin heritage, it should be noted, clung to a color-blind universalism and dismissed race as a serious social factor.[26] Jacky Serin—a percussionist and former AGEG member—insisted that drumming brought psychological support to new immigrants and was an outlet for their daily frustration: "Gwoka may have saved a lot of our people who were in psychological perdition in the French territory." He continues: "In the diaspora, you are French but you are black. You are French but you don't play violin or piano. You play the drum! You are French but if you play in the subway, the police comes running after you. . . . So, there is a certain number of things, whether you want it or not, even if you are not in a political movement, you are in a movement of cultural resistance in spite of yourself."

Indeed, *koud tanbou* started to multiply in the French capital: whether in the subway or on the steps of the landmark Sacré-Coeur cathedral, gwoka made Guadeloupean presence in Paris audible, leading to sometimes violent confrontation with the police.[27] In short, as the French state refused to afford them the label "migrant" and denied their racialization, Antillean migrants used "culture"—especially the aural fields of music and language—to home their place in the metropole, to affirm their presence in the face of an alienating political economy. Put another way, the drum and the Creole language were central to the (post)colonial aurality of Guadeloupean migrants in the metropole. Both would come to define zouk, the music that eventually came out of this experience.

It is obvious that BUMIDOM highlights, once again, the internal contradictions and shortcomings of French republican universalism. As Curtius suggests, BUMIDOM displaced the effects and practice of colonialism from the margins to the center of empire. It operated a translation of the modalities of colonialism. France has long insisted on an understanding of race in cultural rather than biological terms, a strategy that buttresses its assimilationist ideology. As David Beriss outlines: "The French nation has been defined, at least in part, against racial thinking. Instead, culture, understood as a shared worldview and common customs, has come to dominate . . . French self-definitions." In theory, being French is defined by one's relationship to the state. From the perspective of the state, race is not an impediment to assimilation of immigrants, but culture—the refusal to assimilate republican values—can be. Republicanism works to minimize cultural differences and to deny the existence of structural racism. Beriss concludes: "Racism in France is not principally defined by attention to color of by the deployment of racial stereotypes (although it is that as well). Instead, racism is understood primarily as an incorrect or unjust invocation of culture."[28] But BUMIDOM destabilized the already-questionable but still-hegemonic ideal of a color-blind and assimilationist French nation by bringing home and making visible France's own long colonial history premised on the racialization of subalterns.

Yet we also need to shift slightly this portrayal of the BUMIDOM. The BUMIDOM was the most potent expression, the strongest symptom, of

Guadeloupe's sudden and structurally violent conscription into a postindustrial modernity.[29] And while under this new guise France's neocolonialism was no less restrictive or exploitative than in its old forms, it also created new economic, social, and political structures that opened novel artistic, economic, and political horizons. I propose, then, that post-departmentalization migrations—whether organized by the French government or not—transposed the practices of creolization, which were reinvented and reinvigorated by the transversal connections made possible by the enduring presence of the colonial rhizome within the metropolitan space. Post-departmentalization migrations opened new "horizons of possibility" at the same time that they perpetuated the structures of power and the imaginary structures that had animated European colonialism.[30] Under a new (post)colonial and postindustrial context, BUMIDOM fostered "secondary" or discrepant creolizations. Understood as the product of conscription, creolization here necessarily involves both tactics of resistance and strategies of accommodation, both fleeing and homing.

Guy Konket's Discrepant Creolizations

Perhaps no musician better illustrates the extension of creolization processes to the French capital than Guy Konket. Indeed, Konket's music, while rooted in the musical traditions of agricultural workers, went through two phases of incorporation of popular musical styles: once in Guadeloupe and a second time in Paris. There are, then, two audible creolization moments in his music, each reflecting a particular social and musical context and each hinting at slightly different political positionings.[31]

Konket was born in Jabrun, in northern Basse-Terre, in the late 1940s. He grew up in a rural environment, surrounded by notable musicians. His mother, Solange Athénaïse Bac—better known as Man Soso—worked on the nearby sugarcane plantation and was a respected gwoka singer.[32] For several years, Man Soso dated the percussionist Carnot, a now-legendary *léwòz* and quadrille musician. When we talked, Konket reminisced about hiding to listen to Carnot and the many musicians who would come visit his mother. Carnot, for his part, remembered Konket's fascination with the drum. At this time, in the late 1950s—and contrary to the affirmation of Lockel and the patriotic camp—gwoka and quadrille coexisted in most rural areas. In fact, it was not unusual for people to dance quadrille inside Man Soso's *kaz a blan* (the typical housing for agricultural workers) while others participated in a *léwòz* outside.[33] In addition to the quadrille and *léwòz* musicians, Konket also remembers that musicians from local dance bands occasionally visited his mother's house. This musical mix—a testimony to the vibrant musical life of midcentury Guadeloupe—had a profound influence on Konket and informed his later musical choices.[34]

Konket started his own recording career in the late 1960s, working for the two most prominent labels in the French Antilles: Henri Debs and Célini. Recorded around the time of the birth of Lockel's *gwoka modènn*, Konket's recordings offered an alternative performance of gwoka's modernity. Whereas Lockel was involved in a self-conscious and ideologically driven effort to tame Western modernity, Konket is perhaps best heard as a chronicler of the experience of modernity in post-departmentalization Guadeloupe. That is to say that I don't hear in Konket's music the same sort of agonistic relationship to Western modernity that is plainly evident in Lockel's, even if Konket's songs also hint at his own ambivalence toward the social transformations then under way. Through his texts and the fluid musical aesthetics of his performances, Konket brushes a complex portrayal of this period of rapid social and economic mutation.

Many of Konket's early songs remain fairly close to the tradition of *léwòz* and wake singing, covering topics such as a fisherman's crime of passion ("Ban klé a Titine") or a cheating dice player ("Jo mayé dé grenndé-la").[35] But in others, Konket offers a gently critical take on contemporary youth culture. For example, "Baimbridge chaud" addresses the opening of a new high school in Baimbridge, a neighborhood of Pointe-à-Pitre. In this performance and others, Konket sung about his own generation, and he brought a breath of fresh air to gwoka at a time when the music was still relatively marginalized. The composer and multi-instrumentalist Christian Dahomay remembers the impact of Konket's music: "When I was young, only old people sang gwoka; and suddenly a youth burst onto the scene. In Baimbridge, it was a revolution."[36] Yet in "Baimbridge chaud," we can also hear Konket's ironic distance from that generation as he mocks female students who have ambitions to become typists and who, when hitchhiking to school, accept rides only from men driving sports cars.[37]

Konket's music soon came to address the social and political situation of Guadeloupe more directly. "Lapli ka tonbé," recorded around 1970, decries the precariousness of agricultural workers who, paid by the task, are at the mercy of heavy rainfall and mechanical failures that disrupt their normal working schedule. Recorded the same year, "La Gwadloup malad" speaks even more directly to the economic ills facing the country: "Wi mé frè, la Gwadloup malad, o. Nou ké trouvé [fo nou trouvé] rimèd, pou nou sové, péyi-la mé zanmi o!" (Yes, my brothers, Guadeloupe is ill. We have to find [we will find, depending on the version] a remedy to save the country, my friends).[38] Remarkably, in this song, Konket doesn't simply identify France as the source of Guadeloupe's ills; rather, he casts the blame more widely, castigating politicians both in France and in Brussels, the seat of the European Economic Community. This is an important marker of Konket's modern take on gwoka: while typically gwoka songs had focused on the local, Konket not only demonstrates a national consciousness typical of the times but also inscribes that national consciousness within a much larger structure. This also indicates that the patriotic consciousness itself was shifting as the EEC's influence started to grow. Anticolonialism could no longer be conceived of simply as a bilateral conflict.

By the early 1970s, Konket had become an important voice of the social movements in Guadeloupe, even if the singer insists that he has always maintained his independence from nationalist organizations. Wozan Mounien highlights Konket's involvement in Guadeloupean social conflicts:

> It was the strike of 1971. Guy Konket was arrested and jailed on charges that he played gwoka on a picket line, that he excited striking workers, and enticed other workers to keep them from reporting to work. That was the motive. So, at that time, he was imprisoned in Basse-Terre and we put together a collective of lawyers, because [about twenty people had been arrested overall.] In addition, you had students striking in support of agricultural workers. So he went and sang in Baimbridge. For the youths, he had become a very popular singer. Because he was popular and because of his ties to the social movement, he was jailed. And that boosted his career further. In a way, he became the gwoka singer of the people.[39]

But if Konket's lyrics and actions matched the zeitgeist, his musical aesthetics offered an alternative to the then-emerging nationalist orthodoxy of Lockel. Although Konket was backed by a typical *boula* and *makè* ensemble on most recordings, he went on to break the traditional mold in two ways. For one, he started to experiment with the call-and-response structure of *léwòz* and wake songs. The clearest example of this happens in "Lapli ka tombé." The song starts with a long response: "Lapli-la tonbé, pa ni travay pou nou, la la, lapli-la tonbé" (It rained, there is no work for us, it rained). Halfway through the performance, and following a short break from the legendary *makè* Vélo, the *répondè* switch to a shorter response, "tandé" (listen), thus accelerating the pace of the exchange with the lead singer and increasing the overall intensity of the performance. Dahomay points to this sort of practice to explain that the modernization of gwoka was not necessarily limited to the introduction of melodic instruments. "Guy was one

3.1. "Faya faya" response

of the first to arrange the chorus in gwoka," he explains. "From then on, the singer-chorus system was destroyed. Not just anybody could sing the response with Guy, because there were arrangements. If you didn't know them, you couldn't sing. He was one of the first to do that.... The modern aspect isn't necessarily limited to Lockel."[40]

Perhaps more striking is a series of recordings made around 1968. In them, Konket's typical gwoka ensemble is joined by a group of biguine musicians, including the famed alto sax player Emilien Antile. I say that these recordings were striking because they belie the strict division of the Guadeloupean musical field into several ideologically incompatible spheres that the AGEG and Lockel preached at the time. But they were actually not exceptional: other well-respected singers such as Dolor, Robert Loyson, and Chabin—all three having reputations as traditional rather than modern gwoka musicians—recorded songs with biguine instrumentation around this time.[41] For Konket, these collaborations were a natural extension of his childhood experiences in an environment where gwoka, quadrille, and biguine coexisted. Where Lockel followed an ideological line, Konket insisted to me that his choices were guided solely by artistic—and potentially commercial—considerations.[42] Moreover, in contrast to Lockel's *gwoka modènn*, Konket's early music was resolutely tonal, as the tonic-dominant pattern of the bass line in "Faya faya" (fig. 3.1) and the bebop-inflected sax solos of Emilien Antile immediately and unambiguously make audible.

These recordings, mixing the common forms of midcentury Guadeloupean popular music, mark a first creolization moment in Konket's music. Whereas for Lockel there existed "three musics," each with its own position vis-à-vis French colonialism (quadrille as a French imperial imposition, biguine as the sound of assimilation, and gwoka as the sound of resistance), Konket insisted that there is only one: "Music is music," he repeated several times when we talked.[43] This first creolization moment, then, is a sonic rebuttal to the ideologically driven fragmentation of the Guadeloupean musical field. Konket's recordings of that period are no less socially conscious or politically aware than Lockel's. In fact, whereas Lockel's songs tended toward what we could call an aesthetic of the *mot d'ordre* (political slogan), as in songs like "Fò zot savé" (You have to know) or "Lévé pèp" (Get up people), Konket's speaks much more directly to the immediate and concrete preoccupations of the moment, with songs that explicitly address the work conditions that unions were denouncing, the rising cost of living, and the repression that striking workers faced.[44] Konket became, as Mounien asserted, the voice of the people. And he did so without the sort of rupture that Mounien identified in Lockel's music; instead, there is an audible continuity here, a recognition that most Guadeloupeans did not experience the various popular genres as bounded and mutually exclusive but rather as part of the same continuum, a continuum that reached back to the plantation and that tacitly understood that every musical style in Guadeloupe—gwoka, quadrille, and biguine—was born of a double process of resistance and accommodation to the colonial order.[45]

Reflecting back on his own music in 2008, shortly before his passing, Konket further embraced an understanding of gwoka as itself a music of fusion, a fusion that, for him, extended beyond the Guadeloupean archipelago. Echoing Mounien and critiquing what he saw as the arbitrariness of Lockel's aesthetic and ideological choices, the singer outlined a profoundly universalist conception of music:

> [Lockel] said: "There is no *do*, there is no *ré*. . . ." There is none of that stuff with Lockel. But music is music. Whatever the scale. Whether it be the music of *guaguanco* in Cuba, in Africa, music is music. That's all. That's the phenomena. That's what Lockel did not understand. Here, you play gwoka music. You go to Cuba, you play Cuban music. But everywhere, there is one music. It is music. But Lockel wanted to say: "No. Specifically, it is our music, with its own scale that is specific." But in gwoka, we sing with *ré*, we sing with *do*, with everything.[46]

He added: "Gwoka is a mix. There are Cuban contributions, there are African contributions. . . . And that's the result." I prodded further and asked him what, in his eyes differentiated gwoka from other musics. His answer remained unwavering: "Lockel wanted to differentiate [gwoka] from other musics through his atonal-modal system. But this music belongs to everybody. There are contributions. There are no differences. If the African listens to it, he likes it. If the French listens to it, he likes. Everyone likes it. That's it."

Konket was, at that time, speaking from within a different problem-space than what had animated his music from the late 1960s through the 1970s. Here was an artist who, not too long before, had enjoyed a modest amount of international attention as he toured and recorded with American sax player David Murray (see chapter 4) and who had grown somewhat accustomed to responding to journalists. Here was an artist, also, who was speaking at a time when the economic, social, and political pressures of the late twentieth century had morphed into something much more diffuse and had lost much of their urgency (although they would explode back to life with the Lyannaj kont pwofitasyon movement the following year). We hear in his response to my questions a latent cosmopolitanism, an effort to reach an audience that extends far beyond the nation. Konket expresses a sort of vernacular universalism, his own version of the poetics of Relation, in which a supposedly universal musical language born from hybridity ("there are Cuban contributions, there are African contributions") allows listeners to build connections across geographical separation and (post)colonial stratification: "If the African listens to it, he likes it. If the French listens to it, he likes. Everyone likes it. That's it." But Konket's music started sounding this cosmopolitanism long before the singer articulated it verbally, when it underwent what I consider a second creolization moment in Paris.

Around 1970, on the same session that produced "La Gwadloup malad" and "Baimbridge chaud," Konket recorded a song in which he, for the first time, mentioned BUMIDOM. Two parents are looking for their daughter: "Zèzèl w kalé?" (Zèzèl, where are you going?), insistently asks the response. The answer remains elusive until, halfway through the song, the singer interjects: "BIMIDOM, BIMIDOM, BIMIDOM, BIMIDOM!"[47] A few years later, the singer himself migrated to Paris: "It was the same thing for everyone. I left to go be with those Antilleans who had forgotten Guadeloupe. And I brought a message to France and elsewhere as well. I left for that reason, you know."[48]

The message was delivered through Konket's lyrics, with songs like "Kyembé rèd" calling out for resistance: "Kyembé rèd, frè. Kyembé rèd surtou pa moli. Kyembé rèd, surtou pa tranblé. Kyembé rèd surtou pa plèrè douvan misyé-la ka kyembé fwèt-la" (Hang on, brother. Hang on, don't give up. Hang on, don't shake. Hang on, don't cry in front of the man who holds the whip). This type of song fueled the French government's distrust of Konket, and in Paris the singer faced the same sort of repression he had experienced in Guadeloupe. He reminisced: "My first concert in France, it was at the Salle Wagram. The rehearsal . . . Five cop cars came to evacuate the venue. Something about a bomb threat. It wasn't true, right? But because I arrived like a revolutionary, with [my message], so right away: 'He's a revolutionary. Why did he come to this country?'"

This revolutionary attitude infused Konket's musical aesthetic as well. By the early 1980s, surrounded by young musicians, the singer adapted.

In Guadeloupe, Konket had already rubbed elbows with musicians who were slightly younger than he was and who embraced more radical politics, musicians such as Joël Nankin who would become one of the island's most renown visual artist but at the time was involved in the revival of carnival groups and who introduced the *chacha* (a calabash shaker used in carnival music) into Konket's group. Nankin was also a radical activist, closer to the GLA than to the UPLG. Konket also engaged with the percussionists of Takouta. Takouta was unlike anything heard before in Guadeloupe: a collective of three young percussionists who, inspired by Rastafarianism, set out to reconnect gwoka with what Michel Halley—one of the group's members—described as an African intensity or power.[49] The musicians of Takouta played gwoka drums, but each drum played a separate ostinato, therefore greatly increasing the rhythmic complexity of the music. They had apprenticed in Jabrun, and some of them worked with Konket in Guadeloupe. Halley reconnected with Konket in the early 1980s.

Perhaps as a result of these encounters, Konket's music became more rhythmically diverse. Whereas he had previously sung mostly on the *toumblak* rhythm, his group now used a greater variety of rhythms, including the *léwòz*, a rhythm that many in Guadeloupe associate with resistance and fighting. For example, on the album *Guy Konket et le Groupe Ka* (1981), which features a guest appearance by Halley, "La Gwadloup malad" is reinterpreted on a *léwòz* ostinato rather than the original *toumblak*.

But the changes did not stop there. Konket hired a young guitarist by the name of Gilbert Coco. Coco was part of a new generation of musicians who were inspired by Lockel and the nationalist movement to pick up gwoka. Dahomay explains:

> Gilbert started to play gwoka around the same time as me. He had been playing in dance bands and was getting tired of *cadence rampas*. He was looking for something new. . . . It was after Lockel's arrival. So [some musicians] went and played jazz. Others started playing soul, music that was much more American, much more rock, you see? And others still, like Gilbert and I, we decided to play gwoka. There was also Georges Troupé and Robert Oumaou. At the time, it was difficult because there was a lot of separatist pressure that said: only one gwoka, Lockel's. . . . *On sèl mizik* (only one music). The pressure was so strong that many didn't have the courage to persevere down that road.[50]

Coco did not adopt Lockel's *gwoka modènn* system. Instead, within Konket's group, he contributed to creating a groove-oriented music. One night in July 2015, I was lucky enough to sit next to the guitarist at a restaurant in

3.2. "YouYou," basic groove

Sainte-Anne. We immediately struck up a conversation. As we talked about his music and his experience playing with Konket, I shared with him that I heard the impact of Fela Kuti's Afrobeat on Konket's music of the period. He immediately concurred: yes, Fela, but also James Brown. Both genres were, of course, themselves already the products of the cross-circulation and cross-fertilization of the black Atlantic, and both were quite popular among Antilleans in Paris.[51] This influence is most clearly audible on songs like "YouYou" with its slow vamp (fig. 3.2), "Bamileké" with its funk groove, and "La tè touné."[52]

This musical transformation marks Konket's second creolization moment. In Guadeloupe, Konket's music had illustrated what ethnomusicologist Marie-Céline Lafontaine called—in a rebuttal of the nationalist orthodoxy—the Creole continuum of Guadeloupean music.[53] In Paris, Konket's music was both a response to the displacement of colonial dynamics and the product of the "minor" transnational connections that the (post)colonial French capital made possible. His musical style evolved to embrace transnational aesthetics but did so selectively, drawing primarily from other styles of black music associated with political resistance and anticolonialism. I hear his music as enacting a form of vernacular, diasporic cosmopolitanism. A recording like *Guy Konket et le Groupe Ka*—as opposed to Lockel's output—is diasporic and cosmopolitan in its engagement with transnational styles and its suggestion of transversal solidarities. At the same time, it is vernacular to the extent that it demonstrates a localization or homing of these transnational styles. The cosmopolitan and the vernacular exist in tension, even in a dialectical relation, with one another; a tension

Discrepant Creolizations / 109

that, at its heart, captures the negotiations of the politics of belonging that were central to Antillean efforts to "home" their place at the heart of the French (post)colonial state.

Sheldon Pollock defines vernacularization in literature as "the conscious decision of writers to reshape the boundaries of their cultural universe by renouncing the larger world for the smaller place." In renouncing the broader musical universe associated with jazz in favor of the smaller, national place, Lockel turned his back on cosmopolitan and even diasporic ethics of belonging. Konket's music, in contrast, marks a gradual opening, an engagement with circles of belonging that extent beyond the nation and that would come to full fruition with his participation in David Murray's "Creole" recordings in the 1990s. Konket's music, then, offers an example of what Homi Bhabha calls "vernacular cosmopolitanism," a negotiation between an "arbitrary sense of the nation and a necessary postcolonial state."[54]

For Françoise Lionnet, creolization opens up the binary between cosmopolitanism and nationalism.[55] Indeed, by foregrounding the dual process of fleeing and homing, I suggest that creolization allows for a synthesis within the dialectical tension between cosmopolitanism and vernacularization, or between cosmopolitanism and nationalism. This second audible creolization moment in Paris is a "continuance"—"the transformative, displacement, even transfiguration of struggle through continuity into something unrecognizable"—of the first in Guadeloupe, itself a "continuance" of the complex mix of *petit marronnage* and accommodation that saw the transformation of music on the colonial plantation.[56] But just as musical creolization on the plantation could give rise to practices as discrepant as quadrille and gwoka, Guadeloupean musicians' dual drive for public recognition of cultural difference and for professional success produced some ambiguous musical results.

Tumblack and Paco Rabanne

Konket was exceptional in yet another way: he was the first musician to arrive in Paris with the explicit goal of living from his music. Everyone else playing gwoka in the French capital had come to work or study, but Konket came to play, to deliver a message. At the time, performance opportunities were very limited for gwoka musicians. In Guadeloupe, the percussionist and composer Robert Oumaou remembers that his group Gwakasonné mainly performed at friends' houses, with a few occasional concerts at the Centre des Arts, Pointe-à-Pitre's largest concert hall, once it opened in 1978. In the 1970s and 1980s, there were hardly any small venues (music clubs or

110 / Chapter Three

restaurants) featuring live gwoka in the archipelago. The situation was only slightly better in Paris. Guy Konket's concert at the Salle Wagram—a venue that can accommodate between 800 and 1,300 people—was exceptional. Other musicians like Erick Cosaque were limited to performing in restaurants and cabarets like the Canne à sucre or for various Antillean associations. Opportunities to perform in bigger venues were scarce.[57]

Yet in the 1970s, as the number of bands performing so-called modern, progressive, or instrumental gwoka multiplied, a few of them found ways to perform regularly outside of the traditional setting of the *swaré léwòz*. They also started to record with remarkable frequency, even if they did so at their own expense. Self-produced albums are still the norm in gwoka.[58] This means that, for the most part, gwoka musicians do not have access to a distributor. Most groups sell their albums directly to audience members at live events or by putting them on consignment in local stores. This situation makes groups with recording contracts stand out. In Guadeloupe, Henri Debs, the island's biggest record producer, recorded very little gwoka in the 1970s and 1980s, the two biggest exceptions being Konket in the late 1960s and early 1970s and the trumpeter Kafé in the early 1980s. It is in this context that we turn to another effort at homing Guadeloupean music in Paris.

Around 1976, a group of Guadeloupean musicians including the percussionists Marcel Magnat and Daniel Losio started performing regularly at the Feijoada, a Martinican-run restaurant near the Hôtel de Ville in Paris. Both Magnat and Losio had been in the French capital for a few years. Both had come to study and were supplementing their income by playing music. Both also had contacts with the AGEG and other nationalist organizations. In our conversations, both expressed sympathies for the nationalist cause but explained that they never formally joined any militant group. At the Feijoada, the two men performed traditional gwoka with a group of friends. The restaurant catered to what the French refer to as *le Tout-Paris*, a crowd composed of famous musicians, actors, designers, and other personalities.[59]

Among the Feijoada's patrons, the group attracted the attention of fashion designer Paco Rabanne. It is not clear whether the designer was then in the midst of or at the beginning of what he described as a love affair with the French Antilles.[60] Regardless, Rabanne invited the group to perform for his upcoming fashion show, an Antillean-inspired collection. He also hired Losio, who had a gift for metal- and woodworking, to design some jewelry for the collection. Most important, he offered to negotiate a recording deal on behalf of the group with Barclay, then one of France's biggest recording companies.

Given the overall economic marginalization of gwoka musicians at the time, the partnership with Rabanne was a boon for the Guadeloupean artists who called their group Tumblack. They recorded an LP with Barclay, played for several of Rabanne's shows, and performed in some of Paris's most fashionable nightclubs.[61] They even opened for Bob Marley's Parisian concerts in June 1978. It is not surprising, then, that both Losio and Magnat remember the group with fondness and are proud to call Rabanne their friend. They describe their relationship with the designer as a fruitful partnership with a generous and respectful patron. They both assured me that neither Rabanne, Eddie Barclay, nor Yves Hayat—who produced the LP and wrote the arrangements for its two hit singles, "Caraïba" and "Chunga funk"—intruded on the group's artistic direction. Thirty years later, their glee is still apparent as they recall playing at the Pavillon de Paris in front of ten thousand people or getting to meet the Rolling Stones. They also proudly remind anyone who would listen that they were the first gwoka artists to have their music registered with the Société des auteurs, compositeurs et éditeurs de musique (SACEM), the French agency responsible for managing music copyrights.

In spite of the musicians' positive recollections, Tumblack raises some important questions. From a practical standpoint, Paco Rabanne all but took ownership of the group. He controlled the rights to their compositions and managed their bookings. Perhaps not surprisingly given his profession, he even provided them with their stage costumes, which brings us to the second issue: the presentation of the group.

Rabanne may have been inspired by the French Antilles, but he saw them through a problematic primitivist gaze. In an interview published in *Hi-Fi* magazine around 1978, he explained that he preferred Guadeloupean over Martinican music because the former had remained closer to Africa, whereas contact with whites resulted in a Martinican music that was too modern for his taste. In contrast, he declared, "Guadeloupean music is the primitive music of the rain forest in all of its power and wild beauty."[62] To capture this essence, the designer insisted that the studio be decorated with tropical plants while the group recorded its album. The same sort of exoticist approach is on display on Tumblack's album cover. Indeed, the cover plays on familiar representations of black physicality and sexuality: the couple's clothing is designed to expose more than it covers, the woman's open legs express her availability, the faces are tensed in an orgasmic grin as bolts of light and a powerful wave shoot from the gwoka.

Musically, the LP is divided, with the first side offering four compositions by the Guadeloupean members of the group. Three of the four numbers are instrumental and, save occasional sound effects, feature only percussion instruments. The song "Jubilé," in contrast, spotlights the voice of Marcel

Magnat, accompanied by a very slow, single drum pulse. The titles of three of the four songs—"Invocation," "Jubilé," "Vaudou"—evoke an imagined Caribbean mysticism. The first side of the album closes with a traditional song, "Parlement." The second side, at first, sounds like a continuation of the first, opening with a *toumblak* mixed with *boulagyèl* vocables. Only occasional bass-guitar slides allude to what's to come: three minutes in most of the polyrhythmic layers fade out, only to be replaced by an insistent bass-drum beat. Gwoka gives way to disco. Indeed, the next two songs on the album, "Caraïba" and "Chunga funk," were composed by Yves Hayat, a veteran of the French disco scene. On these songs, Tumblack is augmented by the rhythm and horn sections of the disco group the Droids, whom Eddie Barclay hired especially for the session. On "Caraïba," the mix of disco grooves, *toumblak* rhythm, occasional *boulagyèl*, funk bass lines, and tight horn arrangements that Hayat conjured makes for effective dance music. On "Chunga funk," the gwoka elements recede further into the background, and the track ends up sounding much more like run-of-the-mill disco, making the return of a very traditional-sounding "Bateau-la passé [*sic*]" on the brief album closer rather jarring.

Where does Tumblack fit among gwoka's contested aural and political field? On the one hand, the group is an extension of the same ideological process of national affirmation that had started with Lockel's *gwoka modènn* nearly a decade earlier. There are important differences, though. Lockel, driven by his staunch Marxist and anticolonial convictions, resisted turning his music into a commodity. On one of the rare occasions when he accepted to speak with me, he offered me one of his recordings. He wouldn't accept a payment from me, explaining that he had never recorded to make money. Tumblack obviously functioned very differently: theirs was music that was carefully engineered to be commoditized. The Guadeloupean musicians continue to be proud of having successfully, even if briefly, homed their place within the music industry. They see themselves as the precursors to the zouk wave that hit France, and much of the world, just a few years later. In our conversation, Magnat pointed out that bassist Pierre-Édouard Décimus decided to start the group Kassav' upon hearing Tumblack and that Kassav's two dancers also started out working with him.

But the commodification of gwoka in metropolitan France raises the specter of colonial exploitation, and both Rabanne and the group soon attracted the ire of the nationalist press. It did not help that, in 1979, as Rabanne prepared to premiere his new Antillean-inspired collection in Guadeloupe, he ran an ad in *France-Antilles* that read: "Paco Rabanne leads the way to help Guadeloupean culture . . . What about you?"[63] In response, the separatist newspaper *Ja Ka Ta* published an article in which an "an aware Guadeloupean artist" compared Rabanne's involvement with Guadeloupean culture—music in particular—to slavery and scathingly denounced the designer's racism. The article was accompanied by artwork depicting a bull fighter (Rabanne was born in Spain) ready to stab a male gwoka player and female dancer. In a caricature of Tumblack's album cover, the two are clad in a loincloth and the dancer's breasts are completely exposed.

In this chapter, we have seen how gwoka in Paris came to confront and reflect the limits of (post)colonial hospitality, the complex, ambiguous, and multileveled play of integration, exclusion, identification, and disidentification within the remnants of the imperial matrix. Animating these (post)colonial entanglements are discrepant creolizations, continuances of the principles of homing and fleeing that emerged on the margins colonial plantation. With the music of Guy Konket, we saw how creolization—employed as an analytical tool—can synthesize the dialectics of nationalism and diasporic cosmopolitanism, suggesting a transcendence of nationalism by sounding lateral solidarities. Yet if creolization involves both accommodation and disruption, Tumblack's example suggests that it cannot bridge the distance between anticolonial nationalism and capitalist cosmopolitanism. Moreover, it reminds us that creolized auralities—even if they take anticolonialism as their starting point—are not immune to being subsumed back into (neo)colonial logics of capitalist exploitation that they may, in fact, never really fully flee. This was true of quadrille and biguine, and one could argue that it has also been true of zouk, a transnational music that has tried to maintain a delicate balance of its national consciousness, its pan-Caribbean horizon, and its global commercial ambitions.[64]

By the early 1980s, the Guadeloupean separatist movement had reached its peak and faced a number of challenges. For one, the election of the socialist François Mitterrand to the French presidency shuffled the political field that had undergirded nationalist demands not only in the French Antilles but also in Corsica and Brittany. Dominique Cyrille explains: "Mitterrand proclaimed that the nation was made out of regions—among which the overseas departments—and each had its specificity. He therefore encouraged the use of regional cultural expressions. These new, and highly effective, cultural politics were part of the socialist project to protect the integrity of the nation and silence discrepant voices."[65] Mitterrand's *politique des régions* opened the door for the promotion and institutionalization of regional cultural forms. The strategy was cunning: in a display of hegemony, the state gave in to some demands in order to maintain its control over peripheral regions. Regionalization thus deprived the Guadeloupean nationalist movement of its most important foil: the French state could no longer serve as a simple, direct, and uniformly antagonistic enemy.[66]

As the *camp patriotique* splintered over whether or not separatist parties should run candidates in local elections, it struggled to articulate a clear and consistent political vision.[67] By the early 1990s, the UPLG had backed away from demanding outright independence in favor of a form of autonomy that it called a "new associated community."[68] Meanwhile, the more radical wing of the separatist camp spawned the GLA, then the Alliance révolutionnaire caraïbe. Unsatisfied with the slow pace of political change, these organizations engaged in a number of violent actions in both Paris and Guadeloupe in the early 1980s. Some of these actions, like the Alliance révolutionnaire's bombing of the French prefecture in Basse-Terre, which injured twenty-three people, may have contributed to alienating most of the Guadeloupean population from the separatist cause. Within a decade, the cunning of France's decentralization combined with the splintering of the *camp patriotique* fueled a rapid weakening of the separatist movement: by 1994, the UPLG's membership was down to about a tenth of its peak enrollment from ten years earlier.[69]

However, by the 1990s, even if it had not achieved political independence, the nationalist movement had managed to dramatically alter the place of both Creole and gwoka in Guadeloupean society. In the following decades, a new generation of musicians would appropriate the *ka* to express new horizons of cultural and political belonging. Meanwhile, cultural activists shifted their strategy from an open confrontation with the French state to the tactics of subversive engagement of the *détour*. It is to these musicians and activists whom we turn in the remaining two chapters to further explore the creolized aurality of Guadeloupean gwoka.

FOUR

Diasporic or Creole Aurality?
Aesthetics and Politics across the Abyss

In 1989, reflecting on twenty years of activity, Gérard Lockel sought to address those listeners who continued to insist on an audible kinship between *gwoka modènn* and jazz: "The high degree of technical proficiency on the different instruments, the fact of being a music of the black diaspora in America constitute points of convergence," he wrote. However, he immediately added: "But the resemblance stops there. These two musics, gwoka and jazz, are built on different bases."[1] In contrast, Guadeloupean trumpeter Franck Nicolas introduced at the turn of the millennium a new music that he dubbed *jazz ka* and described as having a "gwoka basis" but being otherwise "pure jazz." He explains: "I feel black, a descendant of slaves, like the Americans who are like us, who have the same roots. Me, I see my thing in this logic."[2] While Lockel insists on *gwoka modènn* as an "atonal-modal music," Nicolas embraces the tonal and modal harmonic language of modern jazz. Moreover, to Lockel's unadulterated nationalism, Nicolas responds with an embrace of his hybridity: "My mother is French, my father is Guadeloupean. I also claim this side of me. France is half of me; it is my mother."

In addition to Lockel's nationalism and Nicolas's *métissage*, consider yet another perspective.[3] In July 2008, I was interviewing the percussionist Klod Kiavué about his collaboration with the African American jazz saxophonist David Murray. Between 1998 and 2009, Kiavué and Murray worked together on a series of four albums that the journalist Jacques Denis described, in his liner notes for the album *Gwotet* (2004), as the "soundtrack to what Glissant has called 'Creolisation.'" We were sitting at a table on the veranda of Kiavué's house in Grande Savane, and I—inspired as much by Denis's comment as by my then infatuation with *Éloge de la créolité* (*In Praise of Creoleness*)—brought up creoleness. Kiavué replied: "This thing of *créolité*, it has always been a problem for this music. Because not everybody embraces the concept. . . . I don't embrace it." He then got up and went inside to retrieve his dictionary. He opened it and pointed to the definition of *Creole*: "a person of white race, born in the intertropical colonies, especially the Antilles." How could Kiavué, whose rebellious dreadlocks unabashedly signal his pride in his Afro-Caribbean heritage, recognize himself in this definition of *Creole*?

The contrast among the approaches of Lockel, Nicolas, and Kiavué points to a tension present in gwoka's creolized aurality between nationalism, on the one hand, and diasporic and Creole cosmopolitanisms, on the other hand, a tension that the encounter between jazz and gwoka makes audible.

In Guadeloupe, jazz and the so-called contemporary forms of gwoka exist on a sort of musical continuum. They both often use similar instrumentations and feature instrumental, often virtuosic improvisations. And both of them attract middle-class audiences who "listen to music like they read a book"—as the guitarist Marc Bernos once told me—rather than dance to it, as is far more common throughout the Caribbean.[4] Moreover, both jazz and contemporary forms of gwoka are occasionally programmed in the same venues, such as the informal concerts of the Ti Paris (a pizzeria restaurant in Gosier), the privately owned music club LaKasa, and the publicly subsidized Centre culturel Sonis. A number of musicians function at the articulation between these two styles: in addition to those discussed later in this chapter and Marc Bernos, who performs with the group Kriyolio, these include the bassists Marc Jalet and Gérard Poumaroux, as well as the guitarists Alfred Memel and Alex Jabot. Some, like the guitarist Christian Laviso, are most entrenched on the gwoka side of the spectrum, although Laviso has collaborated extensively with the American saxophonists David Murray and Kenny Garret. Others move freely along the spectrum, such as the percussionist Sonny Troupé, whose different projects span the divide between jazz and gwoka: from his duets with pianist Gregory Privat, focused on original compositions and improvisations, to his continued participation in Kimbol, a *gwoka modènn* group first created by his father in the 1980s. As Jalet, Bernos, and Troupé all highlighted in their conversations with me, the main difference between jazz and "instrumental" gwoka lays in the political value given each style. Anything falling in the gwoka category carries the history of Guadeloupean identity militancy. Jazz, in contrast, is free from this political weight, but its cosmopolitanism can be both liberating and a liability. Biguine belongs on this continuum as well, but in Guadeloupe, it has never quite recovered from the critiques of the nationalist movement. Yet local jazz musicians often include a few biguines in their repertoire, and the pianist Alain Jean-Marie—who initiated the "jazzification" of biguine in the late 1960s—maintains his influential presence across the whole spectrum.

In this chapter, I propose that jazz and gwoka have—at different times and in different hands—combined to form diasporic auralities through which contested imaginaries are performed, longings and belongings are negotiated and produced, and discrepant Antillean ways of being are sounded. Put another way, the music of Lockel, Kiavué, and Nicolas illustrates discrepant ways of conceiving their positions as Guadeloupean, as members of the African diaspora, and as French (post)colonial subjects.

These do not need to be mutually exclusive. In fact, they can coexist in the thickness of the (post)colonial experience. During the 2010 Festival Gwoka in Sainte-Anne, I listened to Franck Nicolas's concert with a friend of mine who has deep nationalist sympathies. My friend offered this appraisal, which captured this (post)colonial unease: "As a gwoka aficionado," he shared, "I do not like [this music,] but the jazz fan in me likes it very much." His response is symptomatic of the capacity to "hear double" within creolized auralities. However, whereas Edwin Hill equates "hearing double" with "impaired, unreliable, or faulty perception," I argue that the contradictory impulses of nationalism, diasporicity, and creoleness should not be read as evidence of a putative incoherence within Antillean (post)colonial subjectivity.[5] Rather, the three cases presented in this chapter illustrate a complex and dynamic poetic marked by the strategic interweaving of the trace, opacity, and the abyss. Thinking with these terms borrowed from Glissant's poetics of Relation enables us to articulate nationalism, creolization, and diaspora. While I suggest that the poetics of Relation may illuminate some of the mechanisms that constitute the "practice of diaspora," I am not concerned here with diaspora as a thing in itself; rather, I am interested in what the strategic embrace and rejection of diasporicity and creoleness tell us about Guadeloupean (post)coloniality.[6] I turn to trace and opacity to elucidate the processes of homing and fleeing that Michaeline Crichlow has identified as central operating principles in contemporary processes of creolization. Specifically, trace and opacity allow us to clarify how fleeing and homing—read metaphorically as disavowal and embrace—translate into musical aesthetics, or, vice versa, how the sounds and silences of music reveal complex and open-ended processes of positioning articulated across the abyss of slavery, colonialism, and their aftermaths. But to better situate this problematic, we need to first take an extended theoretical detour.

Theorizing across the Abyss: Diaspora and Creolization

Rèpriz. The choreographer Lénablou once commented to me that "because of its origins, gwoka has always been political." Perhaps one of the most contested aspect of the *ka* relates precisely to its origin. Is the Guadeloupean drum a product of the plantation system or proof that, in spite of that system's brutality, enslaved Africans were able to retain specific African technologies? In other words, is gwoka the product of creolization or of diaspora? Looking at the system used to adjust the tension of the drumhead offers a potential avenue of investigation and interpretation. This approach is attractive because the tension system of the gwoka, using ropes adjusted with wooden keys, distinguishes the Guadeloupean drum from its Caribbean cousins, such as the drums of Puerto Rican *bomba*. Where does this tension system come from? Again, narratives of creolization or diaspora are possible. Many musicians in Guadeloupe point to linguistic evidence to elucidate the origin of their drum. Because the word *zoban*, which denotes the rope-covered hoop around the drumhead is a creolization of the French *hauban* (shroud, or a ship's standing rigging), they argue that the tension system is an adaptation of nautical technology. This interpretation imagines the drum as a colonial creation, an instrument born of the syncretization of European and African technologies on the plantation. The existence of several drums using similar tension systems around the circum-Caribbean (e.g., the *garawoun* of Belize) may confirm this interpretation, or it may invite an entirely different story, one that emphasizes the diasporic spread of West African knowledge in the Americas. In fact, the *soboun* of Benin uses a similar tension system as the gwoka and *garawoun*. Could the gwoka be the American heir to this West African ancestor? This interpretation would support the claim of gwoka musicians who feel a connection to an African heritage as they perform.[7] As an ebullient *tanbouyé* declared to me at a gwoka gathering outside Paris in 2016, "Me, when I sit on the drum: it's Africa!" Ultimately, whether one chooses to emphasize an approach based in creolization or diaspora—whether the gwoka is interpreted as coming from Guinea, the Congo, Dahomey, or the plantation—depends on one's own position and ideological stakes. As with other "traces," the *ka* provides only a connection to a "point of entanglement," although it remains a symbol in which reversion drives (*pulsions de retour*) can be projected.[8]

Diaspora and creolization have emerged as the two privileged models with which to theorize the (post)colonial predicament of the black Atlantic and its residual entanglements. I turn here to existing scholarship on these two concepts to show that Guadeloupean musicians' unease with these terms echo their theoretical fluidity and may, in fact, be informed by some of the connotations the terms carry. Conversely, Guadeloupean musicians' ambivalence toward their diasporicity and creoleness suggests a need to temper academic urges toward overarching—and often overreaching—theorization.

The challenge, in other words, is to bridge the gap between diaspora and creolization as theoretical concepts and diasporicity and creoleness as resulting from, illustrating, or participating in historical, social, political, and cultural processes and praxis.[9] Because Glissant and others have critiqued the identity category of "creoleness" as too static in comparison to the open-ended process of creolization, I want to insist here that the two dyads diaspora-diasporicity and creolization-creoleness are not meant to distinguish dynamic processes from their fixed results; rather, my approach is meant to be thoroughly dialectical, recognizing that creoleness and diasporicity have contingent and unstable meanings and import.[10]

Diaspora and creolization may seem, at first, at odds with each other, especially in their scholarly anthropological treatment. For example, Robin Cohen underscores what he sees as an opposition between creolization, understood as a "'here and now' sensibility that erodes old roots," and diasporic consciousness, which is forever looking for a lost and remote "home."[11] But the theoretical frictions between the two concepts goes further. They can be understood as operating along two axes. The first axis opposes retentionist and creolist approaches within the anthropology of African American culture. The second uses diasporic and creolist models to plot competing racial formations within Caribbean imaginaries and, by association, the contested claims of authenticity attached to various artistic expressions of Caribbean identity and political subjectivity. In what follows, I first outline these competing models and their attendant politics, then propose ways to transcend their dialectical opposition.

Elucidating the first axis, David Scott highlights a profound epistemic contrast between two opposing approaches to the study of African American culture: a retentionist school that asserts Africans' agency in shaping the Atlantic World and the societies that emerged from it, and a creationist—read, *creolist*—approach that stresses "the invention of distinctively Caribbean modes of life and thought."[12] As Scott points out, both schools are grounded in Melville Herskovits's work, from which they then diverged in contrasting ways: one insisted on enslaved Africans' capacity to perpetuate and transmit African culture in the face of colonial oppression; the other was no less committed to a narrative of resistance but challenged "claims of the distinctive 'Africanness' of African American culture." Rather than emphasizing retention as the primary site of cultural resistance, creolists have located enslaved Africans' resistance in their successful efforts to create institutions "on the edges" of the plantation that "would prove responsive to the needs of everyday life under the limiting conditions that slavery imposed on them."[13] In short, while the two approaches recognize that African American cultures are born from the encounter of African and European cultures in the New World under the oppressive regime of plantation colonialism, they differ as to the degree and kind of knowledge that they view transplanted Africans as being able to retain.[14] At any rate, Scott's interest lays not in a positivist debate over the extent of African retentions but in the different political projects implicit in different theoretical studies of the African diaspora. By respectively foregrounding retention or adaptation and creation, these schools ground African Americans' subject positions in contrasting histories and geographies. They imply two contrasting understandings of what it means to be black in the Americas. The former emphasizes a primordial relationship to Africa. In contrast, the latter—while still recognizing a foundational Africanist grammar—understands the plantation as the principal generative locus of African American culture. The first allows for a quest to trace African American culture back to its implicitly premodern points of origin on the African continent, however compromised or frustrated that effort may be. The second only admits a return to the nexus of the colonial plantation, a posture that inscribes African American cultures as "countercultures of modernity."[15]

These opposing approaches were clearly in evidence when, during a May 2017 conference in Guadeloupe, a panel including the Afrocentrist literary scholar Ena Eluther, the creolist linguist Lambert Félix-Prudent, and the choreographer Lénablou. Eluther's presentation was entirely in Creole, to defend the idea that Africa—broadly conceived—constituted the unconscious foundation of the Guadeloupean soul. Félix-Prudent responded with a presentation in French that highlighted Guadeloupean and Martinican Creoles as the syncretic products of French colonialism. As such, both the lexicon and grammar of French Creoles reveal the overwhelming influence of the dominant language, argued Félix-Prudent, explicitly contradicting Eluther. Lénablou, for her part, struck a middle ground, offering an embodied reading of departmentalization as head and feet pulling in opposite directions. These presentations thus offered three ways of understanding contemporary Guadeloupe, each tugging toward different points of origins: Africa and its diaspora, France and the colonial heritage of the plantation, and the unsteady dance of post-departmentalization entanglement.

This panel, during which Caribbean societies were imagined as either extensions of African culture(s) or as New World creations, resonated with the implicit tension of competing "racial projects."[16] This is the second axis of tension between diaspora and creolization. Indeed, for Eluther, as in the works of artists and cultural critiques including Aimé Césaire and Amiri Baraka, and even Paul Gilroy, invocations of diasporicity cannot be extricated from the construction or performance of blackness, albeit in often divergent forms.[17] In contrast, as Stuart Hall emphasizes, creoleness "was never historically, and is not today, fixed racially," which is not to say that creoleness was never racialized.[18] Rather, the adjective *Creole* has participated in several racial projects and been attached to contradictory racial formations. As Palmié points out, in its original meaning, *Creole* served to distinguish Old World populations and their progeny born in the New World, whether one was seeking to differentiate American-born children from their metropolitan Spaniard parents or plantation-born slaves from the *bozales* born in Africa. For Palmié, the term lacked "any notions of explicitly racial or ethnic difference and least of all any form of hybridity or mixedness." However, in considering, for example, the contrast between the words *criollo* (American born) and *peninsular* (Spanish born) in the Spanish colonies, it seems disingenuous to completely divorce early European musings on the impact of climate and geography on colonists' physiology and moral character from their nascent colonial racial project.[19] Moreover, although Palmié is right to point out that the association of creolization with hybridity (as in the writings of Glissant and Hall, but also, and more problematically, in the anthropological embrace of the concept during the 1990s) is a rather recent reinterpretation of the concept, it remains that, from its inception, creolization theory characterizes approaches that are relational and contrastive. As such—and I am aware here that I border on an overgeneralization—it may be more appropriate to conclude that, while diaspora participates in debates about the cultural expression of a black authenticity, creolization has increasingly become associated with "post-authentic cultural plurality" in the discourse of many cultural critics.[20]

Diasporic authenticity and its deconstruction have likewise been at the center of scholarly debates about African American and Caribbean musics, again evincing competing racial projects. In the work of scholars such as Portia Maultsby, Samuel Floyd, Olly Wilson, and Brenda Dixon Gottschild, claims to shared and enduring musical aesthetics rest on the transmission of various Africanisms, specific traits that connect African American musics to African practices.[21] These claims to diasporicity reinforce music's role as a key media through which racial projects are enacted and unto which racial imaginations are projected, masking—or at least downplaying—the play of differences (e.g., geographic, gender, class) that animate diasporic formations.[22]

In contrast, Denis Constant Martin appeals to Glissant and creolization in an effort to transcend jazz's racial imagination. Whereas under the conceptual frame of diaspora, African American musical aesthetics become racial boundary markers, Martin goes in the opposite direction and points to creolization as a process that enables the "absorption, and assimilation, of differences and eventually amounted to transcending the ideological constructions of difference that support any 'racial imagination.'"[23] Martin thus claims that rethinking jazz as a Creole music or even an expression of *le Tout-Monde* enables scholars to reconcile the music's black roots and its subsequent universalization.

It should be clear by now that diaspora and creolization are concepts that, even as they profess to describe a certain social reality, are highly contingent on specific political and epistemic values. So far, I have traced some of the tensions that this creates within Anglophone literature, but these tensions appear magnified if we put Anglophone and Francophone scholarship in dialogue with each other. As Christine Chivallon explains, while French scholars do not shy from writing about what James Clifford calls "centered" diasporas (e.g., Jewish, Greek, Armenian, but also Chinese and Lebanese), they tend to turn to a discourse of migration in their analysis of Antillean societies. For Chivallon, this distinction hinges on different understandings of diaspora: French scholars remain attached to a conception of diaspora that emphasizes historical continuity along with the maintenance of a shared cultural identity and consciousness across multiple geographic locations (a deterritorialized cultural unity); meanwhile, she argues, Anglophone academics—in the persons of Stuart Hall and Paul Gilroy—have transformed the concept to account for mobility, interconnectivity, and hybridity. In two articles on this subject, Chivallon endeavors to shine a light on the particular political project behind Gilroy's *Black Atlantic*.[24] Yet it is remarkable that she does not extend this analysis with a self-reflexive elucidation of the political motivations behind the French attachment to a relatively stable conception of diaspora.

It seems to me that French academics' reluctance to imagine Antillean societies as diasporic has a lot to do with France's ambivalence toward race and racialization.[25] Chivallon herself reveals this much when she critiques black British scholarship in which "Antillean specificities are often lost within 'racial' studies where the category 'black' trumps all other distinctions."[26] Perhaps it is not surprising, then, that British-style diaspora studies, with their focus on race, have not gained as much traction among French intellectual circles as the concept of creolization, with its articulation of cultural and racial hybridity. In fact, for the Canadian sociologist Abdoulaye Gueyle, French scholars have been particularly resistant to studying the African diaspora precisely because the topic threatens the egalitarian—and therefore color-blind—ideals of French republicanism. At the same time, the French have embraced creolization and creoleness, concepts that are much easier to reconcile with the dominant assimilationist ideology.[27] Recall, for example, Bourdieu and Wacquant's denunciation of the unexamined embrace of American-style race studies beyond the specific historical and sociological context of the United States as a product of the "cunning of imperialist reason."[28]

The political inclination of French scholarship also becomes plainly evident when contrasting the startlingly divergent readings of Césaire and Fanon offered by two anthropologists: the French Jean-Loup Amselle and the American Gary Wilder. Both use Césaire and Fanon to explore the tension—within the French (post)colonial state—between the promise of universal republican rights and the uneven application of those ideals. Sympathetic to Césaire and Fanon's arguments, the American anthropologist concludes that we cannot truly grasp the French "imperial nation-state" without confronting "the complex relationship between racism, rationality, and antiracism in French colonial politics." Race, for Wilder, is at the center of the gap between the abolition of slavery and actual, complete, and effective decolonization within the French republic.[29] The contrast with Amselle could not be starker. Indeed, Amselle reads Césaire and Fanon has having contributed to (he even suggests that they may have introduced) constructions of ethnic or racial essentialism in France. He then critiques them for their emphasis on race as a structuring element of French and Antillean societies. For Amselle, this amounts to nothing else than a rejection of "sociological approaches" to our understanding of Antillean societies. In contrast to his American counterpart, then, the French anthropologist insists that class should be given primacy of place and race understood as a product of class distinctions.[30]

It is in this context that we should understand the popularity and impact of Glissant and the authors of *Éloge de la créolité* in French intellectual circles, for these Antillean intellectuals' projects all work to deconstruct racial essentialisms. By emphasizing *métissage* in *Le discours antillais*, Glissant undermines any claims to racial purity and singular origins. The philosopher later amplified this position as he shifted from *métissage* to creolization—which he conceived as an unbounded, unlimited *métissage* that generates "unexpected and unforeseeable results"—and his adoption of the rhizome to displace the metaphor of roots.[31] Furthermore, Glissant characterizes the *pulsion de retour*—diasporic longing for a return to a lost homeland—not only as antithetical to relation but also, and more important, as a violent denial of the creolizing effects of colonialism and slavery.[32] As we will see, his views on the topic became more complex as he further developed his poetics of Relation, but in *Le discours antillais*, Glissant insists on an embrace of creolization as the only viable means to constitute an Antillean community caught between the lure of colonial mimesis and diasporic longing. For their parts, in *Éloge de la créolité*, Bernabé, Chamoiseau, and Confiant purport to displace claims of authenticity from essentialist racial identities to an "ever-evolving *diversalité*," a neologism that, by gesturing at the universality of diversity, remains compatible with French universalist republican claims. In fact, while the creolists—like Glissant before them—nod toward separatist politics, they have been heavily criticized for serving up a "peculiarly French (Caribbean) movement."[33]

But perhaps the French political appropriation of creoleness is most clearly evidenced by the endorsement of Victorin Lurel—former socialist president of the *région* Guadeloupe and a former *ministre des Outre-mer* under President François Hollande—of the short manifesto published by the Guadeloupean philosopher Laurent Farrugia and linguist Hector Poullet under the title *Tous les hommes sont des créoles* (All Men are Creoles). Lurel writes, "I do not know if everyone is Creole but I know that our Republic is rich and proud of its diversity; and if Creoleness—as a universal ideal of reciprocal understanding and mutual respect—can help the human race [*le genre humain*] become what it [already] is, then, why not Creoleness?"[34] This quote perfectly illustrates the complexity of contemporary political positioning in Guadeloupe, mixing in the course of a single sentence a nod to French universal values, a quote from *L'Internationale* (*le genre humain*), and a nod to the separatist motto "to become what we already are" (*devenir ce que nous sommes*).

Moreover, even as Glissant, Chamoiseau, and their fellow Martinican intellectuals endeavor to construct pan-Antillean, pan-Creole, or even universal movements, they are subjected to charges that their ideas remain the product of a political and intellectual history specific to Martinique and do not translate well to the nearby island of Guadeloupe. These critiques emanate as much from literary scholars and anthropologists as they do from some of the people I have spoken with in Guadeloupe.[35] For example, Lénablou once remarked to me as I brought up Glissant that his ideas—and specifically his terminology—speak more to the Martinican than the Guadeloupean experience. The slam poet and novelist Ti Malo likewise pointed out that, in Guadeloupe, "we don't speak of creoleness. We speak of fusion, we speak of encounters between tradition and modernity, we may even create a specific terminology. But we don't turn to the term 'creoleness' to designate [syncretic practices within Guadeloupean culture.]"[36] However, for Ti Malo, there exists a form of what he coined "vernacular creoleness" in

Guadeloupe. He explained: "The term 'creoleness' is nonetheless used in Guadeloupe, outside of the literary field. But, it seems to me that, when we speak of creoleness, it is specifically to claim a double belonging to both Guadeloupe and France; to claim both the Christmas tree and the *pois d'angole*, champagne and rum; to claim both Creole and French. . . . When I have questioned this conception, what came out was that the two cultures are given equal place, are treated on the same plane, with the same consideration, by those who profess their creoleness."[37]

It seems undeniable that Guadeloupeans' ambivalent attitudes toward creolization and creoleness reveal, in part, the long-term impact of distinctive nationalist conceptions in Guadeloupe and Martinique. It should be noted here once again that anti- and (post)colonial Antillean politics have been articulated primarily around class consciousness as well as territorial and cultural distinctions. While Césaire used *négritude* to affirm a form of diasporic cultural nationalism essential to his efforts to expose the gaps in French republican universalism, neither he nor the next generation of Antillean politicians embraced creolization as a unifying principle: neither Martinican nor Guadeloupean nationalisms were constructed as "Creole nationalisms," in contrast to the strategic use of creoleness in Jamaica and Trinidad. To sum up, in the French Antilles, appeals to creoleness, creolization, or diasporicity are laden with multiple levels of connotations, with horizons that range from cosmopolitan intellectual debates to transatlantic politics of racial authenticity and the objections they provoke within national intellectual traditions, and reach all the way to the construction of differentiated national subjectivities.

Faced with this overdetermination, several responses are possible. One may try to curtail the proliferation of meanings and narrow the theoretical and practical definition of each term: creoleness, diasporicity, or the nation. This is the approach that Palmié and Price continue to advocate with regard to creolization, insisting, in short, that their theoretical model describes empirical processes and should supersede less literal usages.[38] Another approach consists of reconciling diaspora and creolization by merging the two concepts, or "creolizing diaspora." This is the line pursued by Michaeline Crichlow, who proposes a renewed understanding of creolization as a dynamic and ongoing process that addresses the "journeys toward the refashioning of self, times, and places, in the intertwinement of global and local processes."[39] In other words, in Crichlow's work, creolization becomes one of the possible local—or rather, localizing or homing—responses to the experience of globalization, an effort to imagine and articulate new political subjectivities routed through global power structures and modern governmentality. Crichlow's approach is not entirely novel: in many ways, it echoes Hall and Gilroy's embrace of hybridity and creolization. Nonetheless, Crichlow's work opens the door for an investigation of the dynamic embrace of creoleness and diasporicity in global, relational, and fluid processes of (post)colonial subject making. Furthermore, it does so by responding to many of the pitfalls outlined in the previous paragraphs. First, by decentering creolization from the plantation and by recognizing Caribbean subjects as always-already participating in global economic and political networks, it redeems creolization theory for the contemporary era, liberating the concept from the "early rapid synthesis" model that has limited its temporal and geographic application. Yet by maintaining its focus on Caribbean subjectivities and the specific structures of power in which they are implicated, it avoids the kind of overgeneralized and depoliticized use of creolization that Palmié denounced.[40] Second, by operating a "creolization of diaspora," Crichlow responds to long-held criticisms that diasporicity has too often been conceptualized in homogenizing and deterministic ways.[41] In short, Crichlow's work enables us to reengage creolization and diaspora across the multiple horizons—from global to local, from academic to vernacular—through which Guadeloupean musicians perform their subjectivity.

However, Crichlow's work operates on a highly philosophical plane. In the remainder of this chapter, I turn to the encounter between jazz and gwoka as a way to bridge the distance between Crichlow's theoretical considerations and their practical manifestations. Indeed, the ideological projects that surround gwoka, the different claims put on the music, invite a reconsideration of the conceptual separation between nationalism, creolization, and diaspora. Here, rather than simply focus on terms that, as we have seen, offer little conceptual clarity, I want to further explore diasporicity and creoleness as participating in processes of embrace and disavowal, of homing and fleeing. To do so, I foreground the interplay of trace and opacity across the—memorial and sonic—abyss of the black Atlantic. Although Guadeloupeans have been reluctant to embrace the work of Martinican philosopher Édouard Glissant, references to his poetics of Relation are becoming more frequent on the island (see chapter 5), and I propose that they offer a productive vocabulary with which to understand Guadeloupean (post)coloniality.

We need to start by considering the role of creolization and diaspora within Glissant's philosophy. Although Glissant started out relying on metaphors of *métissage* (crossbreeding or cross-fertilization), he later critiqued what he perceived to be the overly deterministic character of *métissage* and embraced creolization instead. Glissant conceived of creolization as an unbounded, unlimited *métissage* or hybridity that generates "unexpected and unforeseeable results." Within the poetics of Relation, creolization came to animate what Glissant termed the *chaos-monde* (or chaos-world).[42] Chaos, in Glissant's philosophy, draws from chaos theory. Thus, the *chaos-monde* is unpredictable, but it isn't chaotic in the common sense of the term: it isn't unruly, disorderly, or confusing.

The trace, opacity, and abyss articulate the relation between the specificity of the Caribbean diasporic formation and Glissant's efforts to build an ambitious, vernacular yet universalist, philosophy of creolization. For Glissant, a trace refers not only to a remnant, an impression, or a memory but also to the ways this memory serves to connect the present to the past. Glissant's and Derrida's conceptualizations of the trace seem, to me, closely related. For Derrida, the trace always involves its own potential disappearance or deletion; thus, it does not allow for a return to a point of origin, an original experience or thought from which it is constitutionally distant. Likewise for Glissant, the trace cannot serve to reconstruct a historical teleology; rather, it highlights the futility of desires for a return or reversion to a mythical point of pure origin.[43] It should be obvious, then, that Glissant does not mean for the trace to be reduced to a simple matter of African retention. On the contrary, traces allow for a return to the "point of entanglement" and a projection into the future.[44] For Glissant, creolized musics such as jazz—which he repeatedly singles out—are "fertilized" or "recomposed" traces. "Music," he writes, "is a trace that exceeds [or surpasses; French *dépasse*] itself." In other words, as music performs the trace, it actualizes it; thus by "exceeding" its trace, music performance also contributes to its destruction. There is a transcendental quality to the trace that allows it to function as the basis of an intersubjective consciousness. The trace, concludes Glissant, puts people—all people—in Relation.[45]

Within the poetics of Relation, the trace should not be considered independently from opacity. If the trace makes possible new forms of intersubjective connections, then opacity avoids the risk that the self be lost in the process. Opacity is an ethical demand for the right *not* to be understood. Opacity, then, breaks the dialectical construction of subjectivity, making it impossible to ever truly know either the Other or the Self.[46] Instead, it foregrounds the "dense materiality of peoples," a fertile but uncertain ground through which it becomes possible to imagine "all the cultures as exercising at the same time a liberating action of unity and diversity."[47] Thus, opacity functions as a counterpart to the trace in informing nondialectical forms of intersubjectivity while also avoiding solipsism. For Glissant, opacity forms the ethical basis of the *chaos-monde*.

By introducing the concept of the *gouffre* (abyss) in the evocative opening of *Poétique de la Relation*, Glissant "anchors" Relation in the rupture of forced removal from Africa. Glissant puts the experience and memory of the abyss at the core of a diasporic intimacy, a form of brotherhood of the abyss.[48] He celebrates the abyss as a "matrix" and the "unknown memory" of the diasporic break as the "silt" from which "metamorphosis" of creolization could grow. But he goes further. The abyss, for Glissant, eventually affords new knowledge. He explains: "Not solely a specific knowledge, appetite, suffering, and ecstasy of a specific people, . . . but knowledge of the Whole which grows from having frequented the abyss and which, within the Whole, frees the knowledge of Relation."[49] In other words, just as he had done with the trace, Glissant intimates a transcendental power to the recognition of the "abyss," a key aspect of overcoming the local and historical specificity of creolization and moving toward the universal ethics of the poetics of Relation.

The vernacular universalism of the poetics of Relation may be more than any ethnographic study can sustain. We run here into the challenge of bringing Glissant's work into anthropology: his writings have gone from description, from a model *of* (post)coloniality, to prescription, to a model *for* a universal decolonized ethics.[50] Nonetheless, trace, opacity, and abyss afford us tools with which to deconstruct evocations of diasporicity or creoleness, reaching beyond their superficial contradictions in order to glimpse the complex ontological positionings that jazz and gwoka make audible.

To recapitulate, the challenge here is to listen to the sounds produced by the encounter of jazz and gwoka along with the discourses that surrounds these musics in order to better understand how these auralities participate in Guadeloupean musicians' construction of themselves as historical and political subjects. Listening for the play of traces and opacity, for the strategic embrace and disavowal of creoleness or diasporicity, helps us move beyond narratives of resistance and overcoming and intimates the erasures and foreclosures that accompany (post)colonial positionings. Exploring these diasporic auralities also enables us to pursue another fundamental issue: to what extent can we assume a confluence between a radical political movement emerging from a majority Afro-descendant population, on the one hand, and black radical politics, on the other hand? Additionally, to what extent can we assume that black musical aesthetics—however we choose to define them—are necessarily expressive of black radical politics? Returning to Lockel's *gwoka modènn* and the Guadeloupean nationalist movement suggests some answers.[51] In the pages that follow, I outline gwoka's participation in three types of diasporic auralities. First, I revisit Lockel's *gwoka modènn* to explicate his diasporic refusal. Second, I explore the collaboration between David Murray and the Gwo Ka Masters to tease out a "diasporization" of creoleness. Finally, I turn to the music of Jacques Schwarz-Bart to illustrate the creolization of diaspora. All three examples, I argue, express different poetics of belonging and illustrate different strategies used by Guadeloupean musicians to position themselves as (post)colonial subjects.

Gérard Lockel and Diasporic Refusal

How should we hear *gwoka modènn*? As a nationalist symbol? As the radical sounds of equally radical black politics? Or as another node within jazz's diasporic cosmopolitan networks? Conversely, how do we hear Lockel's sustained efforts to distance his music from jazz? In chapter 2, I suggested that the move illustrates a form of diasporic refusal. I elaborate on this point now by dwelling on the tensions between class solidarity and racial consciousness and between diasporic refusal and diasporic cosmopolitanism.

As discussed previously, although the Guadeloupean separatist movement participated in the transnational circulation of anticolonial ideologies, it was never truly "cosmopolitan," if we understand cosmopolitanism as an ethics aimed at supranational civic equality.[52] Nonetheless, like other communist revolutionary movements, the *camp patriotique*'s socialist internationalism intersected with a steadfast cultural nationalism. In addition to its seemingly contradictory drives of civic internationalism and cultural nationalism, the Guadeloupean nationalist movement also contained an unresolved tension between class consciousness and racial solidarity. Even as organizations within the *camp patriotique* chose to emphasize Afro-Creole cultural practices, they refrained from equating Guadeloupean identity with blackness, preferring to foreground class solidarity. Thus, in the AGEG's report, gwoka is presented as a national music, equally practiced by the island's different ethnic groups, including its sizable Hindu community. Nevertheless, many of the members of the *camp patriotique* had, like Fanon, experienced racial discrimination in France.[53] Racial awareness informed their anticolonial stance. In spite of the emphasis by the AGEG and other nationalist organizations on class rather than racial solidarity, then, their focus on Afro-Creole cultural expressions—such as the Creole language and gwoka—allowed for a racialized reinterpretation of Guadeloupean identity. For example, the powerful yet polysemic symbolism of the *nèg mawon* quickly escaped control by the nationalist orthodoxy: this was a figure who not only resisted slavery and stood in defiance of capitalist oppression; it was also a figure whose blackness begged to be reclaimed.

In the 1980s, the anthropologist and cultural activist Dany Bébél-Gislert captured a number of testimonials that perfectly demonstrate that the tension between cultural and racial definitions of Guadeloupean identity was not simply a matter of theoretical musings. For example, eighteen-year-old Claire explains: "A Guadeloupean is someone who is born here, whatever his race may be. It is my language, Creole, that shows that I am Guadeloupean. Haitians, Dominicans are not stranger to me. Martinicans are. Their ways are different than ours." Juliette, a seventeen-year-old, responds: "Guadeloupeans are *nègres*, the descendants of African slaves. They speak Creole." But then, she complicates matters, enlarging the ethnic and racial definition of national belonging: "There are Indians, *chabines*, *nègres*." Forty three-year old Simone is much more assertive: "Guadeloupean? I am a *nègresse*, my skin is black, I speak Creole: I am not like Europeans. We don't have the same ways of life, the same mores. I am proud of my skin, I feel good in my country. We are free. For me, white people are the foreigners."[54] All these declarations illustrate the irruption of the disputed role of race in what had been, in the nationalist Marxist orthodoxy, a culturally defined national identity.

Lockel's *gwoka modènn* makes these tensions—between race and class, and between nationalism and cosmopolitanism—audible without necessarily resolving them. In 1976, when he released his first album, Lockel insisted on gwoka being the music of enslaved Africans and their descendants, but he also asserted that "the problem of class is fundamental" to understanding the process of assimilation and resistance against it. Gwoka, for Lockel, is first and foremost the music of class struggle. This offers the first explanation for his refusal to claim the jazz mantle. Indeed, in his writings, Lockel is quick to associate jazz with those he derides as an "intellectual and alienated petty bourgeoisie." *Gwoka modènn* was intended to combat this kind of alienation. If gwoka, though, is the proletarian musical expression of class struggle, it is nevertheless black music. Indeed, in his recent autobiography, the guitarist professes a black rhythmic essence reminiscent of the leading figures of *négritude*: "After all that I have witnessed, after many experiences, after all that I have come to understand and all my analysis, I have deducted that the *nègre* is rhythm; I am convinced that *nègre* and rhythm mean the same thing." He concludes, "Gwoka is and must remain a black [*nègre*] Guadeloupean art."[55]

The tensions between class solidarity and racial consciousness in Lockel's nationalist formulation mirrors a tension between diasporic cosmopolitan aesthetics and nationalist ideology in his music. If we understand diaspora as destabilizing the nation—as both Appadurai and Crichlow propose—then Lockel's diasporic refusal makes sense from an ideological perspective.[56] From an aesthetic perspective, Lockel's music activates musical traces that mark national specificity: most obviously the presence of the *boula* in his ensemble or the codification of the rhythms of "traditional" gwoka. Likewise, the guitarist sets up *gwoka modènn's* atonal modality as a boundary marker that sets Guadeloupean music apart from jazz. The claim is often echoed among gwoka musicians and aficionados: you will recall that the disgruntled audience member in Baie-Mahault objected to Dominik Coco's setting of Rupaire's poem precisely because it was tonal. Yet the musical traces that resonate through the anticolonial aurality of *gwoka modènn* can also be heard as exceeding their nationalism and reaching toward an audible diasporic cosmopolitanism through an engagement with transnational, modernist, and decidedly black musical aesthetics. It is easy to imagine that *gwoka modènn's* diasporic traces inspired the reaction of an Antillean audience member who, following Lockel's performance at the Banlieues Bleues festival in 1997, declared somewhat sheepishly to the journalists of Radio France Outre-mer that he thought the music sounded like jazz.[57] Conversely, these traces also allowed the Guadeloupean pianist Yvan Juraver to adopt (and adapt) Lockel's *gwoka modènn* in his own music: having himself embraced jazz's diasporic cosmopolitanism through the recordings of free jazz musicians such as Cecil Taylor or Archie Shepp, Juraver was "in a real search for [himself]" but also experiencing a sort of creative block. He found in Lockel's music a "wind of freedom" that helped him realize the aesthetic potential of gwoka.[58]

In their musical process of anticolonial self-affirmation, Lockel and Juraver engage in a process of homing the aesthetics of diasporic cosmopolitanism to render them more compatible with their nationalist ethics. In his study of Haitian nationalism, Michael Largey describes "diasporic cosmopolitanism" as an elitist embrace of "values" associated with "a shared vision of black nationalism." In the cases he describes, these values encompass the fields of aesthetics and politics: pan-Africanist composers of the early twentieth century recycled musical markers of Afro-Creole folk culture to sound their participation in a "shared vision of black nationalism."[59] *Gwoka modènn* separates these two aspects: short of embracing black nationalism, it builds on diasporic aesthetics but homes them—that is to say, it brings them back home, it localizes or vernacularizes them—in the service of nationalist, and decidedly not cosmopolitan, ethics. This process is achieved by introducing restrictions on a broad set of musical practices that could otherwise be heard as diasporic: for example, cosmopolitan pentatonic scales are rejected in favor of the nationalist "gwoka scale," and polyrhythms are refined

132 / Chapter Four

and redefined on the basis of gwoka's newly codified set of fundamental rhythmic formulas. Largey's Haitian and African American composers engaged in an additive process, using black folk sounds to enrich and destabilize the conventions of Western art music. Theirs was an act of double appropriation—of Western art music and black vernacular traditions—that revealed their distance from the very folk traditions they reclaimed even as they used those traditions to emancipate themselves from the structures of imperialism and institutionalized racism. In contrast, Lockel's homing strategy is reductive: it nationalizes diasporic aesthetics by narrowing their musical language. In so doing, Lockel's musical aesthetics render his music more opaque while his discourse downplays diasporic traces.

In his exploration of jazz cosmopolitanism in Accra, Steven Feld suggests "that jazz cosmopolitanism in Accra is about histories of listening, echoing and sounding, about acoustemology, the agency of knowing the world through sound. Let me suggest that this acoustemology, this sonic knowing, is the imagination and enactment of a musical intimacy."[60] *Gwoka modènn* is, in many ways, a militant acoustemological intervention (although, as I argue in chapter 2, *gwoka modènn* concerns itself primarily with knowledge of the self and thus is really closer to an acoustic ontology). But contrary to the cosmopolitan imagination of Ghanaian jazz musicians, *gwoka modènn* downplays its diasporic histories of listening, echoing, and sounding. Its diasporic aesthetic traces feed into a musical intimacy that looks inward, to the nation, rather than outward, to the diaspora.

Beyond Lockel, since the late 1960s, gwoka has participated in a complex process of racial formation through which the relative blackness of the music has been, and continues to be, contested within narratives of anticolonial resistance. As such, the music is inscribed alternatively within diasporic, nationalist, or creolized spheres, articulating the overlap and tensions among these categories. Already in their 1967 novel *Un plat de porc aux bananes vertes*, Simone and André Schwarz-Bart adopted the unconventional spelling *n'goka* to designate both the Guadeloupean and the Martinican drums. They justified this spelling in an endnote: "We were made aware that 'N'goka' designates, in the Sango dialect of the shores of the Oubangui, the same sort of instrument, with an identical shape and a similar practice [to the 'G'oka']. Considering the history of the slave trade, it seems lucky to find there an unusual example of total filiation: the object, its technique and its name. We bowed to the ancestral truth of the 'gros tambour' [big drum] of the French Antilles and thus adopted this orthography for this heir, distant and yet so faithful, to the old 'N'goka' drums from Central Africa."[61] The Schwarz-Barts' Herskovitsian claim reveals an early expression of diasporic nostalgia, an alternative diasporic *pulsion de retour* to a lost African motherland—note the conflation of both Guadeloupean gwoka and Martinican *bèlè* under the umbrella *n'goka*—to the then-nascent nationalist longing for an autochthonous, precolonial subjectivity.

Today, gwoka remains caught in a similar tension between national specificity, diasporicity, and creoleness. While Joslen Gabaly's *Diadyéé*, the first monograph on Guadeloupean drumming, echoes the Schwarz-Barts' earlier claim and forcefully reaffirms the music as an Afro-diasporic practice, the group Kannida—a well-respected traditional group that has enjoyed some international visibility—celebrates in song the Creole heritage of Guadeloupe, a *soup-a-kongo* (a typical Guadeloupean soup) that mixes a little bit of French, English, and Spanish with a lot of "African."[62] We now turn to a recent encounter between jazz and gwoka to consider music as a site of simultaneously agonistic, evasive, and yet phatic performance of (post)colonial belonging.

Diasporizing Creoleness: David Murray and the Gwo Ka Masters

In 1995, the American jazz saxophone player David Murray, known for his many intercultural collaborations, met Guadeloupean percussionist Klod Kiavué during the Banlieues Bleues festival in Paris, where they both happened to live. This meeting led to an ambitious project gathering musicians from the United States, Guadeloupe, Martinique, and Cape Verde. After a tour and a first album, entitled *Creole*, the two musicians decided to downgrade their ambitions and focus on blending jazz and Guadeloupean gwoka. The group David Murray and the Gwo Ka Masters was thus born. The collaboration lasted about ten years and produced three albums— *Yonn-dé* (2000), *Gwotet* (2003), and *The Devil Tried to Kill Me* (2009)—for Justin Time Records, Murray's record label.

In discussing what made their musical interaction successful, the two musicians pointed to a shared blues aesthetic, a musical trace of their shared memory of slavery. As Kiavué told me, "These are musics, we know the story, musics of slaves descendants. The only difference, as we like to say, one produced the blues of cotton and we have the blues of the sugarcane."[63] The performance of "On jou matin" on the album *Yonn dé* illustrates how a "blues aesthetic" provided a common ground for American and Guadeloupean musicians. Indeed, on the introduction to this performance of his own composition, the vocalist Guy Konket emphasizes melismas and blue notes in dialogue with bassist Santi Debriano before the drums enter on a distinctive *kaladja* pattern. So far, we seem to be navigating the very familiar waters of the black Atlantic. In his classic book, Gilroy argues that, more than the memory of a lost homeland or the retention of cultural practices, it is the shared experience of racialized structures of power that enable diasporic intimacy. But Murray's so-called Creole project gives us an opportunity to move beyond this frame of analyses, beyond the activation of traces to also explore the opacity that puts a limit on the experience of intimacy.

My conversations with Guadeloupean musicians as well as even the most superficial listening of Murray's albums with the Gwo Ka Masters reveal that this diasporic collaboration did not proceed from an easy familiarity. As could be expected, the musicians struggled to develop a common musical language. On the one hand, the Guadeloupean percussionists and singers—undoubtedly influenced by Lockel's ideas—feared that imposing jazz harmonies on gwoka songs would compromise the fundamental aesthetic of their music and failed to convey its *santiman* or feelings. Kiavué told me: "The business of using gwoka rhythms with jazz harmony, it doesn't always work, right? It can work with the blues. . . . But we realized immediately that, if it is just to stick jazz harmonies on gwoka rhythms, it isn't effective. And it doesn't work either, at the emotional level." On the other hand, Murray did not want to reinvent himself as a gwoka musician but rather use his own musical language to bring, as he told me, a "jazz veneer" to gwoka.[64]

There are parallels between the Gwo Ka Masters' work and Murray's earlier collaboration with Senegalese musicians. In an excellent overview of jazz in Senegal, Timothy Mangin highlights the "tension between the primacy of rhythm, as an essential cultural marker of Senegalese identity, and harmony as an identifying marker of jazz and transatlantic modernity." He concludes, "This close relationship between rhythm and meaning marks a nuanced similarity and difference between jazz and Senegalese popular music." We could make a similar argument around the musical markers of Guadeloupean identity. Gwoka musicians' desire to foreground the rhythmic figures of gwoka and—following Lockel—a melodic language that aspires to atonality function in tension with jazz harmonies and structures. In the case of Senegal, Murray himself understood this tension as an encounter between the Senegalese music as "language" and what he calls the "languageness" of African American jazz. He explains: "We have a language inside of our music. In most African music the rhythms are words, expressions, meanings, and codes. Our language [US English]—maybe because our language was never our own—is not in our music, especially now in jazz . . . so we are mixing a languageness with a music that is language. Like, there we have big similarity and great big difference. The differences are bigger than the similarities in that regard."[65]

With this tension in mind, the two musical encounters between Murray and Lockel are fascinating documents. Murray tried to recruit Lockel for his initial Creole project, but the guitarist refused to join an ensemble that would not embrace his own musical aesthetics. Conversely, Murray was unwilling to invest time learning Lockel's vocabulary. Remarkably, the two did agree to meet in the studio, where they produced two tracks: "Guadeloupe Sunrise" and "Guadeloupe after Dark." Through the poetics of improvisation, free of both rhythmic and harmonic constraints, the two musicians enter into a space of Relation where they can engage in dialogue while maintaining their respective opacity. These duets bring to mind Veit Erlmann's comment that diasporic musical performances are "essentially phatic; they do not concern themselves with a meaning but with what goes on when black people converse with one another in certain ways and thereby mark themselves as different."[66] Yet I am not comfortable concluding with him that such performances lead to the experience of a "community of style" or intimate a diasporic cosmopolitan acoustemology. Rather, any sense of community in these collaborations remains evasive. Moreover, the dialogues demonstrate that the black radical aesthetics of avant-garde jazz, while offering a common ground, do not necessarily allow for the utterance of pan-diasporic radical politics: in this instance, they even seem to hinder such an expression, Murray's diasporic cosmopolitanism clashing with Lockel's nationalism.

Murray's complete control of the recording process exacerbated this issue in the Gwo Ka Masters. As Timothy Taylor, channeling Steven Feld, reminds us, "No matter how collaborative and syncretic a musical style sounds, we should always remember the musicians' relationship to the means of production."[67] With each successive album released over the course of a decade, the markers of Guadeloupean specificity have receded further into the sonic mix. The first album featured Guy Konket's voice and compositions, reprising arrangements from the singer's 1980s Paris-based performances.[68] As a result, this album was sung entirely in Creole, and, as with the example of "On jou matin" discussed earlier, an educated listener could fairly easily identify the basic gwoka rhythmic patterns in the mix.

On the next album, *Gwotet*, this aesthetic gave way to the saxophone improvisations of Pharoah Sanders and the group was augmented by a Cuban big band. Because Konket had left the band, the Creole language lost ground, and even the Guadeloupean drums struggled to make themselves heard in the thick texture of the big band. The "jazz veneer" threatened to cover the gwoka base of the music. The group's last album, *The Devil Tried to Kill Me*, took things even further. The musicians recorded in Guadeloupe in 2008 and invited the local quadrille accordionist Négoce to join them. Mixing took close to two years. During this time, Murray decided to get rid of the tracks laid down by Négoce. Instead, he solicited blues singer Taj Mahal and singer Sista Kee to overdub English lyrics based on poems by Ishmael Reed on half the tracks. The result is an album sung almost entirely in English and in which a heavy funk influence masks most of the distinctive Guadeloupean elements.

On the one hand, we could celebrate Murray's long-term interest in the music of Guadeloupe and his desire to bring it more international attention and promote the careers of his Antillean collaborators. This is the perspective that Kiavué and François Ladrezeau, another long-term member of the Gwo Ka Masters, have foregrounded in their conversations with me. But in Guadeloupe, the reception has not always been so generous: many see Murray's work as demonstrative of American imperialism.[69] As the sounds of gwoka recede in the recordings, the "traces of the gap," the abyss, that separate African American and Afro-Caribbean musicians resonate in their absence. The recordings of the Gwo Ka Masters remind us that a "brotherhood of the abyss" need not be transcendental but is more likely to be contingent, insufficient, and agonistic, and yet powerful for the potential that it, briefly, let ring.

Creolizing Diaspora: Jacques Schwarz-Bart's "Territories of the Soul"

Both Lockel's *gwoka modènn* and Murray's Gwo Ka Masters invite us to follow Michaeline Crichlow's advice that we treat diaspora "as a practical and polemological methodology rather than a condition or transfixed state of being" while also recognizing "diasporic communitarian formations as a practice contained within, though also fractured, by their inherent identitarian instabilities."[70] I would like to further Crichlow's model and return to our original problematic by considering a musician whose work sounds the intersection of creolization and diaspora.

The saxophonist Jacques Schwarz-Bart is the son of novelists Simone and André Schwarz-Bart. Simone is from Guadeloupe, and André is Jewish, from Switzerland. Jacques thus inhabits the intersection of two diasporas, a fact on which he often comments.[71] In 2002, Brother Jacques, as he is nicknamed, participated in Franck Nicolas's first album inaugurating the *jazz ka* concept. In 2006, Schwarz-Bart released his first album as a leader, which offered his own take on *jazz ka*. Since then, in addition to appearing alongside African American luminaries such as Roy Hargrove and Meshell Ndegeocello, Schwarz-Bart has released a series of recordings that quite literally sound the African diaspora: a second *jazz ka* album, an album with heavy neo-soul influences, a straight-ahead jazz release, a project on Haitian *mizik rasyn* (roots music), and a collaboration with the Cuban pianist Omar Sosa. This is in addition to his participation in Trinidadian Étienne Charles's *Creole Soul* album and his several encounters with the Gnawa ethnic group of Morocco. Schwarz-Bart's latest project, *Hazzan*, connects the saxophonist's Jewish and Afro-diasporic heritage. In a promotional video for the new album, he explains: "My father presented a character in one of his latest novels. That character strangely resembles who I am. He is a biracial jazz musician and he defines himself as being 200%. Not only half Jewish and half black, but 100% black and 100% Jewish. And this is the way I live my Jewish identity, in dialogue with everything that represents humanity."[72]

As this quote makes clear, Schwarz-Bart refuses to align his music with any one identity, and his interest in gwoka should not be misheard as a nationalist statement. He has declared repeatedly, including in a conversation with me in 2007, that he does not play music to define himself in relation to a community. Instead, he foregrounds what he calls an "emotional identity."[73] Indeed, the traces that animate Schwarz-Bart's music are mostly affective. While many gwoka musicians I spoke with in Guadeloupe accused him of inauthenticity because they could not remember the saxophonist ever attending a *swaré léwòz*, this is of little consequence to a musician for whom musical traces, glimpsed from recordings or reconstituted from the memories of his mom's singing, serve to construct what Nadia Ellis calls "territories of the soul," affective spaces that are "at once imagined and material."[74]

His 200 percent identity is made particularly audible on a musical diptych dedicated to Schwarz-Bart's parents and released on an album with the evocative title, *Abyss*. In the first part, simply titled "André," Schwarz-Bart and the pianist Milan Milanovic engage in a meditative duet, a kind of musical Kaddish to the memory of the saxophonist's recently departed father. The tender laugh of Simone Schwarz-Bart opens the second part in which one of her poems—read in Creole—leads the band to a gentle groove in which a slightly altered *léwòz* pattern anchors an ostinato by the guitarist Hervé Samb. The poem is an ode to the children *ki fèt an doukou pèdu*, who are born around the new moon (*doukou pèdu* means "the lost moon crescent" in Creole), a poetic evocation of the liminality between Old and New Worlds, between cultures. The poem echoes Glissant's musing on the abyss, a liminal and connecting space from which Relation can grow.

Jacques Schwarz-Bart is himself a child of the new moon, a child of the abyss, which he describes as a connective tissue of infinite possibilities. His music combines the multiple strands of his identity: Caribbean, Jewish, French, black, and, for several years now, New Yorker. Listening to his recorded output to date, one is struck by the great aesthetic continuity between the various projects. The emotional focus may shift from Guadeloupean gwoka to US R&B to Haitian Vodou to Jewish music, but there are no breaks in the musical aesthetics, the musical language flowing from one setting to another.

In Schwarz-Bart's music, the diasporic entanglements are diffused. With bands that bring together musicians from New York, Guadeloupe, Haiti, and Senegal, Schwarz-Bart's saxophone and his invocation of both Jewish and Afro-Caribbean spirituality—the jazzman refers to gwoka rhythms as "mystical"—function as points of articulation between several geographic anchors (New York, Guadeloupe, and Haiti, but also Paris, where several of the Guadeloupean musicians he performs with live, and Switzerland, where his father was born) and the several facets of his 200 percent identity. There is no quest for a single homeland—where would it be?—and no simple identity claim. In July 2014, Schwarz-Bart appeared on *Summertime*, the weekly jazz program on French radio station France Inter, to promote his album *Jazz Racine Haiti*. The album is billed as an encounter between Schwarz-Bart's own blend of acoustic jazz and Haitian roots musics, especially, according to the liner notes, the "melodies of voodoo [*sic*] rituals." It was thus perfectly logical for Elsa Boublil, the show's host, to ask Schwarz-Bart about the role of drums in Vodou. Surprisingly, the saxophonist evaded the question and instead redirected the conversation to a recording by Buckshot Le Fonque, Branford Marsalis's hip-hop group. Likewise, earlier in the shows, he had put French Antillean biguine in dialogue with early jazz in New Orleans, highlighting their similarities and denying either style precedence over the other. He repeated this decentering narrative during a concert with his Jazz Racine Haiti group in France in July 2016, when he insisted on establishing Haitian Vodou as the central force behind the birth of both jazz and cubism.

The diasporic "territory of the soul" that Schwarz-Bart inhabits is performed into existence, given material presence in his music and through the bodies of his collaborators. By recentering the black Atlantic around the Caribbean and by claiming belonging into two different diasporas, Brother Jacques operates what Crichlow calls a "creolization of diaspora." Moreover, he offers perhaps an ideal sonic illustration of Glissant's poetics of Relation, a musical body that constructs a (post)colonial artistic universe across the abyss and exceeds nationalist, ethnic, or racial boundaries. Rather than *jazz-racines* (jazz roots), Schwarz-Bart sounds a jazz rhizome.

The aesthetic and ideological distance that separate Jacques Schwarz-Bart's from Gérard Lockel's music epitomize the mutation of an anticolonial stance into a (post)colonial—or more precisely, postnational—way of being. From

Lockel's *gwoka modènn* to Murray and the Gwo Ka Masters' "Creole" project to the *jazz ka* of Nicolas and Schwarz-Bart, we hear musicians who carefully and sometimes ambiguously manipulate sonic traces to "join diaspora" or distance themselves from it.[75] Within gwoka's contested and contesting aurality, joining diaspora or embracing creoleness—no matter how ambiguously or ambivalently—serves as strategies to flee or to home the French imperial nation-state.

The nationalist orthodoxy confronted the abyss of colonialism with a quest to "recover"—from their perspective—a Guadeloupean irreducible selfhood from French Republican assimilationism. Such an approach had no use for creoleness since, first, an embrace of either hybridity or plurality was antithetical to the effort to uncover a national ipseity, and, second, the term *Creole* was already tainted by colonial semantics. This position is made abundantly clear by Lockel's theory of the three cultures (with the pairings French-quadrille, colonial-biguine, and Guadeloupean-gwoka), and it continues to inform Kiavué's ambivalence toward the characterization of his collaboration with Murray as a "Creole" project. At the same time that Lockel sought to protect the national specificity of his music behind an opaque veil of technicity, the audible traces within *gwoka modènn* hint at the continued diasporic resonance—what Radano describes as "the sounding after an unlocatable origin"—within nationalist discourse and music.[76] In a way, then, David Murray and the Gwo Ka Masters offer an amplification of that resonance. But the activation of these sonic traces have come to overcome gwoka's nationalist significance in a wash of diasporic cosmopolitanism defined primarily from a North American perspective. Put differently, Lockel disavowed diasporicity—even as he embraced blackness—for the sake of national specificity. Through his embrace of virtuosic improvisation and his rejection of tonality, Lockel "homed" black radical aesthetics to position himself in opposition to the French political and cultural sphere of influence. The same black radical aesthetics act as a common ground between Murray, Lockel, and the Gwo Ka Masters, but, while they help confirm Murray's own position as a diasporic cosmopolitan, they complicate the efforts by his Guadeloupean collaborators to position themselves musically within or against the French imperial nation-state.

The musicians involved in *jazz ka* participate in a different political and cultural paradigm. Franck Nicolas's first *jazz ka* album came out in 2002, and Schwarz-Bart followed with his own *Soné ka la* in 2006. These albums are the products of an era marked by (post)colonial disenchantment with the promises of nationhood and sovereignty.[77] No longer being invested in fighting for political recognition, these artists can embrace their creoleness, in the sense that Ti Malo describes as "vernacular," that is to say, as a way of affirming their double belonging to both Guadeloupe and France. They use jazz as a medium through which they can straddle the colonial abyss and claim a place within the African diaspora alongside their African American—and, in the case of Schwarz-Bart, Haitian—models and colleagues. While doing so, they also operate a decentering—or a creolization—of diaspora.

There is also a very practical aspect to Guadeloupean musicians' embracing their Afro-diasporicity in France. As discussed in chapter 3, Antilleans in France occupy an ambiguous racial position: too black to be French, too French to be black, racialized within a state that denies race and racism. By embracing their diasporicity, Guadeloupean musicians stake a claim to the geography of black music in France. Indeed, too exotic to be in the French music section and too French to be in the jazz and blues bins, Antillean musicians are generally pushed to the world music bins of record stores such as FNAC. By claiming the jazz mantle, Guadeloupean musicians maneuver themselves into a category that carries more cultural capital and, most important, opens a number of performing opportunities. But this is a constant struggle. In July 2016, I attended a concert by Franck Nicolas at the Petit Journal Montparnasse, a renowned Parisian jazz club. That night, Nicolas displayed his usually stage presence, dapper and full of youthful exuberance, wearing faux-leather pants and a black- and white-checkered skullcap, while cycling through a collection of novelty sunglasses. The concert—a double billing with Martinican pianist Mario Canonge—was part of a music festival ironically titled "C'est pas du jazz" (This isn't jazz) that was aimed at promoting Caribbean jazz artists who too often find themselves shunned by jazz festival programmers. In the spring of 2018, this battle took a tragic turn: Franck Nicolas, having lost his status as *intermittent du spectacle* (a special labor category instituted by the French state to protect musicians and artists working in the gig economy), started a hunger strike to bring attention to Antillean musicians who, like him, find themselves blocked out of performing at jazz venues. Lifting the mask of playful cheerfulness, he explained: "When I send a CD out to a festival, they respond that what I do isn't jazz. Antilleans are only credible when they stick to the role of entertainers, like Francky Vincent or La Compagnie Créole. But I'm tired of the postcard." His denunciation of the discrimination faced by Antillean musicians was very quickly echoed by his peers, from Schwarz-Bart to Canonge to Alain Jean-Marie. The flautist Magic Malik concludes: "The generation of Daniel Humair and Louis Sclavis have appropriated jazz in France. They've done great things, but in the process, the specificity of those approaches coming from the diaspora have been occluded; and it is all the more regrettable because these specificities have influenced American jazz. In France, Antillean jazzmen are stuck in the "Caribbean jazz" category. Artists have no access to the national scene if they come from a colony."[78]

In this context, even if Brother Jacques pointedly informed me that he does not play music to make political or identity claims, there is a political salience to *jazz ka*. In the twenty-first century, gwoka increasingly plays a role as an ever more contested postnational aurality. In the following chapter, we further explore the political aspirations that the sounds of Guadeloupean drums help carry in the wake of disenchantment.

FIVE

Postnational Aurality: Institutional Detour and the Creolization of Sovereignty

National consciousness, which is not nationalism, is alone capable of giving us an international dimension.

—Frantz Fanon, *The Wretched of the Earth*

In July 2013, I sat in a breezy conference room at the Hotel Rotabas in Sainte-Anne, a seaside town on Guadeloupe's southern coast and the site of the annual Festival Gwoka. For the previous few days, I had been attending a colloquium on questions of intangible cultural heritage (ICH) in the Caribbean. The colloquium was organized by Rèpriz, the center for traditional and popular music and dance of Guadeloupe, a local nonprofit organization that was in the midst of driving Guadeloupe's effort to have gwoka recognized as intangible cultural heritage of humanity. The colloquium featured speakers—political representatives, cultural activists, musicians, and scholars—from a number of Caribbean islands and the United States. Among them was the gwoka singer and political geographer Rosan Monza, who had been tasked with outlining the work of the Lyannaj pou gwoka (Alliance for gwoka), the collective responsible for crafting Guadeloupe's application to have gwoka included on UNESCO's representative list of the Intangible Cultural Heritage of Humanity. Monza is a man with an imposing stature. His voice is deep and his affect conveys seriousness and a sense of purpose, but there is often a playful glint in his eyes. Explaining Guadeloupe's political situation to an audience from various Caribbean independent states, Monza presented the French Antillean archipelago as a "nation without a state." He then quickly added, "But it doesn't even matter."

The seemingly offhand comment resonated with complex implications. It took a familiar complaint and destabilized it, but it also played on a hidden transcript that was accessible only to those familiar with Monza's music. Indeed, the lyrics of one of his songs, released slightly over a year prior, declare: "Nou sé on nasyon, san zéta nasyon; nou sé on nasyon, san zétadam . . . nasyon" (We are a nation, a nation without a state; we are a nation, without states of mind [regrets], a nation). In the song lyrics, the statement is then quickly rephrased as a question: Are we a nation, a nation without a state? A nation without regrets? Monza's song and statement provocatively engage the question of Guadeloupe's political status in a new millennium, and the song suggests that the political status of Guadeloupe may matter more than Monza's comment let on. A verse explains: "At the height of the crisis, we come together to dance in sync to the rhythms of globalization / We beat our chests and declare that we are a nation / *Nègzagonaux* [a derogatory term referring to Antilleans living in mainland France] or fully separated French? / We don't want any flag besides the blue, white, and red / even if we pay the price, we have to consume excessively." The song goes on: "We are a tick nation feeding on the back of the state / a nation without tactics / poorly dressed and in bad shape / always whining / But we live comfortably without worrying about tomorrows." Now, the refrain's last line takes on a different meaning: "Nou sé on nasyon san zéta, damnasyon" (we are a nation without a state, damnation).[1]

We cannot assume that Monza is simply recycling nationalist rhetoric here. The song appears on a CD titled *RExistans*. The term is a Creole portmanteau that combines the words *rezistans* (resistance), *existans* (existence), and *re-exister* (to reexist). Monza invented it to capture Guadeloupeans' "tumultuous identity trajectory." Monza explains further: "This invented term carries the ambition of the album to convey another message, 'an dot lèspri ka son' [a wordplay on *lèsplikasyon* (explanation) meaning 'the spirit of the sounds of the drum'] of our human condition caught in the process of a standardizing globalization and to give depth and consistence to our collective Creole imaginary."[2]

In the album liner notes, Monza does reprise some nationalist rhetoric, making an appeal to the spirit of the *nèg mawon* or rhyming *moun d'isidan* (Creole, people from here) with *peuple dissident* (French, dissident people).[3] Otherwise, though, the text dwells in ambiguity, a quality that is performed through a careful choice of equivocal vocabulary, abundant wordplay, and contrasting—if not contradicting—juxtapositions. For example, Monza writes of the need to "defend [Guadeloupean] specificity." He also describes Guadeloupe as being on a "quest for a *fixation identitaire*." That phrase is, again, filled with double entendre. It expresses a quest for a point of attachment or a fixed point of Guadeloupean identity. But when this quest is paired with a reference to Guadeloupe's "plural culture," it emerges as necessarily inconclusive, the idea of a fixed point being oxymoronic to that of plural society. Thus, we can read *fixation identitaire* differently, as connoting a psychological obsession with defining, arresting, and authorizing a singular identity in the face of the impossibility of doing so successfully. Indeed, Monza seems to propose, with his music, a different type of identity, one perhaps closer to the "open specificity" outlined by the authors of the foundational *Éloge de la créolité*.[4] "*RExistans* is the forward march of a people who gives existence and meaning to the inescapable process of creolization toward which our contemporary world is moving and that disturbs the racializing representations of the old nation-states," writes Monza. He later adds: "We owe it to ourselves to tame or accept our ambivalences and perpetual inner struggles as fully constituting traits of our identity." And he concludes his liner notes by calling for a "re-foundation of our social and political pact for a '*rExistans*' that would give meaning and value to our destiny."[5] Through his embrace of hybridity and creolization, Monza, then, espouses an optic that exceeds the leading nationalist ideologies of the postwar period.

Monza's ideological position is audible in his music. His recordings and concerts illustrate the new aesthetics that has come to dominate so-called instrumental or evolutive forms of gwoka in the new millennium. Gone is Lockel's radical modernism. Monza dubbed his music "évolutif ka blues jazz" and intended for it to make audible Afro-diasporic connections. Having played with Monza myself, I have witnessed that this aesthetic is less the product of arrangement and composition strategies emanating from a single mastermind than of an intentional selection of collaborators. On this album, Monza surrounded himself with musicians who bring a mix of traditional gwoka and jazz experiences. "Nasyon" illustrates the overall aesthetics of the album. The song opens with a *menndé* rhythm played by Serge Dorville on *boula* with the subtle reinforcement of Georges Juraver on drum set. The choice of the *menndé* is likely symbolic as well as aesthetic. One of the seven basic rhythms of gwoka, the *menndé* is often described as combative, an exuberant rhythm of struggle and resistance. After four repetitions of the rhythmic ostinato, the two are joined by the bass of Gérard Poumaroux and an opening piano improvisation by Dominic Bérose. Dorville is a renowned "traditional" percussionist, but the latter two musicians have long straddled the line between jazz and gwoka in Guadeloupe, and Poumaroux is a longtime collaborator of Franck Nicolas. The bass ostinato—with its regular movement from C to D—and the piano improv establish the D-minor vamp on which the song is based. The vamp is thickened by the interwoven finger-style guitar ostinati of Jean Tamas (playing acoustic) and Marc Bernos (electric), a mix reminiscent of Ali Farka Touré's music. Monza sings over this ostinato, but, in perhaps the most significant departure from Lockel's music, the arrangement includes brief instrumental interludes in which the static harmony gives way to a chord progression in D minor and a very "jazzy" improvisation by Marc Bernos.

Monza's music, like his intervention during the 2013 ethnomusicology colloquium, participates in a problem-space that is best understood as a "continuance" of the concerns and contexts that animated the nationalist movement of the late twentieth century. Homi Bhabha, building on Fanon's insight, proposes that post-liberation national consciousness is a "continuance"—in the sense of transformation or displacement—of the anticolonial national consciousness. It needs to take on an international or transnational dimension because it can exist only within an international structure. Yet, writes Bhabha, all acts to singularize national consciousness within an international structure are "partial, limited and unstable."[6] Even if we cannot truly speak of a post-liberation moment in Guadeloupe, it is to this unstable aurality, which I call both Creole and postnational, that we now turn our attention.

Rèpriz. "Because of its creation, gwoka has always been political," affirmed Lénablou. What does it mean for gwoka to be political in the twenty-first century? In this chapter, I explore how, in the wake of disenchantment with the nationalist project, the creolized aurality of gwoka functions as a creative space from which new artistic and political poetic formations emerge. As musicians—such as Monza, Dominik Coco, or the group Soft—find new ways to "home" cosmopolitan aesthetics, to "domesticate" globalization, and to "tame" or embrace their "ambivalences and perpetual inner struggles," they come to sound relational modes of belonging that enable them to reconcile their positions as both Caribbean and French. This new generation's Creole postnationalist take on gwoka—marked by strategic audible entanglements—found its political expression in the campaign of activists and musicians who worked together within the Lyannaj pou gwoka. Successfully led by a well-known nationalist militant, the campaign managed to have gwoka—once heralded as a symbol of anticolonial struggle—recognized as part of France's cultural heritage and diversity. I argue that, far from antithetical to the music's politics and poetics, the work of the Lyannaj represents, nearly seventy years after *départementalisation,* another instantiation of the *détour.* By forcing the recognition of Guadeloupe's cultural specificity within the French state on an international stage, both Lyannaj pou gwoka and the new forms of *gwoka évolutif* cement the emergence of a Creole postnational citizenship: cognizant of its limited

Postnational Aurality / 147

economic autonomy, Guadeloupeans are nonetheless ready to capitalize on their limited cultural sovereignty to redefine, or rather, creolize, their relation with France and enter into new modes of regional collaborations.

The Postnationalist Problem-Space

As I detail below, both Rèpriz (Center for Traditional Music and Dance of Guadeloupe) and the Lyannaj pou gwoka are in various ways the products of the Guadeloupean separatist movement. Yet they function now within a problem-space that is very different from that which originally animated nationalist organizations. Weakened by the French state's decentralizing policies—which, since the 1980s, have gradually granted regional and departmental governments more autonomy and thus fulfilled many nationalist demands—as much as by internal splintering, the separatist movement never managed to transform its labor organizing into an outright anticolonial nationalist uprising. By the early 1990s, the UPLG was forced to contend with a general feeling of "disenchantment with nationalism" among its base.[7] It responded with a proposal to transform Guadeloupe into a "new associated collectivity," a complicated road map that was, for all intent and purposes, a retrenchment from separatist demands toward an autonomist proposal. That proposal didn't get much traction. In the twenty-first century, as Bonilla so aptly summarizes, independence appears as "a 'future past': a once contemplated but no longer imaginable political action."[8]

No event better illustrates the postnational politics of the new millennium than the general strike of 2009. In January of that year, as the carnival season was about to get under way, Guadeloupe—and later Martinique—were rocked by prolonged general strikes. In Guadeloupe, the strike would last a total of forty-four days. It was initiated by the UGTG, but it quickly grew to involve a coalition of forty-eight other organizations—including not only unions but also political parties and cultural associations, such as carnival groups—within the Liyannaj kont pwofitasyon (LKP), the alliance against profiteering.[9] The LKP's demands were articulated around a central concern with *la vie chère*, the high cost of living on the island, which the LKP revealed to be the product of specific structural conditions resulting from the encounter between neoliberal globalizing economics and the local socioeconomic structure inherited from the colonial period. The LKP was a massive movement with, at its apogee, up to a quarter of Guadeloupe's population marching in protest. In February 2009, as the French state proved incapable of listening and properly responding to the demands of the alliance, the island came to a complete halt: shops, gas stations, and schools were closed; imports ground to a stop when the port shut down; and blockades were erected on all major thoroughfares. As representatives of the French government—blatantly unprepared and unequipped to deal with this situation—deserted the negotiating table, the LKP was as close as Guadeloupe ever came to a popular uprising. Except that, as Bonilla explains, the LKP "did not aim to topple the government, to change the political status of Guadeloupe, or to transform its existing forms of governance." Even though the LKP's leadership skillfully highlighted the neocolonial and imperialist structures behind Guadeloupe's social and economic issues, its demands were articulated from a position of citizenship, a position of belonging to the state rather than around demands for sovereignty.[10]

It is in this context that we must understand the work of a second *lyannaj*, the Lyannaj pou gwoka. As we will see, the demands to have gwoka recognized by UNESCO illustrate the strategic (post)colonial entanglements that define the contemporary postnationalist moment. As a department of France, Guadeloupe does not have a seat at the United Nations, and therefore any action to see its culture recognized by UNESCO must first be vetted by France's Ministère de la culture. More than the LKP, the Lyannaj pou gwoka worked within the structure of the French state to carve out some cultural sovereignty, albeit limited.

It might be helpful here to pause and clarify what I mean by *Creole postnationalism*. By using the term *postnationalism*, I do not mean to suggest that the nation is "dead as a political and analytic category" or even that, in the twenty-first century, nationalism has ceased to play a significant role in shaping Guadeloupean politics and musical practices.[11] Rather, I follow the lead of John Carlos Rowes, Lauren Berlant, and others who argue that, even as the meaning and significance of nationalism and the nation-state is evolving, the nation and national symbols continue to "provide an alphabet for a collective consciousness or national subjectivity."[12] Moreover, I echo Puri's own insightful comment that the *post*—in *(post)colonialism* or *postnationalism*—"marks an imperfect break with the past in terms of which it continues to define itself, unable to achieve an affirmative, coherent naming of the present."[13] Postnationalism, then, is best understood as a "continuance" of nationalism. In the 1970s, the centripetal pull of nationalism sought to define a Guadeloupean nation that was both geographically and culturally bounded. I argue that, in the new millennium, postnationalism preserves the nation as a desirable community but submits it to centrifugal forces that inscribe it within regional, diasporic, and transnational networks. In twenty-first-century Guadeloupe, musicians, dancers, and cultural activists use the musical symbols of the nation developed in the preceding decades and reinterpret them to offer a vision of the nation that is no longer predicated solely on a longing for an independent state. I therefore understand postnationalism as a set of strategies and imaginaries that does not negate the pull of nationalist modes of solidarity. It is a poetics informed by both fleeing and homing—by the *détour*—that imagines new forms of solidarity and alternative forms of governance.

Many social scientists, political theorists, and cultural critics have pointed out over the past twenty years that the global neoliberal regime has done much to undermine the classic Westphalian model of the sovereign nation-state. Ours is an age of "Empire," write Hardt and Negri, an era in which "sovereignty has taken a new form, composed of a series of national and supranational organisms united under a single logic of rule."[14] This new global order is perhaps nowhere felt more acutely than in the (post)colonial world, and specifically in the Caribbean, where "nominally independent nations . . . have repeatedly had their political and economic sovereignty challenged through military invasions, electoral interference, security legislation, and the multiple barriers placed on international trade with other countries in the Global South."[15] To this list, we should also include the demands of international tourism and the impact of all these factors on Caribbean ecosystems.[16] For many (post)colonial states, neoliberalism and neocolonialism converge. It is not surprising, then, that political activists in the nonsovereign Caribbean have turned away from nationalist demands for the establishment of an independent state. Instead, they are capitalizing on new strategic entanglements with their metropolitan centers in order to bring about social change as well as establish new modes of cultural and political representation. It is these strategies that I consider postnational.

Beyond these global considerations, I associate creolization and postnationalism as a response to two postcolonial critiques of the nation as an ontological category. First, as Joshua Jelly-Schapiro rightly underscored, Caribbean nations overflow their state's geographic borders. Indeed, many Jamaican, Trinidadian, and Dominican citizens reside in global metropolises in North America and Western Europe. We have likewise seen that studies of the French Antilles cannot ignore the "third island," the Antillean diaspora in metropolitan France. Any study of Caribbean nationalism must therefore be transnational and the Creole postnation is necessarily a "transnation."[17] However, contrary to Jelly-Schapiro's essay, mine is not simply an effort to deterritorialize or decenter the nation. Rather, I align my conception of the Creole postnation with Crichlow and Northover, who recognize creolization processes as "entangled with emancipatory projects" that involve an (re)imagining of place not only from geographic but also ontological perspectives. They continue, "*Creolization* processes were, and are, emancipatory projects tied to the imagining and making of modern subjects and the homing of modern freedom."[18]

This links with the second (post)colonial critique of the "nation," one that addresses more directly imperial nation-states. Stuart Hall writes of British (post)colonial subjects: "'British' most of us were, at one time—but that was long ago and, besides, as Shakespeare said, 'the wench is dead.' 'English' we cannot be. But tied in our fates and fortunes with 'the others'—while steadfastly refusing to have to become 'other' to belong—we do, after all, have a stake, an investment—in this phase of globalization—in what I might call 'the post-nation': but only if it can be re-imagined, re-invented to include us."[19]

Thus, in the age of Empire, the postnational disenchantment with sovereignty is coupled with an effort to redefine citizenship. Anti- and postcolonial discourse has often involved a desire to redefine the terms under which (post)colonial populations "belong" to their metropolitan nation-state, not only in terms of their political participation but also in terms of culture. In other words, demands that the metropolitan state abandon its policies of dominance and assimilation and embrace its plurinationality illuminate another aspect of postnationalism.

In the (post)colonial Caribbean, then, Creole postnationalism can help us conceptualize demands for alternative forms of governance *within* the metropolitan state. In the 1970s and 1980s in Guadeloupe, anticolonial nationalism was based on a demand for sovereignty. In the new millennium, Creole postnationalism—as a form of (post)colonial nationalism—has shifted gears. If domesticating modernity once meant creating a new home space outside the metropolitan state, it now entails efforts to reshape the metropolitan state to be more hospitable. These postnational strategies of decolonization seek forms of partial sovereignty without completely challenging the authority of the French state. In a conversation with Bonilla, Guadeloupean union leader Raymond Gama captured the difference between nationalist and postnationalist attitudes: "You can have independence and be *dans la merde*. . . . We want to transform our lives even if it's under the French flag. The nationalists were guided by one single idea—not a desire for social change, but a desire for the nation. We do not cling to the nation. We want sovereignty but only if it comes with social transformation."[20]

Witness, also, this declaration that Martinican writer Patrick Chamoiseau made—perhaps symbolically if not ironically—on the state-owned radio station France Culture. The intervention is worth quoting at length because it perfectly captures the complexities of my understanding of post-nationalism and its ambiguities:

> We live in a territorial aberration. This being said, we have to put this territorial aberration in perspective because, today, we can conceive of entities that are not purely territorial. . . . Given our reality, we are born of Relation, we are born from a process of creolization and creolization leads to Relation. . . . And when you are the product of Relation, it is not the territory that defines belonging; rather belonging is defined through currents, solidarities, memorial sensitivities, historical sensitivities. . . . Therefore, we can simultaneously belong to the Caribbean, to the Americas and we can maintain friendly and fraternal relations with France and Europe because of our history. . . . I am a separatist and I often say: France's best friends are separatists. Simply because they want a true relation with France, not subjugation under, but a genuine relation with France, that is to say where partnerships can emerge, where the autonomy of thought, creation, and creativity is mutual and fosters fecundity. . . . That is the object of our struggle. It no longer is the old demands of a nationalist rupture with borders and a flag. . . . It is not a declaration of independence but a declaration of inter-dependence. . . . To exist fully in the Caribbean, in the Americas, in France, in Europe, in the world. And with that, to be put in Relation is truly an act of blossoming and freedom. The new act of freedom today is a declaration of inter-dependence.[21]

I propose Creole postnationalism, then, as a way of moving beyond the apparent contradiction of being a French citizen and feeling Guadeloupean, of being a sovereign people of a nonsovereign nation. In the next section, we turn our attention to musicians who have invested the liminal creative space of the Creole postnation to express this interdependence, this difficult quest to find a (post)colonial model between independence and dependence.

Sounding a Postnational Aurality

Today, in Guadeloupe, as in metropolitan France, gwoka participates in this new (post)colonial and postnational aurality. Contrary to the quadrille, which is hardly played anymore, the traditional forms of drumming have not fallen into folklore. Every Saturday, a pedestrian street in Pointe-à-Pitre sees the gathering of drummers from Akiyo Ka who attract a vibrant community of listeners, dancers, and street vendors (see figure 5.1). *Swaré léwòz* are generally well attended, and nearly every municipality has its own private gwoka school where one can learn to play the drum and dance.

5.1. Photo of gwoka in the Rue piétonne, Pointe-à-Pitre, 2007. François Ladrezeau, foreground.

Some—like Akadémiduka, Sakitaw, or Kamodjaka—have become veritable institutions. A few traditional groups—Kannida foremost among them—have found an audience outside the archipelago, even if their professional occupations (the group is headed by brothers who run a body shop) keep them from more extensive touring. The cultural nationalist movement of the 1970s and 1980s has also fueled a revival of carnival drum groups, called *gwoup a pò*, and some of those have become massive organizations, gathering thousands of people for each of their *déboulé* (parade). And while the annual Festival Gwoka struggles financially, it refuses to compromise its gwoka-centered program or Creole-only policy simply to attract foreign tourists, and yet it continues to attract an audience of several hundred people every night.

All this being said, gwoka does not, by any stretch of the imagination, have a preponderant presence in the Guadeloupean soundscape, which, musically speaking, is dominated by the cymbal beats of *konpa* and the heavy bass of dancehall emanating from cars and businesses. Yet Guadeloupean artists working in these styles, like the dancehall superstar Admiral T, claim gwoka as a source of inspiration. In addition to the different versions of *jazz ka* discussed in the previous chapter, the sounds and rhythms of gwoka have found their way in dancehall and hip-hop (through the work of Exxos and Star Jee) and electronic music (Rico Toto, based in Paris). Gwoka may not be the most popular form of music on the archipelago today but the claim that it has become the *potomitan* (central pillar) of Guadeloupean music may be only a slight exaggeration. In all these different hybridizing variations, gwoka accumulates different meanings on top of its nationalist base.

Perhaps no musical group better sounds the new Creole postnationalism in Guadeloupe than Soft. Created in 2002, Soft has taken the Guadeloupean music scene by surprise. Twenty years after the advent of zouk and at a time when Guadeloupean music was increasingly dominated by the electronic sounds of *konpa* and dancehall, Soft found nearly unprecedented popular success by playing only acoustic instruments, centering their rhythm section on gwoka, and singing politically and socially conscious lyrics in Creole. Three months after the release of their first album in 2006, the group had already sold more than ten thousand copies in Guadeloupe alone, rivaling some of zouk's biggest hits.[22] In the following five years, Soft would release two equally successful recordings and consistently fill concert venues in Guadeloupe, Martinique, and France. And after an eight-year hiatus, the band released its fourth album in December 2017.

Singer-songwriter Fred Deshayes, saxophonist Philippe Sadikalay, and bassist Joël Larochelle form the core of the group. In addition, Soft's recordings and concerts generally feature the violin of Julie Aristide, the voice of Maxence Deshayes (Fred's brother), and the work of a number of percussionists. Over the years, Didier Juste, Sonny Troupé, and the late Charlie Chomereau-Lamotte have taken turns performing with the band. With the exception of Chomereau-Lamotte, who, in fact, played in Lockel's first group back in 1969, all these musicians were born after Lockel had moved back to Guadeloupe. They are a new musical and political generation, the sons and daughters of the postwar nationalist activists.

Although Soft is a collaborative enterprise, Fred Deshayes contributes the majority of the group's repertoire and sets the tone of its overall philosophy. A former law professor at the Université Antilles-Guyane (now Université des Antilles), Deshayes has a sharp understanding of Guadeloupe's political and social situation, as well as the ways politics have shaped Guadeloupean music. Deshayes's ideology and musical aesthetics are a product of the cultural and political activism of his parents' generation. His father belonged to GONG and was witness to the violent repressions of May 1967, which only strengthened his nationalist and anticolonialist convictions. In one of our many conversations, Fred Deshayes reminisced—with critical good humor—about his father's doctrinaire revolutionary Marxism: "When

I was young, I told my father: 'It's kind of good that in Guadeloupe we have bridges and stuff like that . . .' He told me: 'Yes, the French build bridges so that they can better transport the troops of repression.'"[23] Deshayes has paid tribute to his father's activism by recording one of his songs, "Lavi fofilé" (Frayed life), which has a clear anticolonial and separatist message.[24] Fred Deshayes's own song "Gouté Gwadloup" (Taste Guadeloupe) also makes clear that his ideology and artistry are rooted in the work of the previous generation. He sings: "An ka gouté tè a Gwadloup pou i pé rakonté / Avan mwen té di dé jenn té ka filé on lidé / Avan mwen sé nonm doubout / Jenn a GONG ké mèt anwout / Po yo té vanté konsyans konsi konsyans pé pran difé" (I taste the Guadeloupean soil so that it tells me / Before me there were youths who worked out an idea / Before me there were men standing up / The youths from GONG who blew on our conscience as if to set it ablaze).[25]

Like the nationalist orthodoxy of the 1970s, Deshayes puts gwoka at the center of his expression of Guadeloupeanness and of his musical creative process. When working on a new composition, Deshayes generally starts by working out riffs and melodies that would fit a particular gwoka rhythm. From there, he develops a melody and write the lyrics. In 2009, Deshayes explained to me that, with his music, he was seeking "what we [Guadeloupeans] can give the world, what is essentially Guadeloupean, what can't be found anywhere else, the phrasing that can only be found here. That's what I'm looking for"[26]—a declaration of intent that is strikingly close to Lockel's own motivations. But Deshayes is actually very critical of Lockel and his music. During our conversations, he denounced repeatedly what he saw as Lockel's normative, "Soviet" approach.[27] For him, *gwoka modènn* lacks feeling. "Those who speak about atonal music," he explained to me, "are trying to prescribe something. That's why I call [*gwoka modènn*] a learned music."[28] For Deshayes, *gwoka modènn* failed to capture the musical qualities that most Guadeloupeans enjoy and replaced them with an intellectual, politically driven concept. Here Deshayes once more echoes his father who thought that the patriotic camp's focus on gwoka was misguided and that biguine would have had a broader popular appeal.

The most cursory listening to Soft's music makes clear that the group is far from a mere extension of the nationalist aurality of the 1970s. For one thing, its members grew up in a different aural environment than that of their parents, one defined by the deregulation of FM airwaves in the early 1980s. Until then, radio broadcasting in France was limited to state-owned stations, and although pirate radios sprouted throughout France in the 1970s—often in support of leftist social movements—they were regularly raided and their equipment confiscated by the conservative government.

Things changed with the election of the socialist François Mitterrand, who had himself relied on pirate stations during his campaign. The liberalization of the airwaves was progressive, but its impact was quickly felt in Guadeloupe. In 1981, Luc Reinette launched Radyo Inité (Radio Unity). A year later, Radyo Tanbou (Radio Drum) started broadcasting and quickly established itself as the voice of the patriotic camp. Still on the air thirty years later, Radyo Tanbou broadcasts a mix of talk programming and music, in which gwoka—both traditional and modern—features prominently. Deshayes remembers how the new radio station shaped his childhood soundscape:

> They had a song that they played all the time. In fact, it was a kind of jingle: "Lindépandans! Lindépandans!" It was a *toumblak chiré* [fast]. "Lindépandans!" [imitates drumming] *Toukoutou ta! Toukoutou ta!* "Lindépandans!" They played it all the time. It was like a jingle that played throughout the day. And then, there was a song that became a sort of nationalist anthem, by Gérard Lockel. "Gwadloupéyen, Gwadloupéyenn! Gwadloup an danjé. Nou pé pa rété kon sa. Fò nou mèt tout fòs an nou adan on sèl konba pou nou rézisté. Dé jou an jou, lenmi ka anvay nou; fò nou fè atensyon, tan ka pasé. Gwadloupéyen, Gwadloupéyenn . . ." You see? And it played all the time. Everyday! And I was raised in this atmosphere.[29]

But the liberalization of the airwaves that made Radyo Tanbou possible also brought new local subsidiaries of metropolitan radio stations to Guadeloupe. These stations targeted the youth market with the latest zouk hits alongside French and American pop. This, too, has had a profound impact on Soft's music. Deshayes explains: "I want to explore my deepest roots, but I want to do so [now]. When I was twelve or fifteen, I listened to Lionel Richie. I can't erase that from my life." He concludes: "One cannot ignore outside influences. You wouldn't be the same [without them]. One cannot be in a constant state of virginity. In music, virginity doesn't exist. There is only the authenticity of feeling."[30] And so, when I asked Deshayes about his musical influences, he listed a mix of gwoka singers (Chabin and Robert Loyson), jazz musicians (Miles Davis, Ron Carter, George Benson), 1980s R&B icons (Michael Jackson, Lionel Richie, and the songwriter Rod Temperton), as well as biguine and calypso musicians, styles of music that his father was also particularly fond of. Soft has, in fact, recorded music that pays tribute to all of these styles: Loyson's song "Jean Fouyé," the soca-inspired "Frenchi," the Caribbean-flavored R&B of "Change My World," some *konpa*, and a number of biguines. All of this has occurred around a core repertoire of original songs in which the rhythms of gwoka are always present, if not explicitly so. It is the combination of all these musical elements that I hear as a Creole postnationalist aesthetic.

This aesthetic is also heard in Deshayes's approach to guitar playing. While the singer tends to downplay his guitar skills, he explained to me that his playing is greatly influenced by Western African music, especially *kora* playing and the guitar stylings of musicians like Salif Keita and the bassist Richard Bona. He also pointed out that he plays on nylon strings, a choice influenced by the sound of Brazilian and Haitian guitarists. Finally, Deshayes admitted to practicing classical guitar exercises, but never for very long: he joked that, being a composer at heart, he lacks the patience to focus on specific exercises and ends up trying to develop them into new compositions.[31]

Overall, Soft's music echoes the aesthetics and concerns of early zouk, a parallel that Deshayes has intentionally cultivated: "I don't keep the traditional structures of gwoka because I don't play gwoka. Me, I would say that [our music] is not gwoka. It is based on gwoka. Rather than picking up zouk where Pierre-Édouard [Décimus] left it with Kassav', I go back to where he started from. And there, he started from the rhythms of carnival and the rhythms of gwoka. And me, I started off from the same point to regenerate my music."[32] Like zouk, Soft's music is anchored in the rhythmic alphabet of Guadeloupe, which is mixed with pan-Caribbean influences, something especially audible while Charlie Chomereau-Lamotte was in the group. Deshayes praised the percussionist as having an "encyclopedic knowledge of Caribbean rhythms." He added: "He [brought] some musics, some rhythms, some ways of playing that rocked our childhood. And it's all part of our culture." But unlike zouk's performance of modernity through the embrace of electronic instrument, Soft cultivates a nostalgic ethos by foregrounding acoustic instruments. Zouk was first and foremost a dance music. *Zouké* means "to party" in Creole, and zouk has never lost sight of that spirit, even when its songs carry an explicit political message. In contrast, while a few people dance to Soft when the band performs in Guadeloupe, the majority of the audience—mainly people in their thirties and older—stands or sits, listens, and often sings along. Soft's gentle aesthetics—like most folk music, whether the American folk songs of Bob Dylan or the Cuban tradition of *nueva trova*, but also, and importantly, like the tradition of French chanson—allow for a greater focus on the lyrics. "Lyrics matter a lot in my songs," explained Deshayes. "I endeavor to give our music some compositions that are dignified; that are popular but have a certain value."[33]

The song "Krim kont la Gwadloup" typifies the sounds of the current Creole postnationalist aurality.[34] The song is based on the *menndé* rhythm

5.2. "Krim kont la Gwadloup," basic vamp

and the guitar plays an E-minor vamp that matches the rhythm of the *boula* (figure 5.2). The minimal harmonic movement in this example reflects Deshayes's desire to preserve what he sees as the simplicity of popular and traditional music. The melody of the song is a recitation around the pitch B, with each phrase ending with a descent down to the tonic E, through a minor pentatonic scale. As Deshayes explained, this melodic construction was inspired by Robert Loyson's frequent use of a similar device.[35]

The song's lyrics are typical of Deshayes's socially conscious writing, but they clearly depart from the nationalist rhetoric of the 1970s. Lockel pushed Guadeloupeans to take up arms against their colonial oppressor. Konket sang that Guadeloupe was sick and blamed that on the inaction of French and European politicians. Cosaque exposed the abusive nature of French migration policies. In contrast, in "Krim kont la Gwadloup," Deshayes turns the accusatory gaze inward, on Guadeloupeans themselves. The song is a denunciation of neocolonialism, but it also indicts the selfishness of those who refuse to share their wealth to help others, of the Guadeloupean youths who complain that they have no future but do not try to better themselves, and of the idealism and aloofness of Guadeloupean intellectuals. Deshayes concludes: "Mwen menm pa méyè ki on dot / Si zot vlé, zot pé gadé avi an zot / Pas lè an vwé ka'y ka pasé / Sé nou menm fò nou pousuiv pou krim kont la Gwadloup" (I am no better than anyone else / If you want you can keep your own opinion / Because when I see what's going on / It is ourselves that we have to sue for crimes against Guadeloupe).

In a follow-up on their album *Konfyans* (Trust), which came out after the LKP, Deshayes offered equally sharp criticism for his fellow citizens. In "Révolution," he asks: "Es w pé konprann on pèp gwadloupeyen ka palé ka di bétiz ka rété la ka soufè?" (Can you understand a Guadeloupean people who speak nonsense and who stay where they suffer?).[36] Echoing a discourse that has become so frequent around Guadeloupe that it borders on cliché, the song goes on: "Nou di mésyé kolonyalis / nou di mésyé esklavajis / nou di fwansé sé linjistis" (We say these people are colonialists / we say these people are slave-traders / we say that the French are unjust). However, when the singer asks, "Revolution?" the rest of the group responds, in French rather than Creole: "Non, non, non, non." Live performances highlight the satirical nature of the song. When performing at the 2010 Festival Gwoka, Deshayes asked each member of the group, in turn, if he or she would be available to start the revolution the following week. Julie Aristide answered that she could not do the revolution on Monday because of her yoga class, Joël Larochelle was not available on Tuesday because he had a *konpa* rehearsal, Philippe Sadikalay's karaoke outing conflicted on Wednesday, and Maxence Deshayes had signed up for swimming lessons at the pool on Thursdays. The lead singer brought the point home: "Tout moun vlé chanjé la sosyété / Oui mais pas trop vite / Oui mais pas tout de suite" (Everybody wants to change society / Yes, but not too quickly / Yes, but not right away). The singer asks the question in Creole and answers in French, underscoring that, underneath all the separatist discourse and regardless of how much they complain, many Guadeloupeans remain attached to some aspects of life under French rule.

Deshayes summed up this postnationalist problematic in an interview for the French daily *Le Monde*:

How do we, Guadeloupeans, live in this vast ensemble that is the French nation? We are legally French but we have a feeling of belonging to something different. This has nothing to do with political belief, it is simply a different way of being. I do not feel "black" either, it doesn't mean anything! My community is composed of East Indians, whites, blacks: they're all Guadeloupeans. I feel closer to a *blanc péyi* [sic, Guadeloupean-born whites] or to Guadeloupean Indians than to African Americans. Teenagers' imagination isn't turned towards Europe. They sing Jamaican dancehall in both Creole and English. . . . My grandmother was light-skinned and didn't really like black people. All of this is part of our reality. Questions remain. We have a customizable identity. A Guadeloupean person is pro-European when it benefits them, that is to say when France makes decisions that bother them; pro-French when Europe is embarrassing; and profoundly Guadeloupean when they meet a *métro* [French person] who bothers them. We do all this quasi-instinctively.[37]

Within the postnationalist problem-space, Deshayes proposes a Guadeloupean identity that is relational, performative, and strategically oppositional. Although not everyone in Guadeloupe would follow Deshayes's racial positioning, the strategic negotiations of identity that he outlines here point to a fragmented, unstable, creative, and open ended—in other words, creolized—approach to the performance of identity.[38]

Indeed, in a significant departure from the nationalist hard line, Deshayes embraces his creoleness. He explained to me once that the "universe of the gwoka" expressed Guadeloupean difference but on a foundation that was *métissée* (hybrid), with contributions from both Africa and France. Likewise, when I asked him to define what it meant to be Guadeloupean, his answer moved past an effort to define the Guadeloupean nation to settle on an expression of Guadeloupean creoleness:

> What's a Guadeloupean? What I can tell you is that being Guadeloupean is, on principle, at least in my mind, without distinction of race, class, or origin. You can be Guadeloupean and white or Guadeloupean and Indian. It has nothing to do with that. The difficulty in defining the word Guadeloupean is the problem with the word nation more broadly. There are two conceptions: either you define the nation as a willingness to live together or you define it with objective criteria. . . . What makes us Guadeloupean? I don't know. The fact that we say we are, that's evident. And the fact, I don't know, that we share Creole references. Because Creole is not only a language: I do not speak Creole, I am Creole. That is to say that I speak Creole and French. I am Creole in my way of living, in my tastes. . . . There. I am unable to tell you what a Guadeloupean is and it is a great difficulty for many people. But I believe that difference has to be felt.[39]

Key to Deshayes's understanding of a Guadeloupean Creole postnationalist subjectivity is establishing difference within the French nation-state. Significantly, my conversations with Deshayes suggest that "difference" in this case shouldn't be understood as a nationalist quest to define a Guadeloupean essence:

> The truth is, that between a French person and myself, you can see the difference. As soon as we meet, it is undeniably evident. When a French person arrives in Guadeloupe, they see that they are not at home; and a Guadeloupean who arrives in France can tell that he is not at home. I don't say this to mean that they have to go back home, I simply say that the difference they feel reminds them of where they came from, that is to say that they are not French. If they were French, they wouldn't see the difference. At least, they wouldn't feel the difference with so much bitterness and pain.[40]

In his foregrounding of the encounter, Deshayes expresses here something that is akin to Glissant's opacity, the "irreducible density of the other," a "non-reducible singularity."[41] For Glissant, essence expresses a closing off, a folding back onto oneself or the group; opacity, in contrast, is necessarily relational. One is opaque to someone else (or to oneself). Glissant writes: "The opaque is not the obscure, but it can be and be accepted as such. It is the non-reducible, which is the strongest guarantee of participation [in the poetics of Relation] and confluence."[42]

When I asked Deshayes to define gwoka, his answer painted gwoka as somewhat opaque, an irreducible musical difference. "I don't know [what it is]. I've never asked myself that question. I've never needed to ask that question. I've wondered that about zouk, about biguine, but not about gwoka." When I pressed him as to why, his answer returned to a process of relational differentiation: "Because zouk is in competition with other things. So we have to distinguish zouk from *konpa*, for example. We have to distinguish biguine from other things, most notably gwoka. Because when I compose, since I don't know how to do the biguine *waché* [the characteristic syncopated accents of biguine], do I really play biguine? . . . For gwoka, I've never really needed a definition. It's like I've always known what it was."[43]

The recognition of the opacity of gwoka, and of Guadeloupeanness, allows Deshayes to place his music in relation to other genres, without fear of losing its Guadeloupean specificity and without desire to privilege any one cultural heritage. "I am Guadeloupean," affirms Deshayes, "and I express myself through an art form that is inferior to no other." As if responding to Glissant's belief that creolization requires elements of equal value, Deshayes adds, "Since we are of equal dignity [with other musical genres], our exchanges are easier and better accepted."[44]

While contrasting Soft's performance of Guadeloupean subjectivity with Lockel's, Deshayes points to a paradox in *gwoka modènn*: "It seeks to express difference. However, one doesn't need that if one is different. The person who seeks difference is, in fact, engaged in a process that reveals that he feels similar. It is when you feel similar [to other people] that you seek to be different. The person who is different does not need to talk about his difference since he is different. . . . Difference is like existence. It cannot be demonstrated, it has to be experienced. . . . And art is this way. It expresses difference without needing to be complicated."[45]

Gwoka's opacity shouldn't simply be taken for granted. Just as Glissant recognized that *négritude* operated a necessary reversal of cultural hierarchy that restored a greater parity between French and Afro-diasporic francophone literatures, my analysis of Lockel's music pointed to its role in combatting assimilationist mimesis. If artists like Soft or Dominik Coco can build a postnationalist, cosmopolitan, pan-Caribbean aurality that takes gwoka as its starting point, it is thanks to the work of nationalist artists—Lockel foremost among them—who restored gwoka's opacity.

In fact, both Lockel's and Deshayes's work are marked by nostalgia. Lockel and the AGEG, while claiming the mantle of modernity, actually illustrate what Svetlana Boym identifies as "restorative nostalgia." For Boym, restorative nostalgia is the appendage of nationalist movements, who "do not think of themselves as nostalgic; they believe that their project is about truth." Restorative nostalgia "proposes to rebuild the lost home and patch up the memory gaps." Boym contrasts this tendency with "reflective nostalgia," which "dwells in *algia*, in longing and loss, the imperfect process of remembrance." Reflective nostalgia addresses itself to the "irrevocability of the past and human finitude. *Re-flection* suggests new flexibility, not the reestablishment of stasis. The focus here is not on recovery of what is perceived to be an absolute truth but on the meditation on history and passage of time."[46] I see a strong parallel between Boym's taxonomy of nostalgic tendencies and what Glissant has theorized as *retour* (reversion) and *détour* (detour or diversion). "Reversion," writes Glissant, "is the obsession with the One: being should not be altered. To revert is to consecrate permanence and non-relation."[47] Nationalism is enmeshed with restorative nostalgia, with the longing for an idealized home, a reversion to a bounded singularity freed of corrupting outside influences. Restorative nostalgia and reversion are central to Lockel's anticolonial aurality. In contrast, Soft's music sounds a form of reflective nostalgia. It evokes the past not as something that can be reverted to, but as "heritage," as "sa papa té lésé an tèt aw, pou timoun aw pé révé" (that which your dad left in your head so that your child can dream," as Deshayes sings in "Leritaj" (Heritage).[48] Reflective nostalgia is consistent with Soft's postnationalist embrace of creolization, which itself dwells in the liminal, in the point of entanglement. "But art is like this," declared Deshayes. "It expresses itself, and it expresses difference, without needing complexity. And here, it is the universe of the gwoka that is different, that is fundamentally *métissé*. . . . Gwoka is a Guadeloupean music. Good. But we have never been Guadeloupean without being French. That doesn't exist."[49] Soft's reflective nostalgia, then, is a dwelling in the liminal space and time of the encounter, of creolization. As he concludes his meditation on the *détour*, Glissant professes: "The *Détour* [diversion] can only be a fruitful ruse if it is fertilized by the *Retour* [reversion]: not a reversion to the fantasy of origin, to the immutable unicity of Being; but a return to the point of entanglement from which we were diverted by force. It is there that we must put in practice

162 / Chapter Five

the components of Relation, or perish."[50] In the next section, we turn our attention to the work of the Lyannaj pou gwoka, itself an effort marked by reflective nostalgia and the Creole postnationalist politics of the *détour*.

Postnational Aurality and the Politics of the *Détour*

Starting in 2004, Félix Cotellon, president of the center for traditional music and dance on Guadeloupe, spearheaded a grassroots campaign to see *gwoka* recognized on the UNESCO's Representative List of the Intangible Cultural Heritage of Humanity (ICH). In April 2014, the French Comité du patrimoine ethnologique et immatériel forwarded Guadeloupe's application to UNESCO, and, in November, the Intergovernmental Committee for the Safeguarding of ICH added *gwoka* to the ICH list, going as far as to cite the application as exemplary. Since then, Cotellon and Rèpriz have continued to work to translate this institutional success into regional action.

This apparently smooth process should not mask the controversies and contradictions that have surrounded Guadeloupe's bid for inclusion. Indeed, Cotellon's initiative originally polarized the gwoka community and revealed, once again, the music as a nexus of contestations.[51] The pushback against the ICH project should have been expected given *gwoka*'s poetic and political overdetermination, to reprise Deshayes's formulation. Because applications to the UNESCO's heritage lists must be submitted by member states and given Guadeloupe's status as an overseas department of France, its application had to come from the French government. This created a series of conundrums. With the validation of the UNESCO, the music once mobilized to resist French colonialism has been listed as representative of French culture. Why did Cotellon, a former *cadre* (member of the leadership team) of the UPLG, pursue this outcome, which, on the surface, seemed to contradict nearly forty years of nationalist activism? Conversely, why did France promote the inscription of a music that is so very closely associated with the separatist efforts in one of its former colonies, something that flies in the face of its unitary republicanism?

In what follows, I elucidate the patrimonialization of gwoka as a postnationalist continuance of the nationalist efforts of the late twentieth century.[52] I focus on Félix Cotellon, whose long personal involvement in separatist activism amplifies the "dissonance" inherent to the creation and promotion of heritage.[53] I explore this dissonance as it resonates within what Anna Tsing calls a "zone[] of awkward engagement, where words mean something different across a divide even as people agree to speak."[54] I find Tsing's metaphor particularly helpful because the latest efforts to patrimonialize gwoka bring together actors who, historically and at first glance, represent divergent and even contradictory ideological traditions. The metaphor illuminates the postnational problem-space as a zone of positive power in which Guadeloupean separatist nationalism rubs against French republicanism. Specifically, even as every actor strategically presents the Guadeloupean project as purely "cultural," I uncover a complex entanglement of culture and politics where appeal to "diversity" functions as an "empty signifier" that can simultaneously bolster French hegemony and serve as a tool of contestation against it.[55] This, I conclude, is symptomatic of the politics of the *détour*, a manifestation of a broader process of creolization of the political.

The patrimonialization of gwoka takes its roots in the nationalist efforts to revitalize, codify, and homogenize drumming practices in post-departmentalization Guadeloupe. Today, the widely accepted idea that gwoka represents a nearly timeless inheritance from the plantation (or Africa) and a continued expression of resistance attests to the success of the nationalist campaign. One individual emerged from this period of intense nationalist activism to play a central role in furthering the institutionalization of gwoka in the following decades. In 1978, Félix Cotellon started organizing *gwoka modènn* concerts in coordination with a youth soccer tournament held in July on the beach in Sainte-Anne. Cotellon was born in the seaside town and had recently returned home upon finishing law school in Bordeaux. While in Bordeaux, he had risen through the ranks of the AGEG and become a dedicated activist. Back in Guadeloupe, Cotellon had joined the UPLG. The football tournament and concerts were part of the separatist party's efforts to reach out and recruit new members. By 1988, the musical events came to eclipse the tournament. In keeping with the nationalist cultural platform, the concerts focused exclusively on *gwoka* performances, mixing its traditional and contemporary expressions. The Festival Gwoka was born and Cotellon would remain its president until 2009.[56] Through his long-term involvement in nationalist organizations, as well as his formal training in law, Cotellon has gathered a large amount of social and cultural capital. He has been able to use this capital to shape the zone of awkward engagement through which the institutionalization of *gwoka* has taken place, first through the festival and later through the UNESCO bid and its implementation.

The Festival Gwoka has played an important role in promoting the ICH project in Guadeloupe. The UNESCO Convention for the Safeguarding of the Intangible Cultural Heritage was drafted in 2003, and, as early as 2004, Cotellon was thinking about its significance for France's overseas departments. That year, two years before France even adopted the convention, the

164 / Chapter Five

Festival Gwoka—under Cotellon's leadership—invited Chérif Khaznadar, president of the cultural committee of the French delegation to UNESCO, to present on the subject.[57] In 2005, Cotellon oversaw the creation of Rèpriz, the Center for Traditional Music and Dance of Guadeloupe, which received UNESCO accreditation in 2007. In July of that year, the center organized an ethnomusicology conference alongside the festival on the intangible cultural heritage of the Caribbean. Every year since, the Festival Gwoka has featured discussions of various aspects of the convention. In 2010, Cotellon used the festival to give a special presentation during which he outlined the text of the ICH convention and its potential for the gwoka community. The 2011 festival was an all-out effort to boost support for the inscription of *gwoka* on the ICH list and to recruit members of the *gwoka* community who would work for nearly a year within the Lyannaj pou gwoka (Alliance for gwoka) to draft the application file. In July 2013, Rèpriz again brought together musicians, cultural activists, academics, and state representatives from Brazil, the Dominican Republic, Grenada, Guadeloupe, Saint Lucia, Trinidad and Tobago, and the United States for a three-day ethnomusicology symposium to foster regional cooperation on issues related to intangible heritage.[58]

Although Cotellon was central in spurring and driving the ICH project, the Guadeloupean bid would not have succeeded if it were solely the work of a single individual. In fact, the success of the Lyannaj pou gwoka rests in part on the fact that the group managed to present itself as representative of the gwoka community as a whole. As outlined earlier, the Lyannaj pou gwoka started to take shape in July 2011, when members of Rèpriz, led by Cotellon and the ethnomusicologist Dominique Cyrille, used the festival to recruit people who would work together to draft Guadeloupe's application to UNESCO. Although Cotellon had started discussing the project with festival participants and attendees as early as 2007, it was only in 2011 that members of the gwoka community took full measure of Cotellon's plan. Historian and gwoka artist Marie-Héléna Laumuno explained to me that she, like other practitioners, became aware of the project during the 2011 festival, when Cotellon started to recruit people to work on the application file.[59] She pointed to a meeting organized by Rèpriz at the Hotel Rotabas in Sainte-Anne on July 10, 2011, as a flash point. I was present at this meeting: the climate in the cramped conference room was tense as Cotellon and Cyrille's pitch was met with a mix of support, questions, and hostility. In the following days, weeks, and months, Cotellon, Cyrille, and a small group of early supporters—including the Festival Gwoka's charismatic master of ceremonies Patrick Solvet—successfully used the festival as a bully pulpit

Postnational Aurality / 165

to recruit for the Lyannaj and to gather signatures on a petition to support the Guadeloupean bid. I myself joined the Lyannaj in July 2011 even though I was not scheduled to remain in Guadeloupe. Throughout the following year, my long-distance involvement allowed me to remain informed of the latest developments while simultaneously staying on good terms with friends who opposed the ICH project.

From September 2011 to March 2012, a group of roughly forty musicians, dancers, academics, and cultural activists worked together within the Lyannaj to draft Guadeloupe's application. Significantly, the Lyannaj brought together people from both sides of the traditional-modern divide: modern singers like Monza and Deshayes sat alongside more traditionally minded practitioners like the dancer Jacky Jalème. In addition to their committee work, members of the Lyannaj met with civic leaders (mayors and municipal council members) as well as cultural organizations in Guadeloupe, in metropolitan France, and even in London to enlist their support for the project. They organized public debates on the topic of intangible cultural heritage, intervened in the local media, and organized two *swaré léwòz* to disseminate information and recruit support. At every step, Rèpriz and the Lyannaj collected signatures and official declarations in support of the project. Thanks to these outreach efforts, and although it grew from the vision of a single individual, the Lyannaj has all the trappings of an effective grassroots campaign.

The prospect of seeing *gwoka* recognized by UNESCO carried with it many hopes but also elicited real fears. Unsurprisingly, given his political convictions and his central role in institutionalizing traditional musics, Cotellon became a catalyst for criticisms of the project. Indeed, several people used the ICH project as an opportunity to settle old scores. Several musicians I spoke with reacted negatively to the ICH project in order to express their overall dissatisfaction with Cotellon's position as a kind of cultural broker. Some questioned his qualifications to deal with gwoka as a UNESCO expert, since he is not himself a gwoka musician.[60] It did not help that Rèpriz had, up to that point, focused many of its activities on other musical practices such as quadrille, *bèlè*, maritime songs, and Indo-Guadeloupean traditions. Others denounced what they saw as a preferential treatment of certain artists who seemed to get more frequent booking at the Festival Gwoka as well as more direct support from Rèpriz. Finally, some people questioned Cotellon's motivations, suspecting that he was driven by a desire for personal gain or, at least, that the initiative was meant to attract funding for Rèpriz. These reactions and conspiracy theories are not merely anecdotal. They also speak to the misgivings of a population that is used to

166 / Chapter Five

dealing with a system of domination that cannot be apprehended, that is both everywhere and nowhere, that—as Glissant points out—assimilation has kept invisible.[61]

Beyond the personal rancor were real anxieties. As soon as the Lyannaj pou gwoka started its work, another group—the Kolektif pou gwoka (Collective for gwoka)—emerged to challenge its efforts. Their sometimes-raucous critique of the Lyannaj channeled the unease that many had with what they perceived as a betrayal of gwoka's nationalist ethos. As the percussionist Klod Kiavué and I chatted on the subject one afternoon, he admitted that he simply could not swallow the idea of France grabbing hold of the music used to express resistance against colonialism.[62] The ICH project came about too quickly for those who felt that the nationalist restorative project was not only unfinished but also still under threat. Indeed, at the heart of nationalist restorative nostalgia is a perceived menace to one's essential way of being. As Boym points out, restorative nostalgia imagines "home" as a space to be restored but also as a space that is "forever under siege, requiring defense against the plotting enemy."[63] This is the "home" of "Lindépendans," Lockel's anthem in which Guadeloupe is in urgent danger of an enemy invasion. Failing to protect this national home can lead only to a sense of loss and alienation. This is exactly what members of the Kolektif pou gwoka feared. Marie-Line Dahomay—a gwoka vocalist, historian, and central figure in the Kolektif—summed up their position:

> Gwoka has never been recognized as a French tradition. However, with the convention, it will come to be recognized throughout the world as a French practice. . . . So this is a problem for gwoka practitioners who, very often, have followed a separatist path, who have followed a nationalist path, even if they've abandoned it later. But they still maintain this image of gwoka as a Guadeloupean practice that was born in Guadeloupe and has nothing to do with French culture. People even say that gwoka is our identity. They even go further and say that it is the soul of Guadeloupe, you see? So, nobody would place their soul outside of their own home.[64]

To the nationalist concerns of the Kolektif, the Lyannaj offered a post-nationalist position. Laumuno shared with me that she had originally been suspicious of the Lyannaj's project but later came to embrace it. She, too, wanted to stay true to the music's nationalist heritage. For this reason, she insisted on being a member of the working group responsible for drafting the paragraph defining gwoka in the application: "I insisted that, in the definition, in the first line—even if we didn't keep it in the first line—that we say that gwoka is rooted in the Guadeloupean territory. That, I really insisted on that because to say that gwoka is French would be to betray the whole history of this drum music that has been decried, that has been marginalized. It would be a betrayal. It has to be said: the roots are in Guadeloupe."[65] Indeed, the application submitted to UNESCO identifies gwoka as "music, dance, and songs representative of Guadeloupean identity." Section D of the application, identifying the music's "geographical location and range," opens with the statement: "The gwoka's roots are in Guadeloupe," even if it opens up this geographic range to include "wherever Guadeloupeans live."[66]

Dancer and educator Jacky Jalème—who has long-established ties to Cotellon and the Festival Gwoka—had a more obviously postnationalist response to the Kolektif's fears: "I have been a nationalist militant, so I am not afraid. I am not afraid to go meet the other. . . . It isn't by shutting borders that we will move forward. . . . It isn't a problem if a Chinese person plays the drum. We need to stop freaking out. Here, we play everybody's music. . . . We are part of globalization. How can we make ourselves known?"[67]

For Jalème, letting France carry the project to seek UNESCO recognition for gwoka does not necessarily lead to a loss of identity. Jalème recognizes that forty years of cultural nationalist work has done much to restore gwoka's opacity. Laumuno, in contrast, sees in the ICHC a tool through which the music can be protected from any claim on it by outsiders:

> If there is a music that is ours, it is gwoka. And I think that the time had come to say so since there are no organizations to protect musical style. There are organizations who protect musical works but there are no organization that protect musical styles. Music belongs to everybody. So I told myself, even if someone plays it, a Chinese person (because we spoke of the Chinese a lot), a Japanese person, well, they would know that they practice something that belongs to Guadeloupe. And for me, that was the only place where we could say this. Maybe it won't be institutionalized, but it will be officialized, almost! Almost![68]

Both Jalème and Laumuno see the work of the Lyannaj and its reliance on French state institutions as illustrative of new (post)colonial entanglements and ambitions. Jalème pointed to the fact that the French state owns the local TV channel, but no one has refused to go perform on the air. Why, then, fear French support in sponsoring the inscription of gwoka on the ICH list? Laumuno, in our conversation, was quick to point out that Guadeloupeans "want to remain French, but only materially." They maintain a "relationship with France that is very ambiguous. . . . It is a relationship

168 / Chapter Five

that is fundamentally material." Outside of this material sphere, Laumuno insist that there is a cultural nation waiting to affirm itself politically: "This cultural nation functions, in my mind, as a substitute for this nation that would be, we can say, political. And the framework for this nation is gwoka." I asked her, "So, this inscription does not contradict the nationalist movement of the seventies and eighties?"

"No, no," she responded.

"Is it a continuation then?"

"Yes. That is to say, when we need France, we use it. Period. It's that simple." Laumuno continued: "Even if we know that this inscription has to be carried by France, we see it as accessory. For us, it is more about Guadeloupe-UNESCO. It is about Guadeloupe reaching the international institution. For us, it seems important that we go speak directly to that institution."[69]

Laumuno and Jalème's remarks point to the Lyannaj as a *détour*, a literal move to search elsewhere for recognition and legitimization. Laumuno, lifting the veil on colonial double consciousness, explains: "Because you know, often, maybe it is because we are on an island, maybe because of our status, but often it is the 'elsewhere' that comforts us in the idea we have of ourselves. Once the 'elsewhere' recognizes that what we have is strong, tough enough that we can lean on it, at that moment, we will realize that we can lean on it and that we can make it a tool." The *détour* is constitutive of Creole postnationalism, an ambivalent double citizenship that reconciles a strictly political and material belonging to the French state and a cultural belonging to a Guadeloupean nation within that state.[70]

As my conversations with Jalème and Laumuno illustrate, diffusion, representation, and visibility have been central motivations behind the work of the Lyannaj. Indeed, as he outlined the benefits of having gwoka recognized by UNESCO, Cotellon kept referring to the idea of *reconnaissance*, which here connotes both "recognition" and "valorization."[71] *Reconnaissance* is a sort of dialectics, a way to seek outside recognition to affirm one's existence. There is still, in the documents released by the Lyannaj, a drive to help Guadeloupeans shed what remains of their assimilationist prejudices. Indeed, we read in the dossier presenting the project to local collectivities that gwoka's inscription on the ICH list would "allow Guadeloupeans to look at their music differently." Moreover, the inscription would represent "an opportunity to tell the world that gwoka is simultaneously a musical and a social expression; that it creates a space where identities are affirmed, constructed, and expressed, a space of political contestation and solidarities."[72] Monza captured the postnationalist dialectics in his intervention during the 2013 symposium: "We at least have something to give, to offer to the world and I believe that gwoka could be, in any case, a tool that will define us and make us visible." If, for Monza, "it doesn't matter" that Guadeloupe is a nation without a state, it is because the ICHC gives nonindependent nations, ethnic minorities, and citizens of microstates a platform to increase their visibility.

Reconnaissance is also highly practical, an intervention in the political economy of world music. If the Lyannaj performs a *détour*, it is out of a simple and practical necessity to seek channels of diffusion for gwoka musicians. Both Jalème and Laumuno recognized that France already provides gwoka musicians with many performance opportunities and occasional financial support in the form of subventions. Likewise, speaking about the Lyannaj's goals during the ethnomusicology symposium in July 2013, Rosan Monza highlighted that through the UNESCO's publications, information about gwoka would become available in many libraries and archives. Importantly, it would also become available to concert promoters, thus making it easier for Guadeloupean musicians to promote themselves on the global music market. Most pointedly, with a clear definition of gwoka available through UNESCO, Guadeloupean musicians would no longer need to subsume their music into more cosmopolitan musical genres, such as jazz, in order to be recognized.

The postnationalist stance also translates into a desire for greater and more direct integration into the Caribbean. Indeed, as nonsovereign territories, Guadeloupeans and Martinicans have, until very recently, faced great difficulties in engaging directly with their neighbors.[73] Members of the Lyannaj argued that joining the UNESCO list would allow for the development of new modes of collaboration with neighboring states—such as Saint Lucia, Cuba, and Trinidad—that have ratified the convention. In July 2013, Rèpriz organized its three-day Caribbean ethnomusicology symposium precisely in hopes of leveraging the ICH convention to increase interregional cooperation. Importantly, for Cotellon and Monza, creoleness, especially Creole heritage, can provide the basis for this regional cooperation. There was a revealing exchange that July when Saint Lucian playwright Travis Weekes challenged Monza: "I note the emphasis on the gwoka as an expression of Guadeloupean national identity. I've heard it and I've heard you say it. . . . My issue is, I recognize within what you have and the gwoka a lot of stuff, dances, and drumming patterns and so on from where I come from, in St. Lucia. . . . But to what extent are you also saying that what you're doing is Caribbean, is an expression of the Caribbean folk? That's my question."

Monza answered: "Yes, Caribbean in the sense that Glissant has of the word," and added, "We are the fruit of a plural identity." In the case of both the Lyannaj and Soft's music, if gwoka makes Guadeloupe a nation, then it is gwoka's creoleness that inscribes Guadeloupe in the Caribbean. Embracing their creoleness, Guadeloupean cultural activists are able to use the intangible cultural heritage convention as a tool to weave transnational links that are not mediated by the metropole. The *détour* through UNESCO makes possible the activation of minor transnational networks.

I see the work of the Lyannaj, then, as a manifestation of Creole postnationalism and the *détour* as its most significant symptom. When considering the Guadeloupean project as a *détour*, I do not mean to suggest that the Lyannaj was a deliberate effort to trick the French government; rather, it is best understood as a political mode of relation that, in the imperial nation-state, has always-already been integral to the relationship between the metropolitan center and the (post)colonial margins. Of course, culture and politics are always-already enmeshed within processes of patrimonialization and the UNESCO convention is well recognized as a status-conferring tool equally useful to established nation-states and would-be nations.[74] But just as departmentalization was an ambiguous ruse that left open the question as to who tricked whom, the Lyannaj is potentially both a *maskò*—a feint, an act of subversion—and a reaffirmation of the French state's hegemony.

We enter here into the complex entanglement of politics and culture that traverse the Guadeloupean bid, France's own political and cultural legacies, and the very nature of the ICH convention. The Guadeloupean initiative created a conundrum that, in some ways, was specific to a (post)colonial, nonsovereign territory, but it also magnified the problematic faced by all French regions that would like to see their cultural heritage recognized by UNESCO. As Laurent-Sébastien Fournier explains:

> The selection of the cultural elements fit to be acknowledged as ICH in the terms accepted by UNESCO often leads to struggles between the local and the national levels. Local tradition bearers who seek state acceptance of their proposal have to show that these proposals are compatible with the universalistic ideals of the French nation. If the proposed cultural elements look too specific or too local, they might not be accepted by the state. However, if they do not appear sufficiently special, UNESCO might reject them. Accordingly, the decisions concerning the definition of intangible cultural heritage in France are compromises between local and national views.[75]

In addition, Fournier points out that, in France, any regional application to see one of its traditions recognized by UNESCO "would be denied legitimacy as a genuine cultural initiative" if it could be demonstrated that the people filing the demand belong to regionalist organizations.[76] In other words, if a project were to give any hints of being motivated by political rather than cultural considerations, the French state would likely refuse to forward it to UNESCO.

Yet the case of the *fest-noz* from Brittany seems to belie Fournier's point. Indeed, like gwoka, the *fest-noz*'s revival in the 1970s was largely due to its instrumentalization in the hands of regionalist activists.[77] In 2012, when UNESCO added the *fest-noz* to the ICH list, it did so on the basis of an application that unambiguously foregrounded the tradition as a marker of regional specificity. What Fournier fails to acknowledge is the extent to which such forms of regional activism—which promote regional cultural diversity without threatening what the French call the "integrity of the territory"— actually align with the *politique des régions* of François Mitterrand in the 1980s, partially in response to the regionalist movements in Corsica and Brittany. The French state's support of regionalist ICH projects can, in this way, be read as an exercise of hegemonic power.

In addition, regional ICH projects play into the French state's performance of its cultural diversity. This is especially true for the (post)colonial overseas departments. Françoise Vergès explains: "The colonies that have become France's 'overseas' territories . . . are systematically given a marginal role in French history. They are only integrated into the official or governmental discourse to the extent that they contribute to the 'wealth of France,' that they represent an 'asset' in their quality as spaces with an 'exceptional biodiversity' or as cultures that confirm the joyous and harmonious 'diversity' of the French Republic."[78]

Nonetheless, there is a difference between regionalism and outright separatism. It remains remarkable that an organization like Rèpriz, headed by a well-known nationalist activist, has managed to successfully petition the French government to sponsor its application to see its national symbol added to one of UNESCO's heritage lists. As a longtime cultural activist, Cotellon understood well that gwoka's prominence during the political and social struggles of the late twentieth century is essential in establishing its significance for the Guadeloupean population. Indeed, the music's role during the nationalist struggle of the 1970s and 1980s is openly referenced in the application file that the Lyannaj prepared. In the section of the application presenting the bearers of the tradition, one can read this summary of gwoka's history:

> Until the 1950s the bearers of this tradition were mainly small farmers. From the 1970s, by including Gwoka in most of their demonstrations, the new leaders of the identity and nationalist movement, including many intellectuals,

172 / Chapter Five

students and secondary school pupils, aroused a passion for this expression. They encouraged the gradual spread of the practice of Gwoka to the Guadeloupean population. In the 1980s, the newly-created schools and associations were henceforth mainly responsible for the transmission of Gwoka. In the 1990s, the new practitioners, recognising the knowledge that some singers, dancers and drummers of the 1950s had, venerated them as *Maître-Ka* [Master Ka].

Yet Cotellon understood equally well that, if the Guadeloupean bid came to be too closely associated with nationalist politics, it would have been doomed to failure, especially in the wake of the LKP. A difficult balance was needed, and the texts produced by the Lyannaj carefully avoid explicitly linking the alliance's proposal with either current or future debates on the political status of the department. The Lyannaj's message is carefully crafted: a cultural grassroots campaign, not an act of political maneuvering. In keeping with the spirit of the ICH convention, Cotellon and the Lyannaj have repeatedly framed the Guadeloupean bid within broader concerns over cultural diversity and sustainability.[79] For example, in 2012, Cotellon invited the economist Jean-Michel Lucas to come speak about sustainable cultural development and the Agenda 21 for Culture for the opening of the Festival Gwoka.[80] Such an approach recognizes the potential of the ICH convention as a useful tool of negotiation for the (post)colonial world but avoids too narrow a focus on the particular status of Guadeloupe as a French overseas department.

Ernesto Laclau highlights the importance of empty signifiers in political practice. Laclau identifies "any term which, in a certain political context becomes the signifier of the lack" as an empty signifier, a concept he borrows from Lacanian psychoanalysis. He adds, "Politics is possible because the constitutive impossibility of society can only represent itself through the production of empty signifiers."[81] Laclau points to "order" as a classic example but diversity functions equally well. In France, where the state has shun multiculturalism in favor of republican universalism, the term captures the antinomy of a nation that imagines itself as one, homogeneous, and universal and simultaneously desires a rich, diverse—that is to say, multiple—cultural heritage. *Diversity*, then, acts as an empty signifier that allows for a recognition of the Guadeloupean claim of cultural difference and its reframing or folding within France's cultural world. In other words, through the rhetoric of diversity, Guadeloupean culture—encapsulated metonymically in gwoka—can exist as bounded, unique, and separate from France's dominant culture and also as an integral part of it. *Diversity* is the empty signifier through which the *détour* can operate.

The work of the Lyannaj, then, is a *détour* with all the ambiguity that Glissant gave to the concept. It is an effort to seek elsewhere a "possible solution to the unsolvable" issue of continued metropolitan dominance.[82] Denied actual sovereignty, and so a seat at the United Nations, members of the Lyannaj were forced to work through the French state to reach UNESCO. In the age of Empire, the *détour* has become international. Guadeloupean separatists realized in the 1990s that they would not be able to achieve independence. Since then, their efforts have shifted, and the Lyannaj pou gwoka, and its success, are both illustrative of cultural activists' new post-nationalist goals and as a culmination of sorts of their past nationalist efforts.

The Lyannaj pou gwoka illustrates what Barnor Hesse calls the creolization of the political.[83] Because the French Republic—like other (post)colonial Western liberal democracies—has never existed without its empire, it has always had to balance politics of metropolitan enfranchisement and colonial exclusions.[84] In other words, once modern European nation-states are reframed as nation-empires, it becomes evident that the colonial politics of exclusion and disenfranchisement have been constitutive of liberal democracy. This understanding actually restores synthesis to an otherwise incomplete dialectical model that focuses only on thesis (republicanism) and antithesis (colonialism). In this sense, European liberal democracy has always-already been creolized "by virtue of its modernity and coloniality."[85] Hesse suggests that while—or rather, *because*—the exclusion of black colonial subjects was central to the liberal democratic project, the resulting political systems always-already contained within them the potential for the emergence of a black politics of disruption. And yet the example of the Lyannaj—and of Guadeloupe's Creole postnationalist politics in general—shows that these politics of disruption continue to function within the logic of conviviality that has always formed the basis of creolization. They do not seek the "radical rupture" that Glissant upholds as the "extreme tip of the Détour."[86]

And yet the *détour* through both the French state and UNESCO has enabled the activists of the Lyannaj to carve out a new creolized form of sovereignty, one that is no less significant than being only partial. Exploring and manipulating the fissures within a new international order, they have challenged their peripheral relationship to the French state, taking initiative and defining their own cultural policies. They have achieved official recognition from the international community and have dictated their own terms of representation to the world. And finally, they are taking steps to reengage themselves in the cultural politics of the Caribbean. In other words, through the poetics of the *détour*, they have demonstrated the continued potential of a creolized politics. Whether this *détour* will lead somewhere, whether it will help produce the political nation that many in the gwoka community continue to imagine, remains to be seen. And as Monza would say, "It doesn't even matter."

CODA

Bigidi

The preceding chapters have explored the ways in which gwoka participated in evolving auralities that are both contesting and contested. Although the rhetoric surrounding gwoka has emphasized a narrative of resistance, of *grand marronnage*, of flight and escape, the sounds of the music, the steps of the dancers, the conversations of the musicians, the overall sociality that emerges around, with, and through the drum, tells a different story. From the margins of the plantations to the margins of Europe, it is a story of conviviality, of finding ways to exist in a (post)colonial system that denies existence: the existence of its subaltern subjects—that goes without saying— but also its own enduring existence as an imperial nation-state. Imagining the drum as a *téléfonn a nèg mawon* (the maroons' phone) that bypasses the colonial system altogether is a convenient anticolonial and nationalist rhetorical strategy: in Lockel's map of Guadeloupean soundscapes, the drum-playing maroons loom outside and above the geographical boundaries of the archipelago. But the percussionist Klod Kiavué imagines gwoka as central to another form of convivial resistance. In the percussionist's view, as slaves gathered together, sometimes traveling off their plantations, news circulated and solidarities emerged. Gwoka, then, tells a story of resisting from the margins of the system rather a tale of escape and opposition from outside the system. Gwoka's aurality sounds from the "hold" of France's enduring coloniality; or, to put it another way, gwoka makes audible operations that Fred Moten—drawing from Jacques Derrida—describes as "invagination," that is to say, operations of "participation without belonging—a taking part in without being part of, without having membership in a set."[1] Gwoka's aurality sounds a (post)colonial ontology of being neither that nor not-that. The drum, moreover, resounds with the *ratés*—the exploding and intruding noise—of the (post)colony. It makes audible what colonial histories and (post)colonial politics have tried to silence. It is both fleeing and homing. It is fugitive if we understand fugitivity not only as escape, exit, or exodus but as "being separate from settling."[2] Gwoka's aurality, then, has always already been a terrain of creolization, a radical effort to confront and transform—no, to reform—the (post)colonial structure through the poetics of the *détour*.

Gwoka sounds (post)colonial ontologies and epistemologies of movement, of instability. Choreographer Lénablou has long argued through her work that gwoka dance captures a way of being-in-the-world that is specific to the Caribbean experience of French (post)coloniality. French (post)coloniality, for Blou, is captured in the *bigidi*, a stumbling gesture typical of the *léwòz* rhythm. She laid out her basic philosophy following a performance at the Festival Gwoka in Sainte-Anne: "Beyond the *bigidi* that you find in gwoka, the more I work on this, the more I think that it is a philosophy. It is our vision, our 'being *ka*.' It is how we are in relation with the other. Whatever we do, we are in *bigidi*." The *bigidi* is a stumble that never leads to a fall: a reflex movement always averts the fall and returns to body to a temporary stability. Indeed, Blou insisted that: "The most important is that we never fall." The *bigidi* is also a feint performed by a dancer to trip the lead drummer with whom they converse. It is a performance of concealment. Blou concludes that the *bigidi* is an "art of life," an art of both "resistance and resilience." It is, she further theorizes, a "sensation to lose oneself to find oneself."[3] I propose that the *bigidi* embodies the *détour*: feint, stumble, reclaiming of the space. In the *bigidi*, in the embodied experience of gwoka's aurality, the antinomies of Antillean (post)coloniality can be reconciled.

ACKNOWLEDGMENTS

This book marks a temporary point of arrival—only a stopover, I hope—in what has been a long, unpredictable—chaotic, even—disciplinary and personal journey. Through this journey, I have crossed oceans and reinvented myself a number of times: as a musician, as a historical musicologist, as an interdisciplinary scholar, as an anthropologist, as all of these things at once. But also as French, as American. And as not French, as not American, as a migrant. Slowly, one by one, each of these experiences and transformations has brought its own sediment, and slowly new understandings have grown. One never journeys alone, and I want to acknowledge here those who have pushed and pulled me along the way as well as those who have walked along with me.

At Washington University in Saint Louis, Patrick Burke, Craig Monson, John Turci-Escobar, Derek Pardue, and Peter Schmelz were the first to read and help shape my thoughts. But none of this would have been possible without the help and patient guidance of Dominique Cyrille, who then taught at CUNY's Graduate Center. Dominique was the first to send me on my way, putting me in contact with many of the people discussed in this book when I was still simply contemplating working in Guadeloupe. Over the years, she has been a fount of information, guidance, and constructive criticism. Few people know and understand the French Caribbean as well as she does.

Félix Cotellon opened many doors for me when I first arrived in Guadeloupe, going as far as setting up a rather brutal schedule of interviews for me during my initial visit in December 2007. Having arrived to work specifically on the collaborations between jazz and gwoka musicians, I did not realize at the time that I was being conscripted into focusing more pointedly on Guadeloupe's drum music. During my preliminary research on the archipelago,

178 / Acknowledgments

Christian Dahomay, Marie-Line Dahomay, Jacky Jalème, Klod Kiavué, and a number of other folks helped redirect my attention toward gwoka and its politics. In addition to spending countless hours answering my questions, Christian and Jacky also helped me take my first steps toward learning to play and dance gwoka. Others have given me opportunities to further explore gwoka as not only a field of intellectual study but also an artistic practice: Klod, François Ladrezeau, Wozan Monza, who all invited me to share the stage with them; Olivier Vamur, Michel Sylvestre, and the musicians of Horizon, who let me repeatedly crash their rehearsals; and Christian Laviso and Jean-Pierre Phipps, who helped me make sense of Lockel's *gwoka modènn*. Max Diakok and Lénablou, through their artistry, rich conversations, and pedagogy, have awakened the dancer in me and started me down the path to understanding (post)coloniality as an embodied practice. *An vlé di zòt on gwan mési.*

Many people have contributed to this study by meeting with me and sharing their life stories, their music, and their insight. Not all of our conversations appear in this book, although their ideas have done much to shape my understanding. At the risk of forgetting some, I would like to recognize them here: Eric Bordelai, Jean-Fred Castry, Félix Flauzin, Jean-Denis Guembé, Michel Halley, Yves Honoré, Patrick Matthieu, Robert Oumaou, Gérard Poumaroux, Pierre Samba, Franz Succab, Sonny Troupé, Rudy Selbonne, Michel Sylvestre. A very special thank-you to Julie Aristide for her friendship, strong opinions, and quick wits. Much gratitude is also due to Gustav Michaux-Vignes for opening up the music collection at the Médiathèque Caraïbe Bettino Lara in Basse-Terre as well as the staff of the Archives départementales de Guadeloupe. And much admiration goes to Marie-Héléna Laumuno who managed to write three books on gwoka while I struggled to get this one going.

Back in the United States, I have benefited from the mentorship of several people who have guided me on the long path to publishing this book. Perhaps no one has done as much to transform my intellectual frame than Françoise Lionnet and Shu-mei Shih, who ran a wonderful postdoctoral fellowship at UCLA. I hope that the preceding pages do justice to their theoretical acumen and pay tribute to their pedagogical generosity. I also particularly want to thank Jocelyne Guilbault, who has been so supportive of my work since I first approached her as a starstruck graduate student at a Society for Ethnomusicology conference. Ron Radano has been a wonderful colleague and generous mentor since I joined the faculty of the University of Wisconsin. I am grateful for his ability to watch from a distance when he can, offer constructive feedback once he gets involved, and deliver stern

Acknowledgments / 179

admonishment when it is needed. Since we crossed paths at UCLA, Tamara Levitz and Timothy Taylor have both continued to contribute to my own scholarly journey through their friendship, mentorship, and scholarship. Steven Feld was very generous in offering feedback on an early paper that eventually became chapter 4 in this book. His work remains a constant source of inspiration.

I want to thank the students of UC Berkeley for their questions and feedback following a presentation I gave there on what became chapter 2. Intellectual journeys work through dialogues, and your questions prompted me to rethink Lockel's diasporicity. Thank you as well to Matt Sakakeeny, who invited me to share some of my research with students and faculty in the Department of Anthropology and the African Studies Program at Tulane University. This gave me an opportunity to further the conversation on diaspora. Finally, I am grateful for the Center for the Humanities at the University of Wisconsin–Madison for giving me a forum to explore Glissant's theory and the Center for Latin American Caribbean and Iberian Studies for building a Caribbean research community in the Midwest. Thank you as well to the students and faculty of the UW School of Music, who have helped me maintain ties with music research even as I joined an anthropology department. And finally, I am extremely grateful to the graduate students and faculty of the Department of Anthropology who took a chance on a music scholar and have welcomed me into my new academic home. A very special thank-you to Claire Wendland, Maria Lepowsky, Larry Nesper, Amy Stambach, Sissel Schroeder, and Falina Enriquez, who make our department such a wonderful and supportive place to work.

Travel—intellectual as well as physical—is never cheap. I was lucky to receive funding at critical junctures. At Washington University, institutional funding provided support for my first trips to Guadeloupe, and a Mellon-Sawyer fellowship gave me time to finish my dissertation. The Mellon Postdoctoral Fellowship at UCLA provided welcome financial and intellectual support as I launched my academic career. Since joining UW, I have benefited from generous institutional funding to revise and expand my research.

When it came time for this book to start its own journey, I feared that it would not match the excellence of the books that I so greatly admire. I was very thankful—and extremely relieved—when I received the readers' reports. I want to thank them here for their overwhelmingly positive feedback and the many suggestions to strengthen my manuscript. I also want to express my deepest gratitude to Elizabeth Branch Dyson at the University of Chicago Press, who kindly sent me back to the drawing board when this project was not ready, only to embrace it wholeheartedly once it was. Few people have had such an impact on my life and work in so little time.

The journey that made this book possible was also deeply personal, fed by love and encouragement from friends and family. I thank my father, who, unaware of the consequences, first gave me the opportunity to visit the United States and many years later brought Patrick Chamoiseau to my attention. Thank you to my mother and stepfather for their unwavering support since I first decided to leave my country of birth. Marvin Polinsky, who, for nearly twenty years, made sure that I felt at home in my country of adoption and never asked for anything in return, deserves more than my gratitude. I deeply regret that he is no longer among us to see the fruits of the labor he helped start. Erin Brooks was a wonderful partner who accompanied me through a good part of this research and who offered a point of anchor at home even as I traveled. Eventually all the traveling caused our paths to diverge, but I remain grateful for her companionship. I was lucky to meet Raphaëlle Rabanes at one of life's crossroads. We have since then traveled together between France, the United States, and Guadeloupe. Our shared experiences and conversations as much as our shared books gave shape to this manuscript. I look at the road ahead with wonder.

Portions of chapter 4 first appeared in "Creolizing Jazz, Jazzing the Tout-Monde," in *American Creoles: The Francophone Caribbean and the American South*, edited by Martin Munro and Celia Britton (Liverpool: Liverpool University Press, 2012). They are reproduced here with permission of the Licensor through PLSclear. The discussion of the Lyannaj pou gwoka in chapter 5 is derived from "Putting the Drum in Conundrum: Guadeloupean Gwoka, Intangible Cultural Heritage, and Postnationalism," *International Journal of Heritage Studies* 22, no. 5 (2016), https://www.tandfonline.com/doi/abs/10.1080/13527258.2015.1028959.

This book is dedicated to the memory of a few Guadeloupean musicians who left this world while I was still trying to grasp their importance: Charly Chomereau-Lamotte, Guy Konket, Bernier Locatin, Robert Oumaou, René Perrin, Man Soso, and Georges Troupé. *Lonè é réspé pou yo.*

BASIC GWOKA RHYTHMS

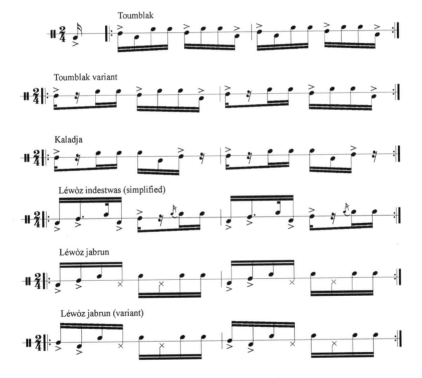

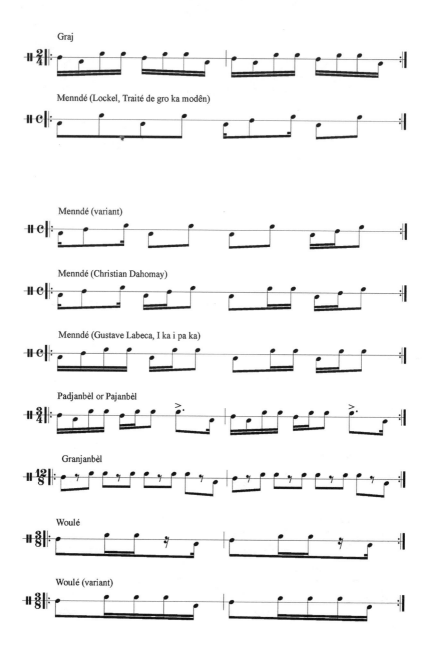

NOTES

INTRODUCTION

1. *Lespri kaskòd*, Golèt Musik DHP 034-2, 2008, CD.
2. Excerpt from "Mwen sé Gwadloupéyen," adapted from the original poem by Coco, my translation.
3. Simon Frith, ed., *World Music, Politics and Social Change: Papers From the International Association for the Study of Popular Music* (Music and Society Series) (Manchester: Manchester University Press, 1991), 2.
4. Jacques Adélaïde-Merlande, *Histoire contemporaine de la Caraïbe et des Guyanes, de 1945 à nos jours* (Paris: Karthala, 2002).
5. Richard D. E. Burton, "The French West Indies *à l'heure de l'Europe*: An Overview," in *French and West Indian: Martinique, Guadeloupe, and Guiana Today*, ed. Richard D. E. Burton, and Fred Reno (London: Macmillan, 1995).
6. Yarimar Bonilla, *Non-Sovereign Futures: French Caribbean Politics in the Wake of Disenchantment* (Chicago: University of Chicago Press, 2015); Ann Laura Stoler, *Duress: Imperial Durabilities in Our Times* (Durham, NC: Duke University Press, 2017).
7. Gary Wilder, *The French Imperial Nation-State: Negritude and Colonial Humanism between the Two World Wars* (Chicago: University of Chicago Press, 2005).
8. Shalini Puri, *The Caribbean Postcolonial: Social Equality, Post-Nationalism, and Cultural Hybridity* (New York: Palgrave Macmillan, 2004).
9. I am, of course, greatly indebted here to Yarimar Bonilla's work *Non-Sovereign Futures*.
10. Stoler, *Duress*, 33.
11. Ellen Schnepel, *In Search of a National Identity: Creole and Politics in Guadeloupe* (Hamburg: Helmut Buske, 2004), 10, 47; Bonilla, *Non-Sovereign Futures*, 204n9.
12. Stoler, "On Degrees of Imperial Sovereignty," in *Duress*, 173–204.
13. Helen Hintjens, "Constitutional and Political Change in the French Caribbean," in *French and West Indian: Martinique, Guadeloupe, and Guiana Today*, ed. Richard D. E. Burton, and Fred Reno (London: Macmillan, 1995), 25; Ferdinand Mélin-Soucramanien, "Les collectivités territoriales régies par l'article 73," *Nouveaux cahiers du Conseil constitutionnel* 35 (April 2012): http://www.conseil-constitutionnel.fr/conseil-constitutionnel/francais/nouveaux-cahiers-du-conseil/cahier-n-35/les-collectivites-territoriales-regies-par-l-article-73.105479.html.
14. Albert Wendt, *Nuanua: Pacific Writing in English since 1980* (Honolulu: University of Hawai'i Press, 1995), 3.

184 / Notes to Pages 5–8

15. I borrow the metaphor of the hold from Christina Sharpe, who deploys it so effectively to write about blackness in her *In the Wake: On Blackness and Being* (Durham, NC: Duke University Press, 2016).

16. Puri, *Caribbean Postcolonial*, 1. I borrow and adapt the concept of audible entanglement from Jocelyne Guilbault's "Audible Entanglements: Nation and Diasporas in Trinidad's Calypso Music Scene," *Small Axe* 9, no. 1 (2005): 40–41.

17. Thomas Turino, *Nationalists, Cosmopolitans, and Popular Music in Zimbabwe* (Chicago: University of Chicago Press, 2000). See also Shannon Dudley, *Music from behind the Bridge: Steelband Aesthetics and Politics in Trinidad and Tobago* (New York: Oxford University Press, 2007).

18. The *mulâtresse* Solitude was a former slave, reputedly born around 1772, who is said to have rallied with the troops of Delgrès in the fight against the reinstatement of slavery in 1802. Pregnant when captured, she was hung the day after she gave birth to a daughter. She now embodies the ideal of the *fanm doubout* (proud and strong woman) in Guadeloupe. She was immortalized in André Schwarz-Bart's novel titled after her. André Schwarz-Bart, *La mulâtresse Solitude* (Paris: Éditions du Seuil, 1972); Laurent Dubois, "Solitude's Statue: Confronting the Past in the French Caribbean," *Outre-mers* 93, no. 350 (2006): 27–38.

19. In Guadeloupe, carnival groups often describe themselves as *mouvman kiltirél* (cultural movements). They parade by walking at a brisk pace to the sounds of shoulder drums. On the LKP, see Bonilla, *Non-Sovereign Futures*, 156–59.

20. Turino offers what remains the foundational text on anticolonial musical nationalism. More recently, McDonald has drafted a convincing study of the complex performative poetics of Palestinian musical nationalism. David A. McDonald, *My Voice Is My Weapon: Music, Nationalism, and the Poetics of Palestinian Resistance* (Durham, NC: Duke University Press, 2013). For studies of musical nationalism in the Caribbean, see Paul Austerlitz, *Merengue: Dominican Music and Dominican Identity* (Philadelphia: Temple University Press, 1997); Dudley, *Music from behind the Bridge*; Michael D. Largey, *Vodou Nation: Haitian Art Music and Cultural Nationalism* (Chicago: University of Chicago Press, 2006); Robin D. Moore, *Nationalizing Blackness: Afrocubanismo and Artistic Revolution in Havana, 1920–1940* (Pittsburgh: University of Pittsburgh Press, 1997); Timothy Rommen, "Nationalism and the Soul: Gospelypso as Independence," *Black Music Research Journal* 22, no. 1 (2002): 37–63.

21. Introduced by Scott, a "problem-space" is a historically contingent discursive context—a context of knowledge and power—that shapes what "the particular questions that seem worth asking and the kinds of answers that seem worth having." As stakes change, so problem-spaces evolve. David Scott, *Conscripts of Modernity: The Tragedy of Colonial Enlightenment* (Durham, NC: Duke University Press, 2004), 4.

22. I am reacting here to the narrow definition of nationalist music that Thomas Turino advanced in *Nationalists, Cosmopolitans, and Popular Music in Zimbabwe*.

23. My understanding of a social field is, of course, indebted to Bourdieu's theory of practice. For an overview of the concept, see Patricia Thomson, "Field," in *Pierre Bourdieu: Key Concepts*, ed. Michael Grenfell (Stocksfield: Acumen, 2008), 65–80.

24. See, e.g., Veit Erlmann, *Reason and Resonance: A History of Modern Aurality* (New York: Zone Books, 2014).

25. Jairo Moreno, "Imperial Aurality: Jazz, the Archive, and U.S. Empire," in *Audible Empire: Music, Global Politics, Critique*, ed. Ronald Radano and Tejumola Olaniyan (Durham, NC: Duke University Press Books, 2016), 139.

Notes to Pages 8–11 / 185

26. Bruno Latour, *Reassembling the Social: An Introduction to Actor-Network-theory* (New York: Oxford University Press, 2005). Moreno, as a student of Rancière's work, has echoed the French philosopher's critique of Bourdieu. See Jairo Moreno and Gavin Steingo, "Rancière's Equal Music," *Contemporary Music Review* 31, nos. 5–6 (2012): 488.

27. Ana María Ochoa Gautier, *Aurality: Listening and Knowledge in Nineteenth-Century Colombia* (Durham, NC: Duke University Press, 2014), 22–23.

28. Crichlow and Northover make this point by taking the work of Richard Burton as symptomatic of this reductive approach. Michaeline Crichlow and Patricia Northover, *Globalization and the Post-Creole Imagination: Notes on Fleeing the Plantation* (Durham, NC: Duke University Press, 2009), locs. 105–8; Richard D. E. Burton, *Afro-Creole: Power, Opposition, and Play in the Caribbean* (Ithaca, NY: Cornell University Press, 1997).

29. Jean Bernabé, Patrick Chamoiseau, and Raphaël Confiant, *Éloge de la créolité (In Praise of Creoleness)* (Paris: Gallimard, 1989); O. Nigel Bolland, "Creolisation and Creole Societies: A Cultural Nationalist View of Caribbean Social History," *Caribbean Quarterly* 44, nos. 1–2 (1998); Kamau Brathwaite, *The Development of Creole Society in Jamaica, 1770–1820* (Oxford, UK: Clarendon Press, 1971); James Clifford, *The Predicament of Culture: Twentieth-Century Ethnography, Literature, and Art* (Cambridge, MA: Harvard University Press, 1988); Ulf Hannerz, "The World in Creolisation," *Africa: Journal of the International African Institute* 57, no. 4 (1987). For a critique of Creole nationalism, see Deborah A. Thomas, *Modern Blackness: Nationalism, Globalization, and the Politics of Culture in Jamaica* (Durham, NC: Duke University Press, 2004). For a similar critique in Trinidad, see Aisha Khan, *Callaloo Nation: Metaphors of Race and Religious Identity among South Asians in Trinidad* (Durham, NC: Duke University Press, 2004); Aisha Khan, "Creolization Moments," in *Creolization: History, Ethnography, Theory*, ed. Charles Stewart (Walnut Creek, CA: Left Coast Press, 2007), 237–53. For a critique of the *créolité* movement, see Mary Gallagher, "The *Créolité* Movement: Paradoxes of a French Caribbean Orthodoxy," in *Creolization: History, Ethnography, Theory*, ed. Charles Stewart (Walnut Creek, CA: Left Coast Press, 2007), 220–36.

30. Stephan Palmié, "Creolization and Its Discontents," *Annual Review of Anthropology* 35, no. 1 (2006): 433–56; Stephan Palmié, "Is There a Model in the Muddle? 'Creolization' in African Americanist History and Anthropology," in *Creolization: History, Ethnography, Theory*, ed. Charles Stewart (Walnut Creek, CA: West Coast Press, 2007), 178–200.

31. Peter Manuel, Kenneth Bilby, and Michael Largey, *Caribbean Currents: Caribbean Music from Rumba to Reggae* (Philadelphia: Temple University Press, 2016), 16.

32. Crichlow and Northover, *Globalization and the Post-Creole Imagination*; Sidney W. Mintz and Richard Price, *The Birth of African-American Culture: An Anthropological Perspective* (Boston: Beacon Press, 1992).

33. Paul Gilroy, *After Empire: Melancholia or Convivial Culture?* (London: Routledge, 2004).

34. Stephan Palmié, "The C-Word Again: From Colonial to Postcolonial Semantics," in *Creolization: History, Ethnography, Theory*, ed. Charles Stewart (Walnut Creek, CA: West Coast Press, 2007), 66–83.

35. Crichlow and Northover, *Globalization and the Post-Creole Imagination*; Édouard Glissant, *Poétique de la relation* (Paris: Gallimard, 1990), 103; Glissant, *Discours antillais* (Paris: Gallimard, 1997).

36. Jean-Pierre Sainton, *Couleur et société en context post-esclavagiste* (Pointe-à-Pitre, Guadeloupe: Éditions Jasor, 2009).

186 / Notes to Pages 11–19

37. Bolland, "Creolisation and Creole Societies"; Khan, *Callaloo Nation*; Khan, "Creolization Moments"; Thomas, *Modern Blackness*.
38. See Jonathan Sterne's critique of the "audiovisual litany" in *The Audible Past: Cultural Origins of Sound Reproduction* (Durham, NC: Duke University Press, 2003), 15.
39. Celia Britton, *Édouard Glissant and Postcolonial Theory: Strategies of Language and Resistance* (Charlottesville: University Press of Virginia, 1999), 21–23; Frantz Fanon, *The Wretched of the Earth* (New York: Grove Press, 2005), 17.
40. Glissant, *Discours antillais*, 260.
41. Britton, *Édouard Glissant and Postcolonial Theory*, 25, original emphasis.
42. Britton, 24, original emphasis.
43. See Fred Moten, *In the Break: The Aesthetics of the Black Radical Tradition* (Minneapolis: University of Minnesota Press, 2003).
44. Glissant, *Discours antillais*, 406.
45. Glissant, 418, 793, my translation.
46. Édouard Glissant, *Caribbean Discourse: Selected Essays*, trans. J. Michael Dash (Charlottesville: University Press of Virginia, 1999).
47. Glissant, *Discours antillais*, 48–57.
48. Britton, *Édouard Glissant and Postcolonial Theory*, 25.
49. Michel-Rolph Trouillot, "Culture on the Edges: Caribbean Creolization in Historical Context," in *From the Margins: Historical Anthropology and Its Futures*, ed. Brian Keith Axel (Durham, NC: Duke University Press, 2002), 202.
50. I adapt here the idea of the tactics of the *détournement* proposed by Michel de Certeau, in *L'invention du quotidien 1: Arts de faire* (Paris: Union générale de l'édition, 1980), 68–75.
51. Crichlow and Northover, *Globalization and the Post-Creole Imagination*, 198.
52. RFO is a conglomerate of TV and radio stations controlled by the French government and broadcast throughout the French overseas departments and territories. In contrast, Radyo Tanbou was created in the 1980s to be the voice of the separatist movement (see chapter 5).
53. Personal interview with the author, Goyave, 22 July 2009.
54. Frédéric Négrit, *Musique et immigration dans la société antillaise* (Paris: L'Harmattan, 2004), 193; Christian Dahomay, *Métòd ka* (Guadeloupe: n.p., 1997), 18. Dahomay's definition, written in French, uses the third-person singular *on*, which carries an ambiguity between the well-bounded English use of *we* (a delineated community) and the abstract, impersonal, pronoun *one*.
55. For an analysis of zouk's beat and genealogy, see Jocelyne Guilbault, *Zouk: World Music in the West Indies* (Chicago: University of Chicago Press, 1993).
56. Dominique Cyrille, "Creole Quadrilles of Guadeloupe, Dominica, Martinique, and Saint Lucia," in *Creolizing Contradance in the Caribbean*, ed. Peter Manuel (Philadelphia: Temple University Press, 2011), 188–208.
57. Jerome Camal, "DestiNation: The Festival Gwoka, Tourism, and Anti-Colonialism," in *Sea, Sun, and Sound: Music and Tourism in the Circum-Caribbean*, ed. Timothy Rommen and Daniel T. Neely (Oxford: Oxford University Press, 2014), 213–37.
58. Carême in Guadeloupe designates two things. First, it refers to the religious season of Lent, informally understood as the period between the end of carnival and Easter during which there is a lull in musical activities. But *carême* is also the name of the dry season, in opposition to *hivernage*, marked by warmer temperatures, more frequent rain falls, and, unfortunately, a higher risk of hurricanes.
59. In mainland France, the weather often demands that *léwòz* be held indoors.

Notes to Pages 22–35 / 187

60. For a taxonomy of participatory music, see Thomas Turino, *Music as Social Life: The Politics of Participation* (Chicago: University of Chicago Press, 2008).

61. "La place de la femme dans le gwoka: De la stigmatisation à la transmission" (public conference at Fort Fleur d'Epée, Gosier, 16 March 2011), http://www.lameca.org/dos siers/femme_gwoka/index.htm.

62. For example, see Lockel's *Traité de gro ka modên* (1981), Jean-Fred Castry's *Gwoka, la méthode moderne* (2005), and Franck Nicolas's *Méthode gammes guadeloupéennes* (2014).

63. Glissant, *Discours antillais*, 803, my translation.

64. Glissant, *Discours antillais*, 401. The notion of *manque* is difficult to translate. In Glissant, it corresponds to a psychological feeling of a general, unspecified yet unfulfilled need. In relation to language, it captures a feeling of always coming short of the mark in one's attempt to master the language that they have appropriated.

65. Steven Feld, *Jazz Cosmopolitanism in Accra: Five Musical Years in Ghana* (Durham, NC: Duke University Press, 2012), 204.

66. Françoise Lionnet and Shu-mei Shih, eds., *Minor Transnationalism* (Durham, NC: Duke University Press, 2005).

67. Brent Hayes Edwards, *The Practice of Diaspora: Literature, Translation, and the Rise of Black Internationalism* (Cambridge, MA: Harvard University Press, 2003).

CHAPTER ONE

1. Joslen Gabaly, *Diadyéé: Gwoka* (Abymes, Guadeloupe: Créapub', 2003), 93, my translation.

2. In Guadeloupe, the word *ballet* generally describes staged gwoka presentations in which dance is used to tell a story.

3. *Petits blancs*, during the colonial period, designated French indentured workers, subsistence farmers, clerks, soldiers, sailors, and low-ranking members of the clergy. The term is still used today to describe their descendants. They are also called *Blancs-Matignon*.

4. Michael Herzfeld, *Cultural Intimacy: Social Poetics in the Nation-State* (London: Routledge, 2004), 26.

5. Barnor Hesse, "Symptomatically Black: A Creolization of the Political," in *The Creolization of Theory*, ed. Françoise Lionnet and Shu-mei Shih (Durham, NC: Duke University Press, 2011), 37–61.

6. David Scott, "That Event, This Memory: Notes on the Anthropology of African Diasporas in the New World," *Diaspora: A Journal of Transnational Studies* 1, no. 3 (1991): 261–84.

7. Lucien-René Abenon, *Petite histoire de la Guadeloupe* (Paris: L'Harmattan, 2000), 32; Frédéric Régent, *La France et ses esclaves: De la colonisation aux abolitions (1620–1848)* (Paris: Grasset & Fasquelle, 2007), 25.

8. On slave demographics, see Régent, *La France et ses esclaves*, 48–51; Nicole Vanony Frisch, "L'origine des esclaves en Guadeloupe," in *Les musiques guadeloupéennes dans le champ culturel afro-américain, au sein des musiques du monde* (Paris: Éditions caribéennes, 1988), 47. Cérol is quoted in Luciani Lanoir-L'Etang, *Réseaux de solidarité dans la Guadeloupe d'hier et d'aujourd'hui* (Paris: L'Harmattan, 2005), 63. Following emancipation in 1848, Guadeloupean planters relied on indentured workers coming from the Congo as well as French trading posts in India as an alternative to an enslaved labor force. This system lasted until the early 1860s. For a critique of African ethnic

188 / Notes to Pages 35–38

categorizations, see Jean-Loup Amselle and Elikia M'Bokolo, *Au cœur de l'ethnie: Ethnie, tribalisme et état en Afrique* (Paris: La Découverte, 1985).

9. Abenon, *Petite histoire de la Guadeloupe*, 51–52.

10. Dominique Cyrille, "Creole Quadrilles of Guadeloupe, Dominica, Martinique, and Saint Lucia," in *Creolizing Contradance in the Caribbean*, ed. Peter Manuel (Philadelphia: Temple University Press, 2011), 199. On this last point, see article 58 in the 1635 version of the Code Noir. Christian Castaldo, ed., *Codes noirs: De l'esclavage aux abolitions* (Paris: Dalloz, 2006), 57.

11. Lanoir-L'Etang, *Réseaux de solidarité*, 62.

12. Cyrille, "Creole Quadrilles," 198.

13. Edwin C. Hill, *Black Soundscapes, White Stages: The Meaning of Francophone Sounds in the Black Atlantic* (Baltimore: The Johns Hopkins University Press, 2013), locs. 112–14.

14. Ronald M. Radano, *Lying Up a Nation: Race and Black Music* (Chicago: University of Chicago Press, 2003), 5.

15. For a description of work songs, see Nicolas Germain Léonard, *Œuvres de Léonard, tome 1* (Paris: Imprimerie de Didot Jeune, 1797). For a description of a funeral wake and funeral in Sainte-Anne, see Abbé Dugoujon, *Lettres sur l'esclavage dans les colonies françaises* (Paris: Pagnerre, éditeur, 1845). It is unclear if *calenda* and *bamboula* refer to the same or different practices in European writing. Both words describe gatherings in which enslaved Africans and their descendants dance to drum music. Whether such gatherings were held solely for entertainment or held a level of spiritual significance was also unintelligible to European eyes and ears. It is also uncertain whether these terms emanated from enslaved Africans, from European imaginations, or from a European reinterpretation of African-derived categories. What is known is that these terms, especially the word *calenda* or *calinda*, circulated through the black Atlantic world. Today, *calinda* or *kalinda* designates a specific tradition of stick fighting in Trinidad that is accompanied by drums, much like *maloyè* in Guadeloupe.

16. Lindon Barrett, *Blackness and Value: Seeing Double* (Cambridge: Cambridge University Press, 1999); Hill, *Black Soundscapes, White Stages*, loc. 346.

17. With its obvious reference to regimes of power, the phrase "listening regime" offers, I hope, a more straight-forward way of describing what Jennifer Stoever as termed the "listening ear." Martin Daughtry's "auditory regime" captures a similar idea. J. Martin Daughtry, *Listening to War: Sound, Music, Trauma, and Survival in Wartime Iraq* (New York: Oxford University Press, 2015), 123–24; Jennifer Lynn Stoever, *The Sonic Color Line: Race and the Cultural Politics of Listening* (New York: New York University Press, 2016), 13–16.

18. Hill, *Black Soundscapes, White Stages*, locs. 350–51.

19. Of course, other senses, such as smell, also participated in the encounter with the racial other. For example, Labat dwells on the smell of enslaved bodies. Jean-Baptiste Labat, *Nouveau voyage aux isles de l'Amerique: contenant l'histoire naturelle de ces pays, l'origine, les mœurs, la religion & le gouvernement des habitans anciens & modernes: les guerres & les evenemens singuliers qui y sont arrivez pendant le séjour que l'auteur y a fait* (Paris: Chez Théodore Le Gras, 1742); Mark M. Smith, *How Race Is Made: Slavery, Segregation, and the Senses* (Chapel Hill: University of North Carolina Press, 2006).

20. Labat, *Nouveau voyage aux isles de l'Amérique*, 466–67; AGEG, *Rapport culturel, 9ème Congrès* (Paris: 1970).

21. Dena J. Epstein, "African Music in British and French America," *Musical Quaterly* 59, no. 1 (1973): 69–71.

Notes to Pages 38–43 / 189

22. Félix Longin, *Voyage à la Guadeloupe: Œuvre posthume* (Le Mans: Monnoyer, 1848), 206.

23. Adolphe Granier de Cassagnac, *Voyages aux Antilles françaises, anglaises, danoises, espagnoles; à Saint Domingue et aux États-Unis d'Amérique. Première partie, Les Antilles françaises* (Paris: Dauvin et Fontaines Librairies, 1842), 214–15, my translation.

24. Saidiya Hartman, *Scenes of Subjection: Terror, Slavery, and Self-Making in Nineteenth-Century America* (New York: Oxford University Press, 1997), 22.

25. Léonard, *Œuvres de Léonard*, 187, my translation.

26. Martin Munro, *Different Drummers: Rhythm and Race in the Americas* (Berkeley: University of California Press, 2010), 16–21.

27. Lanoir-L'Etang, *Réseaux de solidarité*, 64–78.

28. César de Rochefort, *Histoire naturelle et morale des Iles Antilles de l'Amérique* (Rotterdam: Chez Arnout Leers, 1665), 342, my translation. There is a caveat here: Rochefort seems to have gleamed much of his knowledge of the Antilles from previous writings, especially Du Tertre's book, and Labat himself denounced him to be an unreliable source. The point, though, seems consistent with descriptions found in other texts.

29. Munro, *Different Drummers*, 20.

30. Ronald Radano, "Black Music Labor and the Animated Properties of Slave Sound," *boundary 2* 43, no. 1 (2016): 173–208.

31. Labat, *Nouveau voyage aux isles de l'Amérique*.

32. Hartman, *Scenes of Subjection*, 42.

33. On the use of African-derived music and dance as a justification of slavery, see Cyrille, "Creole Quadrilles," 201.

34. Labat, *Nouveau voyage aux isles de l'Amérique*, 464.

35. Labat, 465.

36. Dugoujon, *Lettres sur l'esclavage dans les colonies françaises*, 73; Jean-Baptiste Du Tertre, *Histoire générale des isles de S. Christophe, de la Guadeloupe, de la Martinique et autres dans l'Amérique* (Paris: Jacques Langlois, 1654); Rochefort, *Histoire naturelle et morale des Iles Antilles de l'Amérique*; Labat, *Nouveau voyage aux isles de l'Amérique*, 464; Léonard, *Œuvres de Léonard*, 206–7.

37. Léonard, *Œuvres de Léonard*, 212. On mutual-aid societies, see Lanoir-L'Etang, *Réseaux de solidarité*, 77–78, 299–313.

38. Lanoir-L'Etang, *Réseaux de solidarité*.

39. On shared characteristics of the Afro-diasporic musics, see Samuel A. Floyd, *The Power of Black Music: Interpreting Its History from Africa to the United States* (New York: Oxford University Press, 1996); Portia K. Maultsby, "Africanisms in African-American Music," in *Africanisms in American Culture*, ed. Joseph E. Holloway (Bloomington: Indiana University Press, 1990), 185–210; Olly Wilson, "The Heterogeneous Sound Ideal in African-American Music," in *New Perspectives on Music: Essays in Honor of Eileen Southern*, ed. Josephine Wright and Samuel A. Floyd (Warren, MI: Harmonie Park Press, 1992), 327–38; Munro, *Different Drummers*, 20.

40. Hill, *Black Soundscapes, White Stages*, locs. 350–51. Michel-Rolph Trouillot, "Culture on the Edges: Caribbean Creolization in Historical Context," in *From the Margins: Historical Anthropology and Its Futures*, ed. Brian Keith Axel (Durham, NC: Duke University Press, 2002), 189–210.

41. Munro, *Different Drummers*, 20.

42. On the difference between resistance and opposition, see Michel De Certeau, *L'invention du quotidien 1: Arts de faire* (Paris: Union générale de l'édition, 1980); Richard D. E. Burton, *Afro-Creole: Power, Opposition, and Play in the Caribbean* (Ithaca, NY: Cornell University Press, 1997).

190 / Notes to Pages 44–50

43. Gérard Lockel, "Lolo Camphrin: Un des derniers grands danseurs de gro ka." *Ja Ka Ta*, February 1978.

44. Cyrille, "Creole Quadrilles."

45. Glissant denounces the danger of this mimetic impulse in *Discours antillais* (Paris: Gallimard, 1997), 41.

46. For an example, see Henri Bangou, *Aliénation et désaliénation dans les sociétés post-esclavagistes: Le cas de la Guadeloupe* (Paris: L'Harmattan, 1997).

47. Dany Bébel-Gislert, *Le défi culturel guadeloupéen: Devenir ce que nous sommes* (Paris: Éditions caribéennes, 1989).

48. David Scott, *Conscripts of Modernity: The Tragedy of Colonial Enlightenment* (Durham, NC: Duke University Press, 2004), 106.

49. Glissant, *Discours antillais*, 48.

50. Josette Fallope, "La politique d'assimilation et ses resistances," in *La Guadeloupe, 1875–1914: Les soubresauts d'une société pluri-ethnique ou les ambiguités de l'assimilation*, ed. Henriette Levillain (Paris: Éditions Autrement, 1994).

51. In the French Antilles, *mulâtre* (Creole, *milàt*) is a class category as much as a racial one, designating specifically the mixed middle class. For a more detailed exploration of Guadeloupean socio-racial categories, see Jean-Pierre Sainton, *Couleur et société en context post-esclavagiste* (Pointe-à-Pitre: Éditions Jasor, 2009).

52. Gary Wilder, *The French Imperial Nation-State: Negritude and Colonial Humanism between the Two World Wars* (Chicago: University of Chicago Press, 2005), 5; Hesse, "Symptomatically Black."

53. Fallope, "La politique d'assimilation et ses resistances," 37–39.

54. Antoine Abou, "L'école et ses débats," in *La Guadeloupe, 1875–1914: Les soubresauts d'une société pluri-ethnique ou les ambiguités de l'assimilation*, ed. Henriette Levillain (Paris: Éditions Autrement, 1994), 59–75; Fallope, "La politique d'assimilation et ses resistances," 38–39.

55. Benedict Anderson, *Imagined Communities: Reflections on the Origin and Spread of Nationalism* (London: Verso, 2006); Elleke Boehmer, "Networks of Resistance," in *The Post-Colonial Studies Reader*, ed. Bill Ashcroft, Gareth Griffiths, and Helen Tiffin (London: Routledge, 2006), 113–15; Thomas Turino, *Nationalists, Cosmopolitans, and Popular Music in Zimbabwe* (Chicago: University of Chicago Press, 2000); Wilder, *French Imperial Nation-State*.

56. Fallope, "La politique d'assimilation et ses resistances," 41.

57. Glissant's distinction between dominant and determining classes in the Antilles sets up a more dynamic model than the dominant-subaltern dichotomy. Glissant, *Discours antillais*, 412.

58. Partha Chatterjee, *Nationalist Thought and the Colonial World: A Derivative Discourse?* (London: Zed Books for the United Nations University, 1986); Partha Chatterjee, *The Nation and Its Fragments: Colonial and Postcolonial Histories* (Princeton, NJ: Princeton University Press, 1993), 6.

59. Michaeline Crichlow and Patricia Northover, *Globalization and the Post-Creole Imagination: Notes on Fleeing the Plantation* (Durham, NC: Duke University Press, 2009).

60. Fallope, "La politique d'assimilation et ses resistances," 41.

61. Glissant, *Discours antillais*; see also Celia Britton, *Édouard Glissant and Postcolonial Theory: Strategies of Language and Resistance* (Charlottesville: University Press of Virginia, 1999), 83.

62. Ellen M. Schnepel, *In Search of a National Identity: Creole and Politics in Guadeloupe* (Hamburg: Helmut Buske, 2004), 69.

Notes to Pages 50–55 / 191

63. Frantz Fanon, *The Wretched of the Earth* (New York: Grove Press, 2005), 182.
64. Édouard Glissant, *Caribbean Discourse: Selected Essays*, trans. J. Michael Dash (Charlottesville: University of Virginia Press, 1999), 18, 47; Britton, *Édouard Glissant and Postcolonial Theory*, 83.
65. W. E. B. Du Bois, *The Souls of Black Folk* (New York: Penguin, 1996); Glissant, *Discours antillais*, 494.
66. Glissant's use of *langage* is entirely his own. The French, in this case, cannot be translated by the English *language*. And while Glissant's distinction between *langage* and *langue* echoes Saussure's, Glissant deploys the two terms in a different, idiosyncratic way.
67. Alex Ury and Françoise Ury, *Musiques et musiciens de la Guadeloupe: Le chant de Karukera* (1991), 40.
68. The *swaré léwòz* is historically most associated with sugarcane workers and is understood as a fairly formal event with specific rules and codes. The *koud tanbou* is an informal gathering during which people play the drum, sing, and dance.
69. Marie-Céline Lafontaine, "Le Carnaval de l''autre': A propos d' 'authenticité' en matière de musique guadeloupéenne: Théories et réalités," *Les temps modernes* 39, nos. 441–42 (1983): 2126–73; Marie-Céline Lafontaine, "Unité et diversité des musiques traditionnelles guadeloupéennes," in *Les musiques guadeloupéennes dans le champs culturel Afro-Américain, au sein des musiques du monde* (Paris: Éditions caribéennes, 1988), 71–92; Carnot and Marie-Céline Lafontaine, *Alors ma chère, moi* (Paris: Éditions caribéennes, 1986).
70. Ury and Ury, *Musiques et musiciens de la Guadeloupe*.
71. Lafontaine, "Le Carnaval de l''autre.'"
72. Ury and Ury, *Musiques et musiciens de la Guadeloupe*, 137.
73. Hill, *Black Soundscapes, White Stages*, loc. 1066.
74. Hill.
75. Hill, locs. 1046–55.
76. Kofi Agawu, "Contesting Difference: A Critique of Africanist Ethnomusicology," in *The Cultural Study of Music: A Critical Introduction*, ed. Martin Clayton, Trevor Herbert, and Richard Middleton (New York: Routledge, 2003), 117–26; Barbara Browning, *Infectious Rhythm: Metaphors of Contagion and the Spread of African Culture* (New York: Routledge, 1998); Hill, *Black Soundscapes, White Stages*, locs. 2119–29. Today, one can unfortunately still hear the word *tam tam* in France and even in its overseas territories. Indeed, I remember a conversation with a customer in a *boulangerie* in Basse-Terre as we both awaited the passing of a downpour. The woman—probably in her forties or fifties and elegantly dressed—informed me that she owned a store that sold natural beauty products. I smiled and commented that there were many medicinal herbs in Guadeloupe. She was quick to set me straight, explaining that she sold only manufactured products from well-known laboratories. She then asked what I did, and I explained that I studied *gwoka*. Her response still resonates in my ear: "Ah, oui, le tam tam de la Guadeloupe." The *petit nègre* and imperial connotations of the term are nonetheless recognized as problematic by many.
77. Hill, *Black Soundscapes, White Stages*, locs. 1999–2000.
78. Munro, *Different Drummers*, 135.
79. Gary Wilder, *Freedom Time: Négritude, Decolonization, and the Future of the World* (Durham, NC: Duke University Press, 2015).
80. Hesse, "Symptomatically Black," locs. 507–9.
81. Chatterjee, *Nationalist Thought and the Colonial World: A Derivative Discourse?*; Certeau, *L'invention du quotidien*, 68–75.

192 / Notes to Pages 55–64

82. Helen Hintjens, "Constitutional and Political Change in the French Caribbean," in *French and West Indian: Martinique, Guadeloupe, and Guiana Today*, ed. Richard D. E. Burton and Fred Reno (London: Macmillan, 1995), 25.

83. Jacques Adélaïde-Merlande, *Histoire contemporaine de la Caraïbe et des Guyanes, de 1945 à nos jours* (Paris: Karthala, 2002), 80–82; Hintjens, "Constitutional and Political Change in the French Caribbean," 24–25.

84. William Miles, "Fifty Years of Assimilation: Assessing France's Experience of Caribbean Decolonisation through Administrative Reform," in *Islands at the Crossroads: Politics in the Non-Independent Caribbean*, ed. Aarón Gamaliele Ramos and Angel Israel Rivera (Kingston, Jamaica: Ian Randle Publishers, 2001), 45–60; Wilder, *Freedom Time*, chap. 5.

85. Wilder, *Freedom Time*, 106–99.

86. Jean-Claude William, "Aimé Césaire: Les contrariétés de la conscience nationale," in *1946–1996: Cinquante ans de départementalisation outre-mer*, ed. Fred Constant and Justin Daniel (Paris: L'Harmattan, 1997), 315.

87. On the politics of departmentalization, see Richard D. E. Burton, "The French West Indies *à l'heure de l'Europe*: An Overview," in *French and West Indian: Martinique, Guadeloupe, and Guiana Today*, ed. Richard D. E. Burton and Fred Reno (London: Macmillan, 1995), 1–19; Hintjens, "Constitutional and Political Change in the French Caribbean"; Abenon, *Petite histoire de la Guadeloupe*. On dependency, see Justin Daniel, "The Construction of Dependency: Economy and Politics in the French Antilles," in *Islands at the Crossroads: Politics in the Non-Independent Caribbean*, ed. Aarón Gamaliele Ramos and Angel Israel Rivera (Kingston, Jamaica: Ian Randle Press, 2001), 61–79. On the BUMIDOM and migration to metropolitan France, see Alain Anselin, "West Indians in France," in *French and West Indian: Martinique, Guadeloupe, and Guiana Today*, ed. Richard D. E. Burton and Fred Reno (London: Macmillan, 1995), 112–18; David Beriss, *Black Skins, French Voices: Caribbean Ethnicity and Activism in Urban France* (Boulder, CO: Westview Press, 2004); Brenda F. Berrian, *Awakening Spaces: French Caribbean Popular Songs, Music, and Culture* (Chicago: University of Chicago Press, 2000). On consumption and neocolonialism, see Glissant, *Discours antillais*, 22–23. See also Burton, cited in Miles, "Fifty Years of Assimilation," 58.

88. Daniel Guérin, *Les Antilles décolonisées* (Paris: Présence africaine, 1956), 13.

CHAPTER TWO

1. Jacques Attali, *Bruits: Essais sur l'économie politique de la musique* (Paris: Presses universitaires de France, 1977), 294; Gérard Lockel, "Lolo Camphrin: Un des derniers grands danseurs de gro ka." *Ja Ka Ta*, February 1978. My translations.

2. Interview with the author, 8 August 2009.

3. I use *invented* here in a nod to Hobsbawm and Ranger's seminal work. Eric Hobsbawm and Terence Ranger, eds., *The Invention of Tradition* (Cambridge: Cambridge University Press, 1983).

4. Thomas Turino, *Nationalists, Cosmopolitans, and Popular Music in Zimbabwe* (Chicago: University of Chicago Press, 2000). See also Shannon Dudley, *Music from behind the Bridge: Steelband Aesthetics and Politics in Trinidad and Tobago* (New York: Oxford University Press, 2007).

5. Édouard Glissant, *Discours antillais* (Paris: Gallimard, 1997), 401, 575.

6. Justin Daniel, "The Construction of Dependency: Economy and Politics in the French Antilles," in *Islands at the Crossroads: Politics in the Non-Independent Caribbean*, ed. Aarón Gamaliele Ramos and Angel Israel Rivera (Kingston, Jamaica: Ian Randle Press, 2001).

Notes to Pages 64–69 / 193

7. Yarimar Bonilla, "Nonsoveriegn Futures? French Caribbean Politics in the Wake of Disenchantment," in *Caribbean Sovereignty, Democracy and Development in an Age of Globalization*, ed. Lewis Linden (New York: Routledge, 2012). I pick up this state-sponsored economic migration in chapter 3.

8. Alain Anselin, "West Indians in France," in *French and West Indian: Martinique, Guadeloupe, and Guiana Today*, ed. Richard D. E. Burton and Fred Reno (London: Macmillan, 1995), 113.

9. Diakok, interview with the author, 27 July 2008.

10. *Man* is Creole for "madam." Man Adeline ran perhaps the best-known folkloric group of the 1950s and provided employment for the famed drummer Vélo.

11. Richard D. E. Burton, "The Idea of Difference in Contemporary French West Indian Thought: Négritude, Antillanité, Créolité," in *French and West Indian: Martinique, Guadeloupe, and Guiana Today*, ed. Richard D. E. Burton and Fred Reno (London: Macmillan, 1995), 138.

12. Anselin, "West Indians in France."

13. Richard D. E. Burton, "The French West Indies *à l'heure de l'Europe*: An Overview," in *French and West Indian: Martinique, Guadeloupe, and Guiana Today*, ed. Richard D. E. Burton and Fred Reno (London: Macmillan, 1995), 5.

14. This situation has largely been reversed now that most government functions are filled with Antillean employees.

15. Burton, "French West Indies *à l'heure de l'Europe*," 5.

16. Ellen M. Schnepel, *In Search of a National Identity: Creole and Politics in Guadeloupe* (Hamburg: Helmut Buske, 2004), 47–54. See also Anselin, "West Indians in France."

17. AGEG, *Nou toujou doubout: Guadeloupe, 1635–1971* (Paris: 1981), 81.

18. Louis Théodore, interview with the author, 3 August 2009.

19. Collectif des patriotes guadeloupéens, ed., *Pour servir l'histoire et la mémoire Guadeloupéenne: Mai 1967* (Sainte-Anne, Guadeloupe: Co.Pa.Gua., 2003), 41.

20. Jacques Adélaïde-Merlande, *Histoire contemporaine de la Caraïbe et des Guyanes, de 1945 à nos jours* (Paris: Karthala, 2002), 84.

21. Théodore, interview with the author, 3 August 2009; Anduse, interview with the author, 3 August 2009; Mounien, interview with the author, 15 July 2009; Cotellon, interview with the author, 29 July 2008.

22. Cotellon, interview with the author, 29 July 2008.

23. Théodore, interview with the author, 3 August 2009; Anduse, interview with the author, 3 August 2009; Thierry Césaire, interview with the author, 23 July 2009; Lucien-René Abenon, *Petite histoire de la Guadeloupe* (Paris: L'Harmattan, 2000), 197.

24. J. Michael Dash, *Édouard Glissant* (Cambridge: Cambridge University Press, 1995), 13.

25. Théodore, interview with the author, 3 August 2009.

26. Abenon, *Petite histoire*, 198; Adélaïde-Merlande, *Histoire contemporaine de la Caraïbe*, 190; Laurent Faruggia, *Le fait national guadeloupéen* (Ivry-sur-Seine, France: n.p., 1968), 39–50.

27. A commission of historians appointed by the French Ministre des Outre-Mer in 2014 and led by Benjamin Stora investigated these events to determine the exact number of deaths. Frustratingly for many in Guadeloupe, the commission concluded that the historical record was too incomplete to allow for any authoritative estimate.

28. In this, May 1967 in Guadeloupe anticipated the same synergy between unions and student organizations that would fuel the uprising of May 1968 in the metropole.

29. Abenon, *Petite histoire*, 198; Adélaïde-Merlande, *Histoire contemporaine de la Caraïbe*, 190; Faruggia, *Le fait national guadeloupéen*, 50–54; Raymond Gama and Jean-Pierre

194 / Notes to Pages 69–74

Sainton, *Mé 67: Mémoire d'un évênement* (Pointe-à-Pitre, Guadeloupe: Société Guadeloupéenne d'édition et de diffusion, 1985); Benjamin Stora, René Bénélus, Jacques Dumont, Serge Mam Lam Fouck, Louis-Georges Placide, and Michelle Zancarini Fournel, *Commission d'information et de recherche historique sur les événements de décembre 1959 en Martinique, de juin 1962 en Guadeloupe et en Guyane, et de mai 1967 en Guadeloupe: Rapport à Madame la ministre des Outre-mer* (Paris: Ministère des Outre-mer, 2016); "Le GONG décapité: Dix-neuf arrestations à Paris et en Guadeloupe pour atteinte à l'intégrité du territoire par la Cour de Sureté de l'État," *France-Antilles*, 13 June 1967, 1. The trials took place the following year. Most of the accused were either acquitted or convicted with light sentences, as French prosecutors were unable to prove that the riots were indeed the result of a separatist conspiracy. Indeed, the Stora commission has since established that French law enforcement and domestic intelligence agency had established before the May 1967 demonstration that GONG did not represent a threat to the government. The trials were fairly widely covered in the French metropolitan press but received little attention from *France-Antilles*.

30. Mounien, interview with the author, 15 July 2009; Théodore, interview with the author, 3 August 2009.

31. Théodore, interview with the author, 3 August 2009.

32. Cotellon, interview with the author, 29 July 2008.

33. On social poetics and cultural intimacy, see Michael Herzfeld, *Cultural Intimacy: Social Poetics in the Nation-State* (London: Routledge, 2004).

34. Braflan-Trobo, *Conflits sociaux en Guadeloupe: Histoire, identité et culture dans les grèves en Guadeloupe* (Paris: L'Harmattan, 2007), 13; Dany Bébel-Gislert, *Le défi culturel guadeloupéen: Devenir ce que nous sommes* (Paris: Éditions caribéennes, 1989), 120–24; Yarimar Bonilla, *Non-Sovereign Futures: French Caribbean Politics in the Wake of Disenchantment* (Chicago: University of Chicago Press, 2015). Mounien, interview with the author, 15 July 2009; Théodore, interview with the author, 3 August 2009. "Pour mieux connaitre l'UGTG," http://ugtg.org/article_59.html.

35. AGEG, *Rapport culturel, 9ème Congrès* (Paris: AGEG, 1970), 2–5; Joseph Stalin, "The Nation," in *Nationalism*, ed. John Hutchinson and Anthony D. Smith (Oxford: Oxford University Press, 1994), 20. Stalin defines the nation as "a historically constituted, stable community of people, formed on the basis of a common language, territory, economic life, and psychological make-up manifested in a common culture." This definition seems strikingly problematic for dealing with the complexities of Caribbean societies that are multilingual, have emerged from a violent historical rupture, and are characteristically unstable.

36. Interview with the author, August 2009.

37. AGEG, *Rapport culturel, 9ème Congrès*, 1, 55–61.

38. "L'UPLG s'explique." *Ja Ka Ta*, June 1980.

39. Bébel-Gislert, *Le défi culturel guadeloupéen*.

40. John Hutchinson, "Cultural Nationalism and Moral Regeneration," in *Nationalism*, ed. John Hutchinson and Anthony D. Smith (Oxford: Oxford University Press, 1994), 122.

41. Hutchinson, "Cultural Nationalism and Moral Regeneration," 123.

42. On the *pulsion de retour*, see Glissant, *Discours antillais*, 44–47; Édouard Glissant, *Caribbean Discourse: Selected Essays*, trans. J. Michael Dash (Charlottesville: University Press of Virginia, 1999), 16–18. On Caribbean nationalisms and hybridity, see Shalini Puri, *The Caribbean Postcolonial: Social Equality, Post-Nationalism, and Cultural Hybridity* (New York: Palgrave Macmillan, 2004); Dudley, *Music from behind the Bridge*, 16.

Notes to Pages 74–80 / 195

43. For a discussion of the maroon in Guadeloupean social activism, see Bonilla, *Non-Sovereign Futures*, 43–62; Braflan-Trobo, *Conflits sociaux en Guadeloupe*, 111–37.

44. My understanding here offers a slight corrective to Burton, who, in my opinion, overstates the role of race in Guadeloupean separatist politics of the 1960s and 1970s. The cultural privileging of blackness may have been implicit, but it was far from the official discourse of anticolonial organizations. Burton, "Idea of Difference," 150.

45. Anduse, interview with the author, 4 August 2009.

46. AGEG, *Rapport culturel, 9ème Congrès*, 10–14.

47. AGEG, 13.

48. Jerome Camal, "From Gwoka Modènn to Jazz Ka: Music, Nationalism, and Creolization in Guadeloupe" (Ph.D. diss., Washington University in Saint Louis, 2011).

49. Anduse, interview with the author, 4 August 2009; Cotellon, interview with the author, 29 July 2008. Gérard Lockel, *Gwo Ka Modènn: 1969–1989, vingt ans de lutte sur le front de la culture guadeloupéenne* (Baie-Mahault, Guadeloupe: ADGKM, 1989), chap. 2.

50. Lockel, *Vingt ans de lutte*; Gérard Lockel, *Gwo-ka modèn* (Baie-Mahault, Guadeloupe: ADGKM, 2011). Chomereau-Lamotte, interview with the author, 9 July 2009. It is interesting to note that the first iteration of the *gwoka modènn* project did not feature the Guadeloupean drum, substituting the more cosmopolitan congas instead.

51. Mounien, interview with the author, 15 July 2009.

52. Cotellon, interview with the author, 29 July 2008.

53. Lockel, "Lolo Camphrin."

54. Anduse, interview with the author, 4 August 2009; Lockel, *Vingt ans de lutte*.

55. Turino, *Nationalists, Cosmopolitans, and Popular Music in Zimbabwe*. For an extended overview of the role of traditional gwoka in Guadeloupean politics, see Marie-Héléna Laumuno, *Gwoka et politique en Guadeloupe: 1960–2003: 40 ans de construction du "pays"* (Paris: L'Harmattan, 2011).

56. Lockel, *Gwo-ka modèn*, 101. A kind of diasporic *lieu commun*, this comment finds sympathetic resonance in Paul Gilroy's and Glissant's embrace of music as a privilege medium for the nonlinguistic creation and diffusion of black Atlantic epistemologies. It is echoed as well Ghanaian artist Ni Noi Nortey's comment to Stephen Feld that "music's strength . . . [is] the way everything can come together politically and spiritually, without reading books." Steven Feld, *Jazz Cosmopolitanism in Accra: Five Musical Years in Ghana* (Durham, NC: Duke University Press, 2012), locs. 2259–60; Paul Gilroy, *The Black Atlantic: Modernity and Double-Consciousness* (Cambridge, MA: Harvard University Press, 1993); Glissant, *Discours antillais*.

57. Lockel, *Gwo-ka modèn*, 105–6.

58. On ethnographic refusal, see Sherry Ortner, "Resistance and the Problem of Ethnographic Refusal," *Comparative Studies in Society and History* 37, no. 1 (1995); Zora Neale Hurston, *Of Mules and Men* (New York: Harper's Perennial Modern Classics, 1935), 2–3.

59. Édouard Glissant, *Poétique de la relation* (Paris: Gallimard, 1990), 203–9.

60. Kofi Agawu, "Tonality as a Colonizing Force in Africa," in *Audible Empire: Music, Global Politics, Critique*, ed. Ronald Radano and Tejumola Olaniyan (Durham, NC: Duke University Press Books, 2016), 337.

61. Lockel, "Lolo Camphrin"; Lockel, *Gwo-ka modèn*, 86.

62. Ronald M. Radano, *New Musical Figurations: Anthony Braxton's Cultural Critique* (Chicago: University of Chicago Press, 1994), 99.

63. Interview with Alza Bordin, 25 July 2009.

64. Lockel, *Gwo-ka modèn*, 78.

196 / Notes to Pages 81–90

65. The tune "Kaladja vivilo" is actually played as a fast *toumblak*.
66. Lockel, *Gwo-ka modèn*, 129.
67. Lockel, *Gwo-ka modèn*, 103.
68. Gérard Lockel, *Traité de gro ka modèn* (Baie-Mahault, Guadeloupe: n.p., 1981).
69. Lockel, private phone conversation with the author, 27 July 2009.
70. Ana María Ochoa Gautier, *Aurality: Listening and Knowledge in Nineteenth-Century Colombia* (Durham, NC: Duke University Press, 2014).
71. Many of the exercises in Lockel's treatise involve large interval leaps. While these are relatively easy to perform on guitar, they are much more challenging to saxophone players.
72. Interview with Alza Bordin, 25 July 2009.
73. Interview with the author, 8 August 2009.
74. Jean Comaroff, and John Comaroff, eds., *Modernity and Its Malcontents: Ritual and Power in Postcolonial Africa* (Chicago: University of Chicago Press, 1993), xii; Turino, *Nationalists, Cosmopolitans, and Popular Music in Zimbabwe*; David Scott, *Conscripts of Modernity: The Tragedy of Colonial Enlightenment* (Durham, NC: Duke University Press, 2004).
75. On *marronnage* as rupture, see Bonilla, *Non-Sovereign Futures*, 40–62.
76. Jerome Camal, "DestiNation: The Festival Gwoka, Tourism, and Anti-Colonialism," in *Sea, Sun, and Sound: Music and Tourism in the Circum-Caribbean*, ed. Timothy Rommen and Daniel T. Neely (Oxford: Oxford University Press, 2014).
77. Gilroy, *Black Atlantic*, 189.
78. Tejumola Olaniyan, "The Cosmopolitan Nativist: Fela and the Antinomies of Postcolonial Modernity," in *Arrest the Music! Fela and His Rebel Art and Politics* (Bloomington: University of Indiana Press, 2004), 163; Michaeline Crichlow and Patricia Northover, *Globalization and the Post-Creole Imagination: Notes on Fleeing the Plantation* (Durham, NC: Duke University Press, 2009).
79. Glissant, *Discours antillais*, 630.
80. The traditional-modern binary has proved enduring in Guadeloupe. One of my first exposures to gwoka was a 2006 page titled "Le gwoka entre tradition et modernité" (Gwoka between tradition and modernity) on the website of RFO (now Guadeloupe 1ère), the local public television station. Moreover, most of the gwoka musicians I have met ascribe to these categories. It is only recently, with the inscription of gwoka on the UNESCO list of intangible heritage (see chapter 8), that we have seen the phrase "contemporary expression" used as a substitute for the category "modern."
81. Ann Laura Stoler, *Duress: Imperial Durabilities in Our Times* (Durham, NC: Duke University Press, 2017), 23.
82. The French commonly uses the adjective *identitaire* rather than the noun *identité*. By limiting the translation to "identity," English puts the emphasis on something stable, whereas *identitaire* leaves open processes and negotiations. In *identitaire*, identity is desired (*discours identitaire*) or ascribed (*replis identitaire*) but not necessarily achieved.
83. Interestingly, on the original recording of this song, different lyrics can be heard: "You have to know, we don't have two musics. We have only one music. Gwoka is the music of the people." These lyrics offer a more direct illustration of Lockel's attempt to delegitimize musics that he considered unpatriotic, biguine most centrally.

CHAPTER THREE

1. Mounien, interview with the author, 15 July 2009.
2. Aihwa Ong, Virginia R. Dominguez, Jonathan Friedman, Nina Glick Schiller, Verena Stolcke, David Y. H. Wu, and Hu Ying, "Cultural Citizenship as Subject-Making:

Notes to Pages 90–97 / 197

Immigrants Negotiate Racial and Cultural Boundaries in the United States," *Current Anthropology* 37, no. 5 (1996): 738.

3. Jocelyne Guilbault, *Zouk: World Music in the West Indies* (Chicago: University of Chicago Press, 1993).

4. Erick Cosaque, *Musique, voix, percussion* (n.p., 1984).

5. The song also echoes another popular Guadeloupean song from the 1970s, "An domi déwò" (I slept outside), which describes the plight of a Guadeloupean migrant lured to the French capital who, upon his arrival, ends up homeless and cold, sleeping in a subway station.

6. Interview with the author, 4 June 2009.

7. Interview with the author, 4 June 2009.

8. Guilbault develops this point with regards to zouk. Jocelyne Guilbault, "Créolité and the New Cultural Politics of Difference in Popular Music of the French West Indies," *Black Music Research Journal* 14, no. 2 (1994): 161–78.

9. Jacques Derrida, *Le monolinguisme de l'autre* (Paris: Éditions Galilée, 1996).

10. Françoise Lionnet and Shu-mei Shih, eds., *Minor Transnationalism* (Durham, NC: Duke University Press, 2005).

11. I am responding here to the abundant literature that has seized creolization to theorize global hybridity, most famously encapsulated by James Clifford's declaration "We are all Caribbean now, living in our urban archipelago." Clifford, *The Predicament of Culture: Twentieth-Century Ethnography, Literature, and Art* (Cambridge, MA: Harvard University Press, 1988), 173. For a critique of that paradigm, see Stephan Palmié, "Is There a Model in the Muddle? 'Creolization' in African Americanist History and Anthropology," in *Creolization: History, Ethnography, Theory*, ed. Charles Stewart (Walnut Creek, CA: West Coast Press, 2007), 178–200; Mimi Sheller, "Creolization in Discourses of Global Culture," in *Uprootings/Regroundings: Questions of Home and Migration*, ed. Sarah Ahmed, Claudia Castañeda, Anne-Marie Fortier, and Mimi Sheller (Oxford, UK: Berg, 2003), 273–94. I borrow the term *continuance* from Homi K. Bhabha, "Unsatisfied: Notes on Vernacular Cosmopolitanism," in *Text and Nation: Cross-Disciplinary Essays on Cultural and National Identities*, ed. Laura García-Moreno and Peter C. Pfeiffer (Rochester, NY: Camden House, 1996), 191–207.

12. Steven Feld, *Jazz Cosmopolitanism in Accra: Five Musical Years in Ghana* (Durham, NC: Duke University Press, 2012), 204.

13. Robert Loyson's classic gwoka song "La canne à la richesse" addresses this issue.

14. Marie-Galante was, and remains, one of the main centers of sugar production

15. Marie-Françoise Zébus and François Causeret, "La canne à sucre résiste en Guadeloupe," *Agreste cahiers* 3 (2007): 2. Today, only two sugar refineries still operate in Guadeloupe.

16. In 1983, the GLA would morph into the Alliance révolutionnaire caraïbe, which claimed a number of bombings in France and Guadeloupe in the early 1980s.

17. Chérubin Céleste, "Chretien, donc indépendantiste: Entretien avec Chérubin Céleste," *Les temps modernes* 39, nos. 441–42 (1983); "Dossier No. 1: Les grandes dates du mouvement syndical." *Ja Ka Ta*, May 1980; UGTG, "Guadeloupe—La grève de 1975 dans l'industrie sucrière," http://ugtg.org/article_449.html.

18. On these topics, see Alain Anselin, *L'émigration antillaise en France: La troisième île* (Paris: Éditions Karthala, 1990); Anny Dominique Curtius, "Utopies du BUMIDOM: Construire l'avenir dans un "là-bas" postcontact," *French Forum* 35, nos. 2–3 (2010): 135–55; Françoise Vergès, *Le ventre des femmes: Capitalisme, racialisation, féminisme* (Paris: Albin Michel, 2017).

198 / Notes to Pages 97–102

19. BUMIDOM also managed the migration of workers from Réunion and French Guiana, but they were accounted for through separate quotas.

20. Vergès, *Le ventre des femmes*, 145.

21. Anselin, *L'emigration antillaise en France*, 103–11.

22. Anselin, *L'emigration antillaise en France*; David Beriss, *Black Skins, French Voices: Caribbean Ethnicity and Activism in Urban France* (Boulder, CO: Westview Press, 2004). There was, until the 1980s, an exception to this: the very central neighborhood of Les Halles was also home to a large community of Antillean migrants.

23. André Fontain, "La Guadeloupe, une caricature de département, dit le député Aimé Césaire au procès des 18," *France soir*, 27 February 1968, reproduced in Collectif des patriotes guadeloupéens, ed., *Pour servir l'histoire et la mémoire guadeloupéenne: Mai 1967* (Sainte-Anne, Guadeloupe: Co.Pa.Gua., 2003), 51.

24. Curtius, "Utopies du BUMIDOM," 149, my translation.

25. Édouard Glissant, *Discours antillais* (Paris: Gallimard, 1997), 52–53.

26. Anselin, *L'emigration antillaise en France*, 107–20.

27. All citations are taken from the roundtable "Gwoka an déwò" at the Festival Gwoka, Sainte-Anne, 13 July 2008. The roundtable was presided over by Félix Cotellon, with the participation of Julien Mérion, Marcel Magnat, Daniel Losio, Jacky Serin, Jacky Aglas, Françoise Ury, and Eric Bordelai.

28. David Beriss, "Culture-as-Race or Culture-as-Culture: Caribbean Ethnicity and the Ambiguity of Cultural Identity in French Society," *French Politics, Culture & Society* 18, no. 3 (2000): 18–47.

29. On modernity as a positive structure of power and a condition of conscription, see David Scott, *Conscripts of Modernity: The Tragedy of Colonial Enlightenment* (Durham, NC: Duke University Press, 2004).

30. I borrow the phrase "horizon of possibility" from Nadia Ellis, *Territories of the Soul: Queered Belonging in the Black Diaspora* (Durham, NC: Duke University Press, 2015).

31. I borrow the phrase "creolization moment" from Aisha Khan, "Creolization Moments," in *Creolization: History, Ethnography, Theory*, ed. Charles Stewart (Walnut Creek, CA: Left Coast Press, 2007), 237–53.

32. *Man* is the Creole word for "Mrs." or "Madam" and a common way to show respect for elderly women.

33. The *kaz a blan* (literally, "white people's house") was used to house agricultural workers on *habitations* (plantations) in northern Basse-Terre. The *kaz a blan* was designed to house several families. Its outer walls were built of concrete. The structure was divided into two rows of back-to-back individual rooms separated by wooden walls. Each room had a door that opened onto a covered gallery. Common kitchens were found at each corner of the structure. The manager of the *habitation* assigned each family one or more rooms according to its needs. Families with more than one room could remove the wooden partitions to create a bigger living space.

34. Mounien, interview with the author, 15 July 2009. Konket, interview with the author and Christian Dahomay, 4–5 August 2008. Carnot and Marie-Céline Lafontaine, *Alors ma chère, moi*. (Paris: Éditions caribéennes, 1986). For an overview of Konket's life and career, see Marie-Héléna Laumuno, *Gwoka et politique en Guadeloupe: 1960-2003: 40 ans de construction du "pays"* (Paris: L'Harmattan, 2011), 76–77.

35. In her book on gwoka and politics, Laumuno offers a political reading of "Jo mayé dé grenndé-la." It is possible that the song functioned as a metaphorical critique of cheating estate managers. Laumuno, *Gwoka et politique en Guadeloupe*, 79. Both songs

Notes to Pages 102–105 / 199

appear on Guy Conquette Groupe avec Emilien Antile, *Patrimwàn, vol. 1* (Henri Debs Production, CDD 26-72-2), CD.

36. This comment is taken from an interview Christian and I conducted with Guy Konket, 4–5 August 2008.

37. "Faya faya" likewise offers a critique of youth culture. "Bravo jinès gozyé" (Congratulations to the youth of Gozier) entones the refrain with a heavy dose of irony. "Baimbridge chaud" appears on *Nostalgie caraïbes: Vélo & Guy Konket* (Disques Célini, Réf. 011-2). "Faya faya" was reissued on Guy Conquette Groupe avec Emilien Antile, *Patrimwàn, vol. 1*.

38. Both songs appear on *Nostalgie caraïbes: Vélo & Guy Konket*.

39. Mounien, interview with the author, 15 July 2009.

40. Dahomay and Guy Konket, interview with the author, 4–5 August 2008.

41. Christian Dahomay was the first to bring this up to me. According to Dahomay, Dolor may have been the first artist to bring gwoka and biguine musicians together in a studio. Unfortunately, I have not been able to verify this information. Dolor did record "Ti fi-la ou té madam" with singer Anzala and Vélo as well as an unidentified saxophonist, probably Robert Mavounzy or Emilien Antile, but I do not have an exact recording date (*Tumbélé! Biguines and Afro-Latin Sounds from the French Caribbean, 1963–1974*). Following Konket's recordings with biguine musicians, Robert Loyson recorded two tracks with biguine musicians, "Jen fouyé, Piè fouyé" and "Nou kalé a Kutumba," for Célini in 1972 (*Nostalgie caraïbes: Robert Loyson*). Konket's recordings with Antile include "Faya faya," "Natali O," and "Si sé kon sa, pa ni rézon." on *Patrimwan, vol. 1*. The songs "Ban klé a Titine" and "Firmin au tribunal" on *Nostalgie caraïbes: Vélo & Guy Konket* find Konket accompanied by an unidentified group featuring alto sax, accordion, bass, *maké*, *boula*, *bwa* (clave), and *chacha*. On "Jo mayé dé grenn dé-la" and "Loto wouj la" (*Patrimwan, vol. 1*), Konket is accompanied by Serge Christophe and Jidor playing gwoka as well as an unidentified bass player.

42. The proliferation of such recordings around this period suggests that record producers may have also pushed in that direction. It is clear from the liner notes that he wrote for the original release of these recordings that Henri Debs—self-proclaimed "savior of Antillean music"—was instrumental in orchestrating and marketing Antile and Konket's collaboration.

43. See chapter 1. See also Gérard Lockel, "Lolo Camphrin: Un des derniers grands danseurs de gro ka." *Ja Ka Ta*, February 1978.

44. Laumuno, *Gwoka et politique en Guadeloupe*, 82–83.Yet the song that most explicitly addresses the difficulties of sugarcane workers is undoubtedly Robert Loyson's "Ji kann a la richès"—and its follow-up "Ji kann a la richès 2" (*Nostalgie caraïbes: Robert Loyson*).

45. For a detailed defense on this perspective published in direct response to the discourse of the *camp patriotique*, see Marie-Céline Lafontaine, "Le Carnaval de l'autre': A propos d' 'authenticité' en matière de musique guadeloupéenne: Théories et réalités," *Les temps modernes* 39, nos. 441–42 (1983): 2126–73; Marie-Céline Lafontaine, "Unité et diversité des musiques traditionnelles guadeloupéennes," in *Les musiques Guadeloupéennes dans le champs culturel Afro-Américain, au sein des musiques du monde* (Paris: Éditions caribéennes, 1988), 71–92. See also Jerome Camal, "From Gwoka Modènn to Jazz Ka: Music, Nationalism, and Creolization in Guadeloupe" (PhD diss., Washington University in Saint Louis, 2011).

46. Interview with the author and Christian Dahomay, 4 August 2008.

200 / Notes to Pages 106–115

47. "BIMIDOM" is the Creole pronunciation of BUMIDOM. *Nostalgie caraïbes: Vélo & Guy Konket* (Disques Célini, Réf. 011-2).
48. Interview with the author and Christian Dahomay, 4 August 2008.
49. Michel Halley, interview with the author, 16 July 2009.
50. Interview with the author, 4 August 2008.
51. Paul Gilroy, *The Black Atlantic: Modernity and Double-Consciousness* (Cambridge, MA: Harvard University Press, 1993), 199.
52. All three from *Guy Konket et le Groupe Ka* (Éditions Bolibana, BIP-96).
53. Lafontaine, "Le Carnaval de l'autre.'"
54. Sheldon Pollock, "Cosmopolitan and Vernacular in History," in *Cosmopolitanism*, ed. Carol A. Breckenridge, Sheldon Pollock, Homi K. Bhabha, and Dipesh Chakrabarty (Durham, NC: Duke University Press, 2002), locs. 197–99; Bhabha, "Unsatisfied," 196.
55. Françoise Lionnet, "Cosmopolitan or Creole Lives? Globalized Oceans and Insular Identities," *Profession* (2011): 24.
56. Bhabha, "Unsatisfied," 191.
57. Robert Oumaou, interview with the author, 30 June 2010; Cosaque, interview with the author, 4 August 2009.
58. The most successful artists can benefit from sponsorship from local businesses and an occasional grant from the French government.
59. This history is based on interviews with Losio (15 July 2010) and Magnat (6 July 2010), as well as their comments during the Festival Gwoka roundtable, "Gwoka an déwò," July 2008. Daniel Losio was also generous in sharing many press clippings and documents about the group.
60. J. F. Pecqueriaux, "Paco Rabanne, à la mode de chez nous." *France Antilles*, 2 June 1979.
61. *Tumblack* (Barclay, Ref. 91.024, 1978).
62. Thanks to Daniel Losio for showing me this article. Unfortunately, Losio had torn the pages out of the magazine, and I have not been able to locate the original, hence the skeletal reference: interview with Paco Rabanne, *Hi-Fi*, ca. 1978, 181–82.
63. Advertisement, *France-Antilles*, 1 June 1979.
64. Guilbault, *Zouk*.
65. "Black Music Diaspora: A French-Caribbean Perspective" (communication for the Center for Black Music Research Serial Conference on the Black Music Diaspora, University of Puerto Rico, 19–20 June 2009). Many thanks to Dominique Cyrille for sharing a copy of her paper.
66. Frédéric Bobin, "Les Indépendantistes, d'outre-mer se muent in gestionnaires," *Le Monde*, 31 October 1994; Ernesto Laclau, *On Populist Reason* (London: Verso, 2007), 83–93.
67. Camal, "From Gwoka Modènn to Jazz Ka."
68. UPLG, *Pour une collectivité nouvelle associée de Guadeloupe: Projet de l'UPLG* (Pointe-à-Pitre: n.p., 1992).
69. Eddy Nedejkovic, "Les Indépendentistes de Guadeloupe tentent d'enrailler le déclin de leur mouvement," *Le Monde*, 22 December 1994.

CHAPTER FOUR

1. Gerard Lockel, *Gwo Ka Modènn: 1969-1989, vingt ans de lutte sur le front de la culture guadeloupéenne* (Baie-Mahault, Guadeloupe: ADGKM, 1989).
2. Interview with the author, 8 July 2010.
3. Although common in French, *métisse* and *métissage* have no exact translations in English. From the Latin *mixtus* (mixed), the terms have a strong connotation of

Notes to Pages 115–120 / 201

biological mixing, something akin to "crossbreeding" or "cross-fertilization." When applied to people, they can carry both negative and positive connotations, from a degrading miscegenation to a mutually enriching creolization.

4. Interview with the author, 8 August 2008.

5. Edwin C. Hill, *Black Soundscapes, White Stages: The Meaning of Francophone Sounds in the Black Atlantic* (Baltimore: Johns Hopkins University Press, 2013), 14. On the lack of a coherent Antillean identity, see Christine Chivallon, "De quelques préconstruits de la notion de diaspora à partir de l'exemple antillais," *Revue européenne des migrations internationales* 13, no. 1 (1997): 149–60.

6. Brent Hayes Edwards, *The Practice of Diaspora: Literature, Translation, and the Rise of Black Internationalism* (Cambridge, MA: Harvard University Press, 2003).

7. As will be clear in a moment, I am well aware of the pitfalls surrounding a superficial quest for African retentions and of assuming a linear transmission of knowledge and technologies from Africa to the Americas. Despite their similarities, there is no historical evidence of a connection between the drums of Benin and those of Guadeloupe. See Stephan Palmié, "Introduction: On Predications of Africanity," in *Africas in the Americas: Beyond the Search for Origins in the Study of Afro-Atlantic Religions*, ed. Stefan Palmié (Leiden: Brill Academic Publishing, 2008), 1–37; Stephan Palmié, *The Cooking of History: How Not to Study Afro-Cuban Religion* (Chicago: University of Chicago Press, 2013).

8. Édouard Glissant, *Discours antillais* (Paris: Gallimard, 1997), 40–57.

9. I expand here the distinction made by Aisha Khan with regard to creolization. Aisha Khan, "Creolization Moments," in *Creolization: History, Ethnography, Theory*, ed. Charles Stewart (Walnut Creek, CA: Left Coast Press, 2007), 238.

10. Édouard Glissant, *Poétique de la Relation* (Paris: Gallimard, 1990), 103; Mary Gallagher, "The *Créolité* Movement: Paradoxes of a French Caribbean Orthodoxy," in *Creolization: History, Ethnography, Theory*, ed. Charles Stewart (Walnut Creek, CA: Left Coast Press, 2007), 220–36.

11. Robin Cohen, "Creolization and Diaspora: The Cultural Politics of Divergence and Some Convergence," in *Opportunity Structures in Diaspora Relations: Comparisons in Contemporary Multilevel Politics of Diaspora and Transnational Identity*, ed. Gloria P. Totoricaguena (Reno: Center for Basque Studies, University of Nevada Press, 2007), 85–112.

12. David Scott, "That Event, This Memory: Notes on the Anthropology of African Diasporas in the New World," *Diaspora: A Journal of Transnational Studies* 1, no. 3 (1991): 261–84; David Scott, *Conscripts of Modernity: The Tragedy of Colonial Enlightenment* (Durham, NC: Duke University Press, 2004), 108.

13. Sidney W. Mintz and Richard Price, *The Birth of African-American Culture: An Anthropological Perspective* (Boston: Beacon Press, 1992), 17; Scott, *Conscripts of Modernity*, 109; Michel-Rolph Trouillot, "Culture on the Edges: Caribbean Creolization in Historical Context," in *From the Margins: Historical Anthropology and Its Futures*, ed. Brian Keith Axel (Durham, NC: Duke University Press, 2002), 189–210.

14. Although the tensions between retentionist and creolist approaches may seem like a rehashing of Herskovits's debates with sociologist Franklin A. Frazier, I insist once again that both approaches build on Herskovits's work and admit to the retention of Africanisms to a much greater degree than Frazier recognized. It also needs to be stressed that discussions surrounding both creolization and diaspora theories have often been accompanied by disputes about the relative homogeneity or heterogeneity of African and European cultures, with all three terms open to debate.

202 / Notes to Pages 120–121

15. Christine Chivallon, "Beyond Gilroy's Black Atlantic: The Experience of the African Diaspora," *Diaspora* 11, no. 3 (2002): 359–82; Paul Gilroy, *The Black Atlantic: Modernity and Double-Consciousness* (Cambridge, MA: Harvard University Press, 1993), 37.

16. Michael Omi and Howard Winant, *Racial Formation in the United States: From the 1960s to the 1990s* (New York: Routledge, 1994), 56.

17. Gilroy, *Black Atlantic*; Stuart Hall, "Cultural Identity and Diaspora," in *Identity: Community, Culture, Difference*, ed. Jonathan Rutherford (London: Lawrence and Wishart, 1990), 222–37; Leroi Jones, *Blues People: Negro Music in White America* (New York: Perennial, 1999).

18. Stuart Hall, "Créolité and the Process of Creolization," in *The Creolization Reader: Studies in Mixed Identities and Cultures*, ed. Robin Cohen and Paola Toninato (New York: Routledge, 2009), 28.

19. Stephan Palmié, "Creolization and Its Discontents," *Annual Review of Anthropology* 35, no. 1 (2006): 438. See also Jorge Cañires-Esguerra, "Creole Colonial Spanish America," in *Creolization: History, Ethnography, Theory*, ed. Charles Stewart (Walnut Creek, CA: West Coast Press, 2007), 26–45; Stephan Palmié, "Is There a Model in the Muddle?"; Stephan Palmié, "The C-Word Again: From Colonial to Postcolonial Semantics," in *Creolization: History, Ethnography, Theory*, ed. Charles Stewart (Walnut Creek, CA: West Coast Press, 2007). On the shifting contour of racism, see Ann Laura Stoler, "Racial Regimes of Truth," in *Duress: Imperial Durabilities in Our Times* (Durham, NC: Duke University Press, 2017), 237–65.

20. Gilroy, *Black Atlantic*; Nicholas Thomas, "Cold Fusion," *American Anthropologist* 98, no. 1 (1996), 12.

21. Brenda Dixon Gottschild, "Crossroads, Continuities, and Contradictions: The Afro-Euro Triangle," in *Caribbean Dance from Abakuá to Zouk: How Movement Shapes Identity*, ed. Susanna Sloat (Gainesville: University Press of Florida, 2002), 3–10; Samuel A. Floyd Jr. and Ronald Radano, "Interpreting the African-American Musical Past: A Dialogue," *Black Music Research Journal* (2009): 1–10; Samuel A. Floyd, *The Power of Black Music: Interpreting Its History from Africa to the United States* (New York: Oxford University Press, 1996); Portia K. Maultsby, "Africanisms in African-American Music," in *Africanisms in American Culture*, ed. Joseph E. Holloway (Bloomington: Indiana University Press, 1990), 185–210; Olly Wilson, "The Heterogeneous Sound Ideal in African-American Music," in *New Perspectives on Music: Essays in Honor of Eileen Southern*, ed. Josephine Wright and Samuel A. Floyd (Warren, MI: Harmonie Park Press, 1992), 327–38.

22. Ingrid Monson, ed., *The African Diaspora: A Musical Perspective* (London: Routledge, 2003); Ronald Radano and Philip Bohlman, eds., *Music and the Racial Imagination* (Chicago: University of Chicago Press, 2001); Ronald M. Radano, *Lying Up a Nation: Race and Black Music* (Chicago: University of Chicago Press, 2003). Ingrid Monson comments: "The participatory, egalitarian, and spiritual qualities of African diasporic musics have frequently been idealized in the ethnomusicological literature with scant attention to intercultural [and, I would add intracultural as well] power stratifications and processes of contestation." The problem has proved persistent: for example, in an otherwise great analysis of intercultural musical collaborations, Jason Stanyek reduces diasporic discrepancies and contestations as mere examples of an Afro-diasporic "heterogeneous sound ideal." Likewise Fischlin, Heble, and Lipsitz's concept of *rifference*—which suggests that, despite many reservations, "ethnic differences" can somehow be "overridden by the aesthetic accomplishment evident in the 'riffing' that denotes profound ideological and cultural differences"—flirts with

idealist naïveté. Jason Stanyek, "Transmission of an Interculture: Pan-African Jazz and Intercultural Improvisation," in *The Other Side of Nowhere: Jazz, Improvisation, and Communities in Dialogue*, ed. Daniel Fischlin and Ajay Heble (Middleton, CT: Wesleyan University Press, 2004), 87–130; Daniel Fischlin, Ajay Heble, and George Lipsitz, "Improvisation and Encounter: Rights in the Key of Rifference," in *The Fierce Urgency of Now: Improvisation, Rights, and the Ethics of Cocreation* (Durham, NC: Duke University Press, 2013).

23. Denis-Constant Martin, "Can Jazz Be Rid of the Racial Imagination? Creolization, Racial Discourse and Semiology of Music," *Black Music Research Journal* 28, no. 2 (2008): 120.

24. Chivallon, "De quelques préconstruits"; Chivallon, "Beyond Gilroy's Black Atlantic."

25. Étienne Balibar and Immanuel Wallerstein, *Race, Nation, Class: Ambiguous Identities* (London: Verso, 1991); David Beriss, "Culture-as-Race or Culture-as-Culture: Caribbean Ethnicity and the Ambiguity of Cultural Identity in French Society," *French Politics, Culture & Society* 18, no. 3 (2000): 18–47.

26. Chivallon, "De quelques préconstruits," 150, my translation.

27. Abdoulaye Gueye, "De la diaspora noire: Enseignements du contexte Français," *Revue européenne des migrations internationales* 22, no. 1 (2009):11–33.

28. Pierre Bourdieu and Loïc Wacquant, "On the Cunning of Imperialist Reason," *Theory, Culture & Society* 16, no. 1 (1999): 41–58.

29. Gary Wilder, "Race, Reason, Impasse: Césaire, Fanon, and the Legacy of Emancipation," *Radical History Review* 90 (2004): 31–61.

30. Jean-Loup Amselle, *L'ethnicisation de la France* (Paris: Nouvelles Éditions Lignes, 2011). The French tendency to contrast racial and "sociological" approaches may surprise American readers. In France, a sociological approach is one that favors class as the primary lens of analysis. Noticeably, this frame does not allow for a consideration of the intersection of race and class. Nonetheless, I should note that French academic engagement with race and racism has shifted in the aftermath of the 2005 riots in France. Amselle represents here one corner of a much more diversified field. See Didier Fassin and Eric Fassin, eds., *De la question sociale à la question raciale: Représenter la société française* (Paris: La Découverte, 2006).

31. Édouard Glissant, *Introduction à un poétique du divers* (Paris: Gallimard, 1996), 16–17; Glissant, *Poétique de la Relation*, 23, 31.

32. Celia Britton, *Édouard Glissant and Postcolonial Theory: Strategies of Language and Resistance* (Charlottesville: University of Virginia Press, 1999), 19; Glissant, *Discours antillais*.

33. Martin Munro and Celia Britton, "Eulogizing Creoleness? *Éloge de la créolité* and Caribbean Identity, Culture, and Politics," *Small Axe* 21, no. 1 52 (2017): 164–68; Gallagher, "*Créolité* Movement." See also Richard Price and Sally Price, "Shadowboxing in the Mangrove," *Cultural Anthropology* 12, no. 1 (1997): 3–36.

34. Laurent Farrugia and Hector Poullet, *Tous les hommes sont des créoles* (Paris: Éditions Art, 2006), http://www.potomitan.info/poullet/kreyol.php

35. Richard D. E. Burton, "The Idea of Difference in Contemporary French West Indian Thought: Négritude, Antillanité, Créolité," in *French and West Indian: Martinique, Guadeloupe, and Guiana Today*, ed. Richard D. E. Burton and Fred Reno (London: Macmillan, 1995); Gallagher, "*Créolité* Movement"; Richard Price, "Créolisation, Creolization, and Créolité," *Small Axe* 21, no. 1 52 (2017): 211–19. I presented my own argument on this topic in Jerome Camal, "Creolizing Jazz, Jazzing the *Tout-Monde*: Jazz, Gwoka, and the Poetics of Relation," in *American Creoles: The Francophone*

204 / Notes to Pages 124–128

Caribbean and the American South, ed. Martin Munro and Celia Britton (Liverpool, UK: Liverpool University Press, 2012).

36. Poullet and Farrugia, in *Tous les hommes sont des créoles*, offer a counterexample.
37. Communication presented during the seminar "Créolité, créolisations, arts et pratiques socioculturelles" (Paris, 25 June 2012). Thanks to Ti Malo for providing a transcription of his presentation on his website (http://www.timalo.com/seminaire -creolites-creolisations-arts-et-pratiques-socioculturelles/) and for directing me to it.
38. In addition to the texts already cited, see Price, "Créolisation, Creolization, and Créolité."
39. Michaeline Crichlow and Patricia Northover, *Globalization and the Post-Creole Imagination: Notes on Fleeing the Plantation* (Durham, NC: Duke University Press, 2009), ix.
40. Palmié, "Is There a Model in the Muddle?"
41. See Tiffany Ruby Patterson and Robin D. G. Kelley, "Unfinished Migrations: Reflections on the African Diaspora and the Making of the Modern World," *African Studies Review* 43, no. 1 (2000): 11–45; Tyler Stovall, "Race and the Making of the Nation: Blacks in Modern France," in *Diasporic Africa: A Reader*, ed. Michael A. Gomez (New York: New York University Press, 2006), 200–218.
42. Andrea Schwieger Hiepko, "Europe and the Antilles: An Interview with Édouard Glissant," in *The Creolization of Theory*, ed. Françoise Lionnet and Shu-mei Shih (Durham, NC: Duke University Press, 2011), 255–61.
43. Jacques Derrida, *L'écriture et la différence* (Paris: Éditions du Seuil, 1967), 334–39; Édouard Glissant, *Introduction à une poétique du divers* (Paris: Gallimard, 1996), 69.
44. Édouard Glissant, *Caribbean Discourse: Selected Essays*, trans. J. Michael Dash (Charlottesville: University of Virginia Press, 1999), 26. In Martinique and Guadeloupe, the French word *trace* also commonly refers to a footpath; thus, metaphorically, the *trace* connects past, present, and future. Stuart Hall echoes Glissant (and Derrida) in his characterization of the Caribbean as "translated societies" that "always bear the traces of the original, but in such a way that the original is impossible to restore. The concept of resonance allows Radano to likewise critically engage with the musicological discourse about African retentions, uncovering the ideological work this kind of historical endeavor performs in the present. Radano, *Lying Up a Nation*; Hall, "Créolité and the Process of Creolization," 29.
45. Derrida, *L'écriture et la différence*, 339; Édouard Glissant, *Tout-Monde* (Paris: Gallimard, 1993), 280; Édouard Glissant, *Traité du Tout-Monde* (Paris: Gallimard, 1997), 18–19. All translations are mine.
46. Britton, *Glissant and Postcolonial Theory*, 21. The poetics of Relation are simultaneously an epistemology (a way of knowing the world, the Other, and the Self), an ethics, and an ontology.
47. Glissant, *Introduction à une poétique du divers*, 71–72, my translation.
48. See, for example, his discussion of Barack Obama as a "child of the abyss" and a product of creolization in Édouard Glissant and Patrick Chamoiseau, *L'intraitable beauté du monde: Adresse à Barack Obama* (Paris: Éditions Galaade, 2009). See also Valérie Loichot, "Creolizing Barack Obama," in *American Creoles: The Francophone Caribbean and the American South*, ed. Martin Munro and Celia Britton (Liverpool, UK: Liverpool University Press, 2012), 77–94.
49. Glissant, *Poétique de la Relation*, 20, my translation.
50. I build here on a distinction made by Aisha Khan, who riffs on an idea introduced by Clifford Geertz. Khan, "Creolization Moments," 238.

Notes to Pages 128–137 / 205

51. These questions were inspired by Gilroy's critical reading of black politics in *Black Atlantic*, 29–40.

52. Anthony Appiah, *Cosmopolitanism: Ethics in a World of Strangers* (New York: W. W. Norton & Co., 2006).

53. Yarimar Bonilla, *Non-Sovereign Futures: French Caribbean Politics in the Wake of Disenchantment* (Chicago: University of Chicago Press, 2015), 24; Frantz Fanon, *Peau noire, masques blancs* (Paris: Points Essais, 1971).

54. Dany Bébel-Gislert, *Le défi culturel guadeloupéen: Devenir ce que nous sommes* (Paris: Éditions caribéennes, 1989), 204–7, my translation. The terms *nègre* and *chabin(e)* refer to Guadeloupean racial categories and are notoriously difficult to translate. See Edwards, *Practice of Diaspora*, chap. 1.

55. Gérard Lockel, *Gro ka modèn* (n.p.: Guadeloupe Disques, 1976); Lockel, *Vingt ans de lutte*; Gerard Lockel, *Gwo-ka modèn* (Baie-Mahault, Guadeloupe: ADGKM, 2011), 87, 179, 243.

56. Arjun Appadurai, *Modernity at Large: Cultural Dimensions of Globalization* (Minneapolis: University of Minnesota Press, 1996), 158–77; Crichlow and Northover, *Globalization and the Post-Creole Imagination*, 184.

57. Magallie Pillal, "Le Gwoka entre tradition et modernité," http://guadeloupe.rfo.fr/article185.html#.

58. Interview with the author, 22 July 2008.

59. Michael D. Largey, *Vodou Nation: Haitian Art Music and Cultural Nationalism* (Chicago: University of Chicago Press, 2006), 18.

60. Feld, *Jazz Cosmopolitanism in Accra*, 49.

61. Simone Schwarz-Bart and André Schwartz-Bart, *Un plat de porc aux bananes vertes* (Paris: Le Seuil, 1967), 222, my translation.

62. Joslen Gabaly, *Diadyéé: Gwoka* (Abymes, Guadeloupe: Créapub', 2003); Kannida, "Kreyòl," in *Kyenzenn* (Label Bleu, 1999).

63. Interview with the author, 24 December 2007.

64. We, of course, should not ignore the implied hierarchy in his statement.

65. Timothy R. Mangin, "Notes on Jazz in Senegal," in *Uptown Conversation: The New Jazz Studies*, ed. Robert O'Meally, Brent Hayes Edwards, and Farah Jasmine Griffin (New York: Columbia University Press, 2004), 241–42.

66. Veit Erlmann, "Communities of Style: Musical Figures of Black Diasporic Identity," in *The African Diaspora: A Musical Perspective*, ed. Ingrid Monson (London: Routledge, 2003), 83–100.

67. Timothy D. Taylor, *Global Pop: World Music, World Markets* (New York: Routledge, 1997), 173; Steven Feld, "Notes on 'World Beat,'" in *Music Grooves: Essays and Dialogues*, ed. Steven Feld and Charles Kiel (Chicago: University of Chicago Press, 1994), 238–46.

68. Compare, for example, the arrangement of "YouYou" on Murray's *Yonndé* with Konket's on Guy Konket, *Guy Konket et le Groupe Ka* (Éditions Bolibana, BIP-96, ca. 1981).

69. Luc Michaux-Vignes, "Le gwo-ka et le dilemme d'être jazzé," http://bananierbleu.fr/1515/le-gwo-ka-et-le-dilemne-detre-jazze/.

70. Crichlow and Northover, *Globalization and the Post-Creole Imagination*, 185.

71. Interview with the author, December 2007. See also Jacques Schwartz-Bart, "Questions sur une vaudou session," *Jazz News* 29 (2014): 52.

72. Jacques Schwarz-Bart, "EPK Hazzan HD (English version), CD by Jacques Schwarz-Bart," posted May 19, 2018, 3:22, https://youtu.be/Xdr4lC5pMP4.

206 / Notes to Pages 137–148

73. Schwartz-Bart, "Questions sur une vaudou session."
74. Nadia Ellis, *Territories of the Soul: Queered Belonging in the Black Diaspora* (Durham, NC: Duke University Press, 2015), 3.
75. I borrow the idea of joining diaspora from Paul C. Johnson, *Diaspora Conversions: Black Carib Religion and the Recovery of Africa* (Berkeley: University of California Press, 2007).
76. Radano, *Lying Up a Nation*, 11, 53.
77. Bonilla, *Non-Sovereign Futures*.
78. Eric Delhaye, "Le jazz français discrimine-t-il les musiciens antillais?" *Télérama*, 25 April 2018, http://www.telerama.fr/musique/le-jazz-francais-discrimine-t-il-les-musiciens-antillais,n5621362.php?utm_campaign=Echobox&utm_medium=Social&utm_source=Facebook&link_time=1524671955#link_time=1524671793.

CHAPTER FIVE

1. Wozan Monza, *RExistans* (Debs Music, 2011).
2. Both quotes in this paragraph come from the liner notes to Monza, *RExistans*.
3. Both Creole and French operate a distinction between *moun* and *pèp* (in Creole) or *gens* and *peuple* (in French). All these terms are commonly rendered as "people" in English but they infer a difference similar to that of "people" as the plural of "person" (*moun, gens*) and "a people" in the singular (*pèp, peuple*). Perhaps the distinction between *folks* and *people* carries some of the same connotations.
4. Jean Bernabé, Patrick Chamoiseau, and Raphaël Confiant, *Éloge de la créolité (In Praise of Creoleness)* (Paris: Gallimard, 1989), 89.
5. Although Dr. Marie-Françoise Sinseau translated the liner notes, the translations presented here are my own.
6. Homi K. Bhabha, "Unsatisfied: Notes on Vernacular Cosmopolitanism," in *Text and Nation: Cross-Disciplinary Essays on Cultural and National Identities*, ed. Laura García-Moreno and Peter C. Pfeiffer (New York: Camden House, Columbia, 1996), 191–207; Frantz Fanon, *The Wretched of the Earth* (New York: Grove Press, 2005).
7. Dany Bébel-Gislert, *Le défi culturel guadeloupéen: Devenir ce que nous sommes* (Paris: Éditions caribéennes, 1989); Yarimar Bonilla, *Non-Sovereign Futures: French Caribbean Politics in the Wake of Disenchantment* (Chicago: University of Chicago Press, 2015), 35–36.
8. Bonilla, *Non-Sovereign Futures*, 36; UPLG, *Pour une collectivité nouvelle associée de Guadeloupe: Projet de l'UPLG* (Pointe-à-Pitre: n.p., 1992).
9. Both *lyennaj* and *liyennaj* (meaning "tie," "connection," "solidarity," and also "alliance" or "network") are commonly accepted spellings. The LKP is generally spelled with the additional *i*, whereas the LPG leaves it out.
10. I hesitate to follow Bonilla in concluding that the LKP illustrates "prefigurative politics through which alternative forms of social and political organization could be both invoked and rehearsed" or "a new template of political possibility" for "an alternative non-sovereign future." Bonilla, *Non-Sovereign Futures*, 150–51.
11. Shalini Puri, *The Caribbean Postcolonial: Social Equality, Post-Nationalism, and Cultural Hybridity* (New York: Palgrave Macmillan, 2004), 6.
12. John Carlos Rowes, ed., *Post-Nationalist American Studies* (Berkeley: University of California Press, 2000); Lauren Berlant, *The Anatomy of National Fantasy: Hawthorne, Utopia, and Everyday Life* (Chicago: University of Chicago Press, 1991), 20.
13. Puri, *Caribbean Postcolonial*, 85.

Notes to Pages 149–156 / 207

14. Michael Hardt and Antonio Negri, *Empire* (Cambridge, MA: Harvard University Press, 2001), xii.

15. Yarimar Bonilla, "Nonsoveriegn Futures? French Caribbean Politics in the Wake of Disenchantment," in *Caribbean Sovereignty, Democracy and Development in an Age of Globalization*, ed. Lewis Linden (New York: Routledge, 2012), 214. See also Shalini Puri, *The Grenada Revolution in the Caribbean Present: Operation Urgent Memory* (New York: Palgrave Macmillan, 2014).

16. Mimi Sheller, *Consuming the Caribbean: From Arawaks to Zombies* (London: Routledge, 2003); Puri, *Caribbean Postcolonial*, 12. The proliferation of sargassum washing up on Guadeloupean beaches dramatically illustrates the impact of global environmental shifts on Caribbean economies, as the toxic seaweed covered entire beaches that would otherwise have been opened to tourists.

17. Joshua Jelly-Schapiro, "'Are We All Creoles Now?' Ethnicity and Nation in a Heterogeneous Caribbean Diaspora," in *Ethnicity, Class, and Nationalism: Caribbean and Extra-Caribbean Dimensions*, ed. Anton L. Allahar (Lanham, MD: Lexington Books, 2005), 23–55. Arjun Appadurai has already argued that, in late capitalism, nationalism needs to be rethought to include transnational imaginings and solidarities. Appadurai, *Modernity at Large: Cultural Dimensions of Globalization* (Minneapolis: University of Minnesota Press, 1996); Appadurai, "Sovereignty without Territoriality: Notes for a Postnational Geography," in *The Geography of Identity*, ed. Patricia Yaeger (Ann Arbor: University of Michigan Press, 1996), 40–58. For a broader discussion of the importance of applying transnational perspective to the study of (post)colonial nationalisms, see Akhil Gupta, "The Song of the Nonaligned World: Transnational Identities and the Reinscription of Space in Late Capitalism," *Cultural Anthropology* 7, no. 1 (1992): 63–79.

18. Michaeline Crichlow and Patricia Northover, *Globalization and the Post-Creole Imagination: Notes on Fleeing the Plantation* (Durham, NC: Duke University Press, 2009), 19, 33, original emphasis.

19. Stuart Hall, "Whose Heritage? Un-Settling the Heritage, Re-Imagining the Post-Nation," in *The Politics of Heritage, the Legacies of "Race,"* ed. Jo Littler and Roshi Naidoo (New York: Routledge, 2005), 35.

20. Cited in Bonilla, *Non-Sovereign Futures*, 3.

21. "Entre mémoire et histoire, un balisage de la Martinique," *La fabrique de l'histoire*, France Culture, 2 October 2013, http://www.franceculture.fr/emission-la-fabrique-de-l-histoire-martinique-34-2013-10-02.

22. Bouziane Daoudi, "Soft, plus dur qu'il n'y parait." *Libération*, 24 November 2007.

23. Fred Deshayes, interview with the author, 12 August 2008.

24. Fred Deshayes, *Fred Deshayes* (Aztec Music, 2011).

25. Soft, *Partout étranger* (Aztec Musique, CM2197, 2007).

26. Interview with the author, 20 July 2009.

27. Interview with the author, 12 August 2008.

28. Interview with the author, 20 July 2009.

29. Fred Deshayes, interview with the author, 12 August 2008.

30. Interview with the author, 12 August 2008.

31. Interview with the author, 20 July 2009. The last time I saw Soft performed, in 2017, Deshayes had significantly shifted to playing an electric guitar.

32. Interview with the author, 20 July 2009.

33. Interview with the author, 20 July 2009.

208 / Notes to Pages 156–164

34. Soft, *Kadans a peyi-la* (Aztec Musique, CM3282, 2005).
35. Interview with the author, 20 July 2009.
36. Soft, *Konfyans* (Aztec Musique, CM2259, 2009).
37. Patrick Labesse, "Fred Deshayes: «La Guadeloupe est responsable de son naufrage»," *Le Monde*, 18 March 2006.
38. Mary Gallagher emphasizes the basic opposition between *créolité* as a static identity and creolization as an open-ended process. Mary Gallagher, "The *Créolité* Movement: Paradoxes of a French Caribbean Orthodoxy," in *Creolization: History, Ethnography, Theory*, ed. Charles Stewart (Walnut Creek, CA: Left Coast Press, 2007).
39. Interview with the author, 12 August 2008.
40. Interview with the author, 12 August 2008.
41. Édouard Glissant, *Discours antillais* (Paris: Gallimard, 1997), 418; Édouard Glissant, *Poétique de la Relation* (Paris: Gallimard, 1990), 204.
42. Glissant, *Poétique de la Relation*, 205–6.
43. Interview with the author, 20 July 2009.
44. Interview with the author, 12 August 2008. Édouard Glissant, *Introduction à une poétique du divers* (Paris: Gallimard, 1996).
45. Interview with the author, 12 August 2008.
46. Svetlana Boym, *The Future of Nostalgia* (New York: Basic Books, 2001), 41, 49.
47. Glissant, *Discours antillais*, 44, my translation.
48. Soft, *Partout étranger* (Aztec Musique, CM2197, 2007).
49. Interview with the author, 12 August 2008.
50. Glissant, *Discours antillais*, 56–57, my translation.
51. For a broader view on the power struggles that accompany processes of patrimonialization, see Christian Bromberger, "'Patrimoine immatériel' entre ambiguités et overdose," *L'Homme* 209 (2014).
52. Following Bendix, I prefer the neologism *patrimonialization*—based on the French *patrimoine*—over terminology referencing "heritage," as is more common in Anglophone literature. Indeed, Bendix draws a helpful contrast between *héritage* and *patrimoine*, linking the former with private property and individual or small group responsibility and defining the latter as "large-scale heritage" for which questions of responsibility are more fluid and contested. Furthermore, the etymology of *patrimonialization* highlights the role of the nation (French *patrie*), an aspect that is central to the argument I develop in these pages but gets lost in the English *heritage*. Regina Bendix, "Héritage et patrimoine: de leurs proximités sémantiques et de leurs implications," in *Le patrimoine culturel immatériel*, ed. Chiara Bortolotto, Annick Arnaud, and Sylvie Grenet (Paris: Maison des Sciences de l'Homme, 2011), 99–121.
53. Brian Graham, G. J. Ashworth, and J. E. Tunbridge, *A Geography of Heritage: Power, Culture, and Economy* (London: Arnold; New York: Oxford University Press, 2000).
54. Anna Lowenhaupt Tsing, *Friction: An Ethnography of Global Connection* (Princeton, NJ: Princeton University Press, 2004), xi.
55. Ernesto Laclau, *Emancipation(s)* (London: Verso, 1996), 36–46.
56. I develop the history of the Festival Gwoka as an example of anticolonial tourism in Jerome Camal, "DestiNation: The Festival Gwoka, Tourism, and Anti-Colonialism," in *Sea, Sun, and Sound: Music and Tourism in the Circum-Caribbean*, ed. Timothy Rommen and Daniel T. Neely (Oxford: Oxford University Press, 2014).
57. Lyannaj pou gwoka, *Présentation du projet: Gwadloup ansanm pour l'inscription du gwoka sur la Liste représentative du patrimoine culturel immatériel de l'humanité de l'UNESCO* (2012), 42. Although France ratified the ICH convention in 2006, it had been

Notes to Pages 164–169 / 209

involved in the Masterpieces of the Oral and Intangible Heritage of Humanity program since 2001.

58. A Cuban participant had been invited but was forced to cancel at the last minute due to delays in processing her visa application.

59. Interview with the author, 18 July 2013.

60. In January 2008, Cotellon was invited to participate in the capacity of expert in the meeting of a UNESCO-sponsored subsidiary committee reflecting on the implementation of the ICHC's operational directives. He has since identified himself as *expert UNESCO pour la sauvegarde du patrimoine culturel immatériel* (UNESCO expert for the safeguarding of intangible cultural heritage).

61. Glissant, *Discours antillais*, 48.

62. Interview with the author, 7 July 2012.

63. Svetlana Boym, "On Diasporic Intimacy: Ilya Kabakov's Installations and Immigrant Homes," *Critical Inquiry* 24, no. 2 (1998): 43.

64. Interview with the author, 6 July 2012. I do not want to dismiss the work of the Kolektif pou gwoka, which has raised many important issues regarding the institutionalization of gwoka, such as the impact it will have on intellectual property rights for gwoka composers. Unfortunately, space constraints keep me from fully dealing with this aspect of the zone of awkward engagement.

65. Interview with the author, 18 July 2013.

66. These quotes are taken from the English language application, compiled and translated by members of the Lyannaj.

67. Interview with the author, 7 July 2012.

68. Interview with the author, 18 July 2013.

69. Interview with the author, 18 July 2013.

70. The concept of postnationalism emerged in the 1990s as scholars considered the impact of globalization on the nation-state as well as the specific consequence of the emergence of the European Union on state sovereignty. See Arjun Appadurai, *Modernity at Large: Cultural Dimensions of Globalization* (Minneapolis: University of Minnesota Press, 1996); Appadurai, "Sovereignty without Territoriality: Notes for a Postnational Geography," in *The Geography of Identity*, ed. Patricia Yaeger (Ann Arbor: University of Michigan Press, 1996): 40–58; Ignacio Corona and Alejandro Madrid, eds., *Postnational Musical Identities: Cultural Production, Distribution, and Consumption in a Globalized World* (Lanham, MD: Lexington Books, 2008); Jürgen Habermas, *The Postnational Constellation: Political Essays*, trans. Max Pensky (Cambridge, MA: MIT Press, 2001); John-Carlos Rowes, ed., *Post-Nationalist American Studies* (Berkeley: University of California Press, 2000). Although very much informed by her work, my own understanding of the term reaches beyond Shalini Puri's stark contrast between of *postnationalism* and *transnationalism*. The entanglement of nationalism, statehood, and sovereignty deserves to be explored further, with attention paid to the specifics of (post)coloniality in addition to the general effects of neoliberalism. Puri, *Caribbean Postcolonial*, 6. For an example of the instrumentalization of heritage as a tool of state making for a nonsovereign territory, see De Cesari, "Creative Heritage: Palestinian Heritage Ngos and Defiant Arts of Government," *American Anthropologist* 112, no. 4 (2010): 625–37.

71. Personal communication, July 2012.

72. Lyannaj pou gwoka, *Présentation du projet*, 22.

73. This changed to a large degree in April 2014 when the Association of Caribbean States conferred the status of associate member on both Guadeloupe and Martinique,

210 / Notes to Pages 170–176

thus making it possible for the islands to represent themselves directly within the association.

74. Marc Askew, "The Magic List of Global Status: UNESCO, World Heritage and the Agendas of States," in *Heritage and Globalisation*, ed. Sophia Labadi and Colin Long (New York: Routledge, 2010), 19–44; Janet Blake, "UNESCO's 2003 *Convention on Intangible Cultural Heritage*: The Implications of Community Involvement in 'Safeguarding,'" in *Intangible Heritage*, ed. Laurajane Smith and Natsuko Akagawa (London: Routledge, 2009), 46; Luc Charles-Dominique, "La patrimonialisation des formes musicales et artistiques: Anthropologie d'une notion problématique," *Ethnologies* 35, no. 1 (2013): 84–86; Barbara Kirshenblatt-Gimblett, "Theorizing Heritage," *Ethnomusicology* 39, no. 3 (1995): 367–80; Barbara Kirshenblatt Gimblett, "Intangible Heritage as Metacultural Production," *Museum international* 56, nos. 1–2 (2004): 52–65; Jessica Roda, "Des judéo-espagnols à la machine Unesquienne: Enjeux et défis de la patrimonialisation musicale," *Cahiers d'ethnomusicologie*, no. 24 (2011): 123–41.

75. Laurent-Sébastien Fournier, "Intangible Cultural Heritage in France: From State Culture to Local Development," in *Heritage Regimes and the State*, ed. Regina Bendix, Aditya Eggert, and Arnika Peselmann (Göttingen: Universitätsverlag Göttingen, 2013), 327.

76. Fournier, 333.

77. Olivier Goré, "Le géosymbole, vecteur de la territorialité régionale : L'exemple du fest-noz en Bretagne," *Norois* 198 (2008): 21–33.

78. Françoise Vergès, *Le ventre des femmes: Capitalisme, racialisation, féminisme* (Paris: Albin Michel, 2017), 13, my translation.

79. This is the common ground that can bring Guadeloupean activists together with the French state.

80. The Agenda 21 for Culture is a program developed and managed by United Cities and Local Governments that promotes culture as the fourth pilar of sustainable development and governance, in addition to the three pillars of environment, social inclusion, and economics promoted by the UNESCO's Agenda 21.

81. Laclau, *Emancipation(s)*, 44.

82. Glissant, *Discours antillais*, 53.

83. Barnor Hesse, "Symptomatically Black: A Creolization of the Political," in *The Creolization of Theory*, ed. Françoise Lionnet and Shu-mei Shih (Durham, NC: Duke University Press, 2011).

84. Gary Wilder, *The French Imperial Nation-State: Negritude and Colonial Humanism between the Two World Wars* (Chicago: University of Chicago Press, 2005).

85. Hesse, "Symptomatically Black," locs. 507–9.

86. Glissant, *Discours antillais*, 56.

CODA

1. Fred Moten, *In the Break: The Aesthetics of the Black Radical Tradition* (Minneapolis: University of Minnesota Press, 2003), 5, 258.

2. Jack Halberstam, "The Wild Beyond: With and for the Undercommons," in *The Undercommons: Fugitive Planning and Black Study*, ed. Stefano Harney and Fred Moten (Wivenhoe, UK: Minor Compositions, 2013), 11.

3. Léna Blou, *Techni'Ka: Recherches sur l'émergence d'une méthode d'enseignement à partir des danses gwo-ka* (Pointe-à-Pitre: Éditions Jasor, 2005), 33.

DISCOGRAPHY

All these recordings were released as CDs, unless otherwise noted. Many are self-published. Some of these CDs are also available through streaming services online.

Coco, Dominik. *Lèspri kaskòd*. Golèt Musik, DHP 034-2, 2008.

Conquette, Guy, with Emilien Antile. *Patrimwàn, vol. 1*. Disques Debs, CDD 26-72-2, n.d.

Cosaque, Erick. *Musique, voix, percussion*. N.p., 1984.

———. *Twa set*. Aztec Musique, CM2226, 2009.

Kan'nida. *Kyenzenn*. Indigo France, 2001. Digital download.

Konket, Guy, and the Groupe ka. *Guy Konket et le Groupe ka*. Éditions Bolibana, BIP-96, n.d.

Lockel, Gérard. *Gwo KA MODÈNN en concert*. N.p., 1997.

Lockel, Gérard. *Gérard Lockel présente des extraits de concerts tirés d'archives de 1969 à 1990*. ADGKM, 2012. 8 CD box set.

Loyson, Robert. *Nostalgie caraïbes*. Disques Célini, 5524.2, 2007.

Monza, Wozan. *RExistans*. Debs Music, 2011.

———. *Maux phrasés*. N.p., WOZ003, 2016.

Murray, David. *Creole*. Justin Time Records, 1998.

Murray, David, and the Gwo-Ka Masters. *Yonn-dé*. Justin Time Records, 2002.

———. *Gwotet*. Justin Time Records, 2004.

———. *The Devil Tried to Kill Me*. Justin Time Records, 2009.

Schwarz-Bart, Jacques. *Soné ka-la*. Universal Music France, 2006.

———. *Abyss*. Universal Music Jazz France, 2008.

———. *Jazz Racine Haïti*. Motéma, 2014.

Soft. *Kadans a peyi-la*. Aztec Musique, 2005.

———. *Konfyans*. Aztec Musique, 2009.

———. *Partout étranger*. Aztec Musique, 2007.

———. *Ti gwadloupéyien*. Aztec Music, 2017.

Tumblack. *Tumblack*. Barclay, 1978. One LP.

Vélo and Guy Conquête. *Nostalgie caraïbes*. Disques Célini, 011-2, 2008.

BIBLIOGRAPHY

Abenon, Lucien-René. *Petite histoire de la Guadeloupe*. Paris: L'Harmattan, 2000.

Abou, Antoine. "L'école et ses débats." In *La Guadeloupe, 1875-1914: Les soubresauts d'une société pluri-ethnique ou les ambiguités de l'assimilation*, edited by Henriette Levillain, 59–75. Paris: Éditions Autrement, 1994.

Adélaïde-Merlande, Jacques. *Histoire contemporaine de la Caraïbe et des Guyanes, de 1945 à nos jours*. Paris: Karthala, 2002.

Agawu, Kofi. "Contesting Difference: A Critique of Africanist Ethnomusicology." In *The Cultural Study of Music: A Critical Introduction*, edited by Martin Clayton, Trevor Herbert, and Richard Middleton, 117–26. New York: Routledge, 2003.

———. "Tonality as a Colonizing Force in Africa." In *Audible Empire: Music, Global Politics, Critique*, edited by Ronald Radano and Tejumola Olaniyan, 334–56. Durham, NC: Duke University Press, 2016.

AGEG. *Rapport culturel, 9ème Congrès*. Paris: AGEG, 1970.

———. *Nou toujou doubout: Guadeloupe, 1635-1971*. Paris: AGEG, 1981.

Amselle, Jean-Loup. *L'ethnicisation de la France*. Paris: Nouvelles éditions lignes, 2011.

Amselle, Jean-Loup, and Elikia M'Bokolo. *Au cœur de l'ethnie: Ethnie, tribalisme et état en Afrique*. Paris: La Découverte, 1985.

Anderson, Benedict. *Imagined Communities: Reflections on the Origin and Spread of Nationalism*. London: Verso, 2006.

Anselin, Alain. *L'émigration antillaise en France: La troisième île*. Paris: Éditions Karthala, 1990.

———. "West Indians in France." In *French and West Indian: Martinique, Guadeloupe, and Guiana Today*, edited by Richard D. E. Burton and Fred Reno. London: Macmillan, 1995.

Appadurai, Arjun. *Modernity at Large: Cultural Dimensions of Globalization*. Minneapolis: University of Minnesota Press, 1996.

———. "Sovereignty without Territoriality: Notes for a Postnational Geography." In *The Geography of Identity*, edited by Patricia Yaeger, 40–58. Ann Arbor: University of Michigan Press, 1996.

Appiah, Anthony. *Cosmopolitanism: Ethics in a World of Strangers*. New York: W. W. Norton & Co., 2006.

Askew, Marc. "The Magic List of Global Status: UNESCO, World Heritage and the Agendas of States." In *Heritage and Globalisation*, edited by Sophia Labadi and Colin Long, 19–44. New York: Routledge, 2010.

214 / Bibliography

Attali, Jacques. *Bruits: Essais sur l'économie politique de la musique*. Paris: Presses universitaires de France, 1977.

Austerlitz, Paul. *Merengue: Dominican Music and Dominican Identity*. Philadelphia: Temple University Press, 1997.

Balibar, Étienne, and Immanuel Wallerstein. *Race, Nation, Class: Ambiguous Identities*. London: Verso, 1991.

Bangou, Henri. *Aliénation et désaliénation dans les sociétés post-esclavagistes: Le cas de la Guadeloupe*. Paris: L'Harmattan, 1997.

Barrett, Lindon. *Blackness and Value: Seeing Double*. Cambridge: Cambridge University Press, 1999.

Bébel-Gislert, Dany. *Le défi culturel guadeloupéen: Devenir ce que nous sommes*. Paris: Éditions caribéennes, 1989.

Bendix, Regina. "Héritage et patrimoine: De leurs proximités sémantiques et de leurs implications." In *Le patrimoine culturel immatériel*, edited by Chiara Bortolotto, Annick Arnaud, and Sylvie Grenet, 99–121. Paris: Maison des sciences de l'homme, 2011.

Beriss, David. *Black Skins, French Voices: Caribbean Ethnicity and Activism in Urban France*. Boulder, CO: Westview Press, 2004.

———. "Culture-as-Race or Culture-as-Culture: Caribbean Ethnicity and the Ambiguity of Cultural Identity in French Society." *French Politics, Culture & Society* 18, no. 3 (2000): 18–47.

Berlant, Lauren. *The Anatomy of National Fantasy: Hawthorne, Utopia, and Everyday Life*. Chicago: University of Chicago Press, 1991.

Bernabé, Jean, Patrick Chamoiseau, and Raphaël Confiant. *Éloge de la créolité (In Praise of Creoleness)*. Paris: Gallimard, 1989.

Berrian, Brenda F. *Awakening Spaces: French Caribbean Popular Songs, Music, and Culture*. Chicago: University of Chicago Press, 2000.

Bhabha, Homi K. "Unsatisfied: Notes on Vernacular Cosmopolitanism." In *Text and Nation: Cross-Disciplinary Essays on Cultural and National Identities*, edited by Laura García-Moreno and Peter C. Pfeiffer, 191–207. Rochester, NY: Camden House, 1996.

Blake, Janet. "UNESCO's 2003 *Convention on Intangible Cultural Heritage*: The Implications of Community Involvement in 'safeguarding.'" In *Intangible Heritage*, edited by Laurajane Smith and Natsuko Akagawa, 45–73. London: Routledge, 2009.

Blou, Léna. *Techni'ka: Recherches sur l'émergence d'une méthode d'enseignement à partir des danses gwo-ka*. Pointe-à-Pitre: Éditions Jasor, 2005.

Bobin, Frédéric. "Les Indépendantistes, d'outre-mer se muent in gestionnaires." *Le Monde*, 31 October 1994.

Boehmer, Elleke. "Networks of Resistance." In *The Post-Colonial Studies Reader*, edited by Bill Ashcroft, Gareth Griffiths, and Helen Tiffin, 113–15. London: Routledge, 2006.

Bolland, O. Nigel. "Creolisation and Creole Societies: A Cultural Nationalist View of Caribbean Social History." *Caribbean Quarterly* 44, nos. 1–2 (1998): 1–32.

Bonilla, Yarimar. *Non-Sovereign Futures: French Caribbean Politics in the Wake of Disenchantment*. Chicago: University of Chicago Press, 2015.

———. "Nonsovereign Futures? French Caribbean Politics in the Wake of Disenchantment." In *Caribbean Sovereignty, Democracy, and Development in an Age of Globalization*, edited by Lewis Linden, 208–27. New York: Routledge, 2012.

Bourdieu, Pierre, and Loïc Wacquant. "On the Cunning of Imperialist Reason." *Theory, Culture & Society* 16, no. 1 (1999): 41–58.

Boym, Svetlana. "On Diasporic Intimacy: Ilya Kabakov's Installations and Immigrant Homes." *Critical Inquiry* 24, no. 2 (1998): 498–524.

———. *The Future of Nostalgia*. New York: Basic Books, 2001.

Braflan-Trobo, Patricia. *Conflits sociaux en Guadeloupe: Histoire, identité et culture dans les grèves en Guadeloupe*. Paris: L'Harmattan, 2007.

Brathwaite, Kamau. *The Development of Creole Society in Jamaica, 1770–1820*. Oxford, UK: Clarendon Press, 1971.

Britton, Celia. *Édouard Glissant and Postcolonial Theory: Strategies of Language and Resistance*. Charlottesville: University of Virginia Press, 1999.

Bromberger, Christian. "'Patrimoine immatériel' entre ambiguités et overdose." *L'homme* 209 (2014): 143–52.

Browning, Barbara. *Infectious Rhythm: Metaphors of Contagion and the Spread of African Culture*. New York: Routledge, 1998.

Burton, Richard D. E. *Afro-Creole: Power, Opposition, and Play in the Caribbean*. Ithaca, NY: Cornell University Press, 1997.

———. "The French West Indies *à l'heure de l'Europe*: An Overview." In *French and West Indian: Martinique, Guadeloupe, and Guiana Today*, edited by Richard D. E. Burton and Fred Reno, 1–19. London: Macmillan, 1995.

———. "The Idea of Difference in Contemporary French West Indian Thought: *Négritude, antillanité, créolité*." In *French and West Indian: Martinique, Guadeloupe, and Guiana Today*, edited by Richard D. E. Burton and Fred Reno, 137–66. London: Macmillan, 1995.

Camal, Jerome. "Creolizing Jazz, Jazzing the *Tout-Monde*: Jazz, Gwoka, and the Poetics of Relation." In *American Creoles: The Francophone Caribbean and the American South*, edited by Martin Munro and Celia Britton, 165–79. Liverpool, UK: Liverpool University Press, 2012.

———. "DestiNation: The Festival Gwoka, Tourism, and Anti-Colonialism." In *Sea, Sun, and Sound: Music and Tourism in the Circum-Caribbean*, edited by Timothy Rommen and Daniel T. Neely, 213–237. Oxford: Oxford University Press, 2014.

———. "From Gwoka Modèn to Jazz Ka: Music, Nationalism, and Creolization in Guadeloupe." PhD diss., Washington University in Saint Louis, 2011.

———. "Putting the Drum in Conundrum: Guadeloupean Gwoka, Intangible Cultural Heritage, and Postnationalism." *International Journal of Heritage Studies* 22, no. 5 (2016): 395–410.

Cañires-Esguerra, Jorge. "Creole Colonial Spanish America." In *Creolization: History, Ethnography, Theory*, edited by Charles Stewart, 26–45. Walnut Creek, CA: West Coast Press, 2007.

Carnot and Marie-Céline Lafontaine. *Alors ma chère, moi*. Paris: Éditions caribéennes, 1986.

Castaldo, Christian, ed. *Codes noirs: De l'esclavage aux abolitions*. Paris: Dalloz, 2006.

Céleste, Chérubin. "Chretien, donc indépendantiste: Entretien avec Chérubin Céleste." *Les temps modernes* 39, nos. 441–42 (1983): 1946–60.

Certeau, Michel de. *L'invention du quotidien 1: Arts de faire*. Paris: Union générale de l'édition, 1980.

Charles-Dominique, Luc. "La patrimonialisation des formes musicales et artistiques: Anthropologie d'une notion problématique." *Ethnologies* 35, no. 1 (2013): 75–101.

Chatterjee, Partha. *Nationalist Thought and the Colonial World: A Derivative Discourse?* London: Zed Books for the United Nations University, 1986.

———. *The Nation and Its Fragments: Colonial and Postcolonial Histories*. Princeton, NJ: Princeton University Press, 1993.

Chivallon, Christine. "Beyond Gilroy's Black Atlantic: The Experience of the African Diaspora." *Diaspora* 11, no. 3 (2002): 359–82.

216 / Bibliography

———. "De quelques préconstruits de la notion de diaspora à partir de l'exemple antillais." *Revue européenne des migrations internationales* 13, no. 1 (1997): 149–60.

Clifford, James. *The Predicament of Culture: Twentieth-Century Ethnography, Literature, and Art.* Cambridge, MA: Harvard University Press, 1988.

Cohen, Robin. "Creolization and Diaspora: The Cultural Politics of Divergence and Some Convergence." In *Opportunity Structures in Diaspora Relations: Comparisons in Contemporary Multilevel Politics of Diaspora and Transnational Identity,* edited by Gloria P. Totoricaguena, 85–112. Reno, NV: Center for Basque Studies, University of Nevada Press, 2007.

Collectif des patriotes guadeloupéens, ed. *Pour servir l'histoire et la mémoire guadeloupéenne: Mai 1967* Sainte-Anne, Guadeloupe: Co.Pa.Gua., 2003.

Comaroff, Jean, and John Comaroff, eds. *Modernity and Its Malcontents: Ritual and Power in Postcolonial Africa.* Chicago: University of Chicago Press, 1993.

Crichlow, Michaeline, and Patricia Northover. *Globalization and the Post-Creole Imagination: Notes on Fleeing the Plantation.* Durham, NC: Duke University Press, 2009.

Curtius, Anny Dominique. "Utopies du BUMIDOM: Construire l'avenir dans un 'là-bas' postcontact." *French Forum* 35, nos. 2–3 (2010): 135–55.

Cyrille, Dominique. "Creole Quadrilles of Guadeloupe, Dominica, Martinique, and Saint Lucia." In *Creolizing Contradance in the Caribbean,* edited by Peter Manuel, 188–208. Philadelphia: Temple University Press, 2011.

Dahomay, Christian. *Métòd ka.* Guadeloupe: n.p., 1997.

Daniel, Justin. "The Construction of Dependency: Economy and Politics in the French Antilles." In *Islands at the Crossroads: Politics in the Non-Independent Caribbean,* edited by Aarón Gamaliele Ramos and Angel Israel Rivera, 61–79. Kingston, Jamaica: Ian Randle Publishers, 2001.

Daoudi, Bouziane. "Soft, plus dur qu'il n'y parait." *Libération* (Paris), 24 November 2007.

Dash, J. Michael. *Édouard Glissant.* Cambridge: Cambridge University Press, 1995.

Daughtry, J. Martin. *Listening to War: Sound, Music, Trauma, and Survival in Wartime Iraq.* New York: Oxford University Press, 2015.

Delhaye, Eric. "Le jazz français discrimine-t-il les musiciens antillais?" *Télérama,* 25 April 2018. https://www.telerama.fr/musique/le-jazz-francais-discrimine-t-il-les-musiciens -antillais,n5621362.php?utm_campaign=Echobox&utm_medium=Social&utm _source=Facebook&link_time=1524671955#link_time=1524671793.

Derrida, Jacques. *L'écriture et la différence.* Paris: Éditions du Seuil, 1967.

———. *Le monolinguisme de l'autre.* Paris: Éditions Galilée, 1996.

Dixon Gottschild, Brenda. "Crossroads, Continuities, and Contradictions: The Afro-Euro Triangle." In *Caribbean Dance from Abakuá to Zouk: How Movement Shapes Identity,* edited by Susanna Sloat, 3–10. Gainesville: University Press of Florida, 2002.

"Dossier No. 1: Les grandes dates du mouvement syndical." *Ja Ka Ta,* May 1980.

Dubois, Laurent. "Solitude's Statue: Confronting the Past in the French Caribbean." *Outremers* 93, no. 350 (2006): 27–38.

Du Bois, W. E. B. *The Souls of Black Folk.* New York: Penguin, 1996.

Dudley, Shannon. *Music from Behind the Bridge: Steelband Aesthetics and Politics in Trinidad and Tobago.* New York: Oxford University Press, 2007.

Dugoujon, Abbé. *Lettres sur l'esclavage dans les colonies françaises.* Paris: Pagnerre, éditeur, 1845.

Du Tertre, Jean-Baptiste. *Histoire générale des isles de S. Christophe, de la Guadeloupe, de la Martinique et autres dans l'Amérique.* Paris: Jacques Langlois, 1654.

Edwards, Brent Hayes. *The Practice of Diaspora: Literature, Translation, and the Rise of Black Internationalism.* Cambridge, MA: Harvard University Press, 2003.

Bibliography / 217

Ellis, Nadia. *Territories of the Soul: Queered Belonging in the Black Diaspora*. Durham, NC: Duke University Press, 2015.

Epstein, Dena J. "African Music in British and French America." *Musical Quarterly* 59, no. 1 (1973): 61–91.

Erlmann, Veit. "Communities of Style: Musical Figures of Black Diasporic Identity." In *The African Diaspora: A Musical Perspective*, edited by Ingrid Monson, 83–100. London: Routledge, 2003.

———. *Reason and Resonance: A History of Modern Aurality*. New York: Zone Books, 2014.

Fallope, Josette. "La politique d'assimilation et ses resistances." In *La Guadeloupe, 1875-1914: Les soubresauts d'une société pluri-ethnique ou les ambiguités de l'assimilation*, edited by Henriette Levillain, 34–47. Paris: Éditions Autrement, 1994.

Fanon, Frantz. *Peau noire, masques blancs*. Paris: Points Essais, 1971.

———. *The Wretched of the Earth*. New York: Grove Press, 2005.

Faruggia, Laurent. *Le fait national guadeloupéen*. Ivry-sur-Seine: n.p., 1968.

Farrugia, Laurent, and Hector Poullet. *Tous les hommes sont des créoles*. Paris: Éditions art, 2006.

Fassin, Didier, and Eric Fassin, eds. *De la question sociale à la question raciale: Représenter la société français*. Paris: La Découverte, 2006.

Feld, Steven. *Jazz Cosmopolitanism in Accra: Five Musical Years in Ghana*. Durham, NC: Duke University Press, 2012.

———. "Notes on 'World Beat.'" In *Music Grooves: Essays and Dialogue*, edited by Steven Feld and Charles Kiel, 238–46. Chicago: University of Chicago Press, 1994.

Fischlin, Daniel, Ajay Heble, and George Lipsitz. "Improvisation and Encounter: Rights in the Key of Rifference." In *The Fierce Urgency of Now: Improvisation, Rights, and the Ethics of Cocreation*, 57–97. Durham, NC: Duke University Press, 2013.

Floyd, Samuel A. *The Power of Black Music: Interpreting Its History from Africa to the United States*. New York: Oxford University Press, 1996.

Floyd, Samuel A., Jr., and Ronald Radano. "Interpreting the African-American Musical Past: A Dialogue." *Black Music Research Journal* (2009): 1–10.

Fournier, Laurent-Sébastien. "Intangible Cultural Heritage in France: From State Culture to Local Development." In *Heritage Regimes and the State*, edited by Regina Bendix, Aditya Eggert, and Arnika Peselmann, 327–40. Göttingen: Universitätsverlag Göttingen, 2013.

Frith, Simon, ed. *World Music, Politics and Social Change: Papers from the International Association for the Study of Popular Music*. Music and Society Series. Manchester: Manchester University Press, 1991.

Gabaly, Joslen. *Diadyéé: Gwoka*. Abymes, Guadeloupe: Créapub', 2003.

Gallagher, Mary. "The *Créolité* Movement: Paradoxes of a French Caribbean Orthodoxy." In *Creolization: History, Ethnography, Theory*, edited by Charles Stewart, 220–36. Walnut Creek, CA: Left Coast Press, 2007.

Gama, Raymond, and Jean-Pierre Sainton. *Mé 67: Mémoire d'un évènement*. Pointe-à-Pitre: Société guadeloupéenne d'édition et de diffusion, 1985.

Gilroy, Paul. *After Empire: Melancholia or Convivial Culture?* London: Routledge, 2004.

———. *The Black Atlantic: Modernity and Double-Consciousness*. Cambridge, MA: Harvard University Press, 1993.

Glissant, Édouard. *Caribbean Discourse: Selected Essays*. Translated by J. Michael Dash. Charlottesville: University of Virginia Press, 1999.

Glissant, Édouard. *Discours antillais*. Paris: Gallimard, 1997.

———. *Introduction à une poétique du divers*. Gallimard, 1996.

218 / Bibliography

————. *Poétique de la Relation*. Paris: Gallimard, 1990.

————. *Traité du Tout-Monde*. Paris: Gallimard, 1997.

————. *Tout-Monde*. Paris: Gallimard, 1993.

Glissant, Édouard, and Patrick Chamoiseau. *L'intraitable beauté du monde: Adresse à Barack Obama*. Paris: Éditions Galaade, 2009.

Goré, Olivier. "Le géosymbole, vecteur de la territorialité régionale: L'exemple du Fest-Noz en Bretagne." *Norois* 198 (2008): 21–33.

Graham, Brian, G. J. Ashworth, and J. E. Tunbridge. *A Geography of Heritage: Power, Culture, and Economy*. London: Arnold; New York: Oxford University Press, 2000.

Granier de Cassagnac, Adolphe. *Voyages aux Antilles françaises, anglaises, danoises, espagnoles; à Saint Domingue et aux États-Unis d'Amérique. Première partie, Les Antilles françaises*. Paris: Dauvin et Fontaines Librairies, 1842.

Guérin, Daniel. *Les Antilles décolonisées*. Paris: Présence africaine, 1956.

Gueye, Abdoulaye. "De la diaspora noire: Enseignements du contexte français." *Revue européenne des migrations internationales* 22, no. 1 (2009): 11–33.

Guilbault, Jocelyne. "Audible Entanglements: Nation and Diasporas in Trinidad's Calypso Music Scene." *Small Axe* 9, no. 1 (2005): 40–63.

————. "Créolité and the New Cultural Politics of Difference in Popular Music of the French West Indies." *Black Music Research Journal* 14, no. 2 (1994): 161–78.

————. *Zouk: World Music in the West Indies*. Chicago: University of Chicago Press, 1993.

Gupta, Akhil. "The Song of the Nonaligned World: Transnational Identities and the Reinscription of Space in Late Capitalism." *Cultural Anthropology* 7, no. 1 (1992): 63–79.

Habermas, Jürgen. *The Postnational Constellation: Political Essays*. Translated by Max Pensky. Cambridge, MA: MIT Press, 2001.

Halberstam, Jack. "The Wild Beyond: With and for the Undercommons." In *The Undercommons: Fugitive Planning and Black Study*, edited by Stefano Harney and Fred Moten, 2–12. Wivenhoe, UK: Minor Compositions, 2013.

Hall, Stuart. "*Créolité* and the Process of Creolization." In *The Creolization Reader: Studies in Mixed Identities and Cultures*, edited by Robin Cohen and Paola Toninato, 26–38. New York: Routledge, 2009.

————. "Cultural Identity and Diaspora." In *Identity: Community, Culture, Difference*, edited by Jonathan Rutherford, 222–37. London: Lawrence and Wishart, 1990.

————. "Whose Heritage? Un-Settling the Heritage, Re-Imagining the Post-Nation." In *The Politics of Heritage, the Legacies of "Race,"* edited by Jo Littler and Roshi Naidoo, 23–35. New York: Routledge, 2005.

Hannerz, Ulf. "The World in Creolisation." *Africa: Journal of the International African Institute* 57, no. 4 (1987): 546–59.

Hardt, Michael, and Antonio Negri. *Empire*. Cambridge, MA: Harvard University Press, 2001.

Hartman, Saidiya. *Scenes of Subjection: Terror, Slavery, and Self-Making in Nineteenth-Century America*. New York: Oxford University Press, 1997.

Herzfeld, Michael. *Cultural Intimacy: Social Poetics in the Nation-State*. London: Routledge, 2004.

Hesse, Barnor. "Symptomatically Black: A Creolization of the Political." In *The Creolization of Theory*, edited by Françoise Lionnet, and Shu-mei Shih, 37–61. Durham, NC: Duke University Press, 2011.

Hill, Edwin C. *Black Soundscapes, White Stages: The Meaning of Francophone Sounds in the Black Atlantic*. Baltimore: Johns Hopkins University Press, 2013.

Hintjens, Helen. "Constitutional and Political Change in the French Caribbean." In *French and West Indian: Martinique, Guadeloupe, and Guiana Today*, edited by Richard D. E. Burton and Fred Reno, 20–33. London: Macmillan, 1995.

Bibliography / 219

Hobsbawm, Eric, and Terence Ranger, eds. *The Invention of Tradition* Cambridge: Cambridge University Press, 1983.

Hurston, Zora Neale. *Of Mules and Men.* New York: Harper's Perennial Modern Classics, 1935.

Hutchinson, John. "Cultural Nationalism and Moral Regeneration." In *Nationalism,* edited by John Hutchinson and Anthony D. Smith, 122–31. Oxford: Oxford University Press, 1994.

Jelly-Schapiro, Joshua. "'Are We All Creoles Now?' Ethnicity and Nation in a Heterogeneous Caribbean Diaspora." In *Ethnicity, Class, and Nationalism: Caribbean and Extra-Caribbean Dimensions,* edited by Anton L. Allahar, 23–55. Lanham, MD: Lexington Books, 2005.

Johnson, Paul Christopher. *Diaspora Conversions: Black Carib Religion and the Recovery of Africa.* Berkeley: University of California Press, 2007.

Jones, Leroi. *Blues People: Negro Music in White America.* New York: Perennial, 1999.

Khan, Aisha. *Callaloo Nation: Metaphors of Race and Religious Identity among South Asians in Trinidad.* Durham, NC: Duke University Press, 2004.

———. "Creolization Moments." In *Creolization: History, Ethnography, Theory,* edited by Charles Stewart, 237–53. Walnut Creek, CA: Left Coast Press, 2007.

Kirshenblatt-Gimblett, Barbara. "Intangible Heritage as Metacultural Production." *Museum International* 56, nos. 1–2 (2004): 52–65.

———. "Theorizing Heritage." *Ethnomusicology* 39, no. 3 (1995): 367–80.

Labat, Jean-Baptiste. *Nouveau voyage aux isles de l'Amerique: Contenant l'histoire naturelle de ces pays, l'origine, les mœurs, la religion & le gouvernement des habitans anciens & modernes: les guerres & les evenemens singuliers qui y sont arrivez pendant le séjour que l'auteur y a fait.* Paris: Chez Théodore Le Gras, 1742.

Labesse, Patrick. "Fred Deshayes: 'La Guadeloupe est responsable de son naufrage.'" *Le Monde,* 18 March 2006.

Laclau, Ernesto. *Emancipation(s).* London: Verso, 1996.

———. *On Populist Reason.* London: Verso, 2007.

Lafontaine, Marie-Céline. "Le Carnaval de l''autre': A propos d' 'authenticité' en matière de musique guadeloupéenne: Théories et réalités." *Les temps modernes* 39, nos. 441–42 (1983): 2126–73.

———. "Unité et diversité des musiques traditionnelles guadeloupéennes." In *Les musiques guadeloupéennes dans le champs culturel afro-américain, au sein des musiques du monde,* 71–92. Paris: Éditions caribéennes, 1988.

Lanoir-L'Etang, Luciani. *Réseaux de solidarité dans la Guadeloupe d'hier et d'aujourd'hui.* Paris: L'Harmattan, 2005.

Largey, Michael D. *Vodou Nation: Haitian Art Music and Cultural Nationalism.* Chicago: University of Chicago Press, 2006.

Latour, Bruno. *Reassembling the Social: An Introduction to Actor-Network-theory.* New York: Oxford University Press, 2005.

Laumuno, Marie-Héléna. *Gwoka et politique en Guadeloupe: 1960-2003: 40 ans de construction du "pays."* Paris: L'Harmattan, 2011.

Léonard, Nicolas Germain. *Œuvres de Léonard.* Vol. 1. Paris: Imprimerie de Didot Jeune, 1797.

Lionnet, Françoise. "Cosmopolitan or Creole Lives? Globalized Oceans and Insular Identities." *Profession* (2011): 23–43.

Lionnet, Françoise, and Shu-mei Shih, eds. *Minor Transnationalism* Durham, NC: Duke University Press, 2005.

220 / Bibliography

Lockel, Gérard. *Gro ka modên*. N.p.: Guadeloupe disques, 1976.

———. *Gwo-ka modèn*. Baie-Mahault, Guadeloupe: ADGKM, 2011.

———. *Gwo ka modènn: 1969–1989, vingt ans de lutte sur le front de la culture guadeloupéenne*. Baie-Mahault, Guadeloupe: ADGKM, 1989.

———. "Lolo Camphrin: Un des derniers grands danseurs de gro ka." *Ja Ka Ta*, February 1978.

———. *Traité de gro ka modên*. Baie-Mahault, Guadeloupe: n.p., 1981.

Loichot, Valérie. "Creolizing Barack Obama." In *American Creoles: The Francophone Caribbean and the American South*, edited by Martin Munro and Celia Britton, 77–94. Liverpool, UK: Liverpool University Press, 2012.

Longin, Félix. *Voyage à la Guadeloupe: Œuvre posthume*. Le Mans, France: Monnoyer, 1848.

Lyannaj pou gwoka. *Présentation du projet: Gwadloup Ansanm pour l'inscription du gwoka sur la liste représentative du patrimoine culturel immatériel de l'humanité de l'UNESCO*. 2012.

Mangin, Timothy R. "Notes on Jazz in Senegal." In *Uptown Conversation: The New Jazz Studies*, edited by Robert O'Meally, Brent Hayes Edwards, and Farah Jasmine Griffin, 224–48. New York: Columbia University Press, 2004.

Manuel, Peter, Kenneth Bilby, and Michael Largey. *Caribbean Currents: Caribbean Music from Rumba to Reggae*. Philadelphia: Temple University Press, 2016.

Martin, Denis-Constant. "Can Jazz Be Rid of the Racial Imagination? Creolization, Racial Discourse and Semiology of Music." *Black Music Research Journal* 28, no. 2 (2008): 105–23.

Maultsby, Portia K. "Africanisms in African-American Music." In *Africanisms in American Culture*, edited by Joseph E. Holloway, 185–210. Bloomington: Indiana University Press, 1990.

McDonald, David A. *My Voice Is My Weapon: Music, Nationalism, and the Poetics of Palestinian Resistance*. Durham, NC: Duke University Press, 2013.

Miles, William. "Fifty Years of Assimilation: Assessing France's Experience of Caribbean Decolonisation through Administrative Reform." In *Islands at the Crossroads: Politics in the Non-Independent Caribbean*, edited by Aarón Gamaliele Ramos and Angel Israel Rivera, 45–60. Kingston, Jamaica: Ian Randle Publishers, 2001.

Mintz, Sidney W., and Richard Price. *The Birth of African-American Culture: An Anthropological Perspective*. Boston: Beacon Press, 1992.

Monson, Ingrid, ed. *The African Diaspora: A Musical Perspective* London: Routledge, 2003.

Moore, Robin D. *Nationalizing Blackness: Afrocubanismo and Artistic Revolution in Havana, 1920–1940*. Pittsburgh: University of Pittsburgh Press, 1997.

Moreno, Jairo. "Imperial Aurality: Jazz, the Archive, and U.S. Empire." In *Audible Empire: Music, Global Politics, Critique*, edited by Ronald Radano and Tejumola Olaniyan, 135–60. Durham, NC: Duke University Press, 2016.

Moreno, Jairo, and Gavin Steingo. "Rancière's Equal Music." *Contemporary Music Review* 31, nos. 5–6 (2012): 487–505.

Moten, Fred. *In the Break: The Aesthetics of the Black Radical Tradition*. Minneapolis: University of Minnesota Press, 2003.

Munro, Martin. *Different Drummers: Rhythm and Race in the Americas*. Berkeley: University of California Press, 2010.

Munro, Martin, and Celia Britton. "Eulogizing Creoleness? *Éloge de la créolité* and Caribbean Identity, Culture, and Politics." *Small Axe* 21, no. 1 52 (2017): 164–68.

Nedejkovic, Eddy. "Les Indépendentistes de Guadeloupe tentent d'enrailler le déclin de leur mouvement." *Le Monde*, 22 December 1994.

Négrit, Frédéric. *Musique et immigration dans la société antillaise*. Paris: L'Harmattan, 2004.

Bibliography / 221

Ochoa Gautier, Ana María. *Aurality: Listening and Knowledge in Nineteenth-Century Colombia*. Durham, NC: Duke University Press, 2014.

Olaniyan, Tejumola. "The Cosmopolitan Nativist: Fela and the Antinomies of Postcolonial Modernity." In *Arrest the Music! Fela and His Rebel Art and Politics*. Bloomington: Indiana University Press, 2004.

Omi, Michael, and Howard Winant. *Racial Formation in the United States: From the 1960s to the 1990s*. New York: Routledge, 1994.

Ong, Aihwa, Virginia R. Dominguez, Jonathan Friedman, Nina Glick Schiller, Verena Stolcke, David Y. H. Wu, and Hu Ying. "Cultural Citizenship as Subject-Making: Immigrants Negotiate Racial and Cultural Boundaries in the United States." *Current Anthropology* 37, no. 5 (1996): 737–62.

Ortner, Sherry. "Resistance and the Problem of Ethnographic Refusal." *Comparative Studies in Society and History* 37, no. 1 (1995): 173–93.

Palmié, Stephan. "Creolization and Its Discontents." *Annual Review of Anthropology* 35, no. 1 (2006): 433–56.

———. *The Cooking of History: How Not to Study Afro-Cuban Religion*. Chicago: University of Chicago Press, 2013.

———. "The C-Word Again: From Colonial to Postcolonial Semantics." In *Creolization: History, Ethnography, Theory*, edited by Charles Stewart, 66–83. Walnut Creek, CA: West Coast Press, 2007.

———. "Introduction: On Predications of Africanity." In *Africas in the Americas: Beyond the Search for Origins in the Study of Afro-Atlantic Religions*, edited by Stefan Palmié, 1–37. Leiden: Brill Academic Publishing, 2008.

———. "Is There a Model in the Muddle? 'Creolization' in African Americanist History and Anthropology." In *Creolization: History, Ethnography, Theory*, edited by Charles Stewart, 178–200. Walnut Creek, CA: West Coast Press, 2007.

Patterson, Tiffany Ruby, and Robin D. G. Kelley. "Unfinished Migrations: Reflections on the African Diaspora and the Making of the Modern World." *African Studies Review* 43, no. 1 (2000): 11–45.

Pecqueriaux, J. F. "Paco Rabanne, à la mode de chez nous." *France Antilles*, 2 June 1979.

Pollock, Sheldon. "Cosmopolitan and Vernacular in History." In *Cosmopolitanism*, edited by Carol A. Breckenridge, Sheldon Pollock, Homi K. Bhabha, and Dipesh Chakrabarty, Durham, NC: Duke University Press, 2002.

Price, Richard. "Créolisation, Creolization, and Créolité." *Small Axe* 21, no. 1 52 (2017): 211–19.

Price, Richard, and Sally Price. "Shadowboxing in the Mangrove." *Cultural Anthropology* 12, no. 1 (1997): 3–36.

Puri, Shalini. *The Caribbean Postcolonial: Social Equality, Post-Nationalism, and Cultural Hybridity*. New York: Palgrave Macmillan, 2004.

———. *The Grenada Revolution in the Caribbean Present: Operation Urgent Memory*. New York: Palgrave Macmillan, 2014.

Radano, Ronald. "Black Music Labor and the Animated Properties of Slave Sound." *boundary 2* 43, no. 1 (2016): 173–208.

———. *Lying Up a Nation: Race and Black Music*. Chicago: University of Chicago Press, 2003.

———. *New Musical Figurations: Anthony Braxton's Cultural Critique*. Chicago: University of Chicago Press, 1994.

Radano, Ronald, and Philip Bohlman, eds. *Music and the Racial Imagination*. Chicago: University of Chicago Press, 2001.

222 / Bibliography

Régent, Frédéric. *La France et ses esclaves: De la colonisation aux abolitions (1620-1848)*. Paris: Grasset & Fasquelle, 2007.

Rochefort, César de. *Histoire naturelle et morale des Iles Antilles de l'Amérique*. Rotterdam: Chez Arnout Leers, 1665.

Roda, Jessica. "Des judéo-espagnols à la machine Unesquienne: Enjeux et défis de la patrimonialisation musicale." *Cahiers d'ethnomusicologie* no. 24 (2011): 123–41.

Rommen, Timothy. "Nationalism and the Soul: Gospelypso as Independence." *Black Music Research Journal* 22, no. 1 (2002): 37–63.

Rowes, John Carlos, ed. *Post-Nationalist American Studies* Berkeley: University of California Press, 2000.

Sainton, Jean-Pierre. *Couleur et société en context post-esclavagiste*. Pointe-à-Pitre, Guadeloupe: Éditions Jasor, 2009.

Schnepel, Ellen M. *In Search of a National Identity: Creole and Politics in Guadeloupe*. Hamburg: Helmut Buske, 2004.

Schwarz-Bart, André. *La mulâtresse Solitude*. Paris: Éditions du Seuil, 1972.

Schwartz-Bart, Jacques. "Questions sur une vaudou session." *Jazz News* 29 (2014): 51–52.

Schwarz-Bart, Simone, and André Schwartz-Bart. *Un plat de porc aux bananes vertes*. Paris: Le Seuil, 1967.

Schwieger Hiepko, Andrea. "Europe and the Antilles: An Interview with Édouard Glissant." In *The Creolization of Theory*, edited by Françoise Lionnet and Shu-mei Shih, 255–61. Durham, NC: Duke University Press, 2011.

Scott, David. *Conscripts of Modernity: The Tragedy of Colonial Enlightenment*. Durham, NC: Duke University Press, 2004.

———. "That Event, This Memory: Notes on the Anthropology of African Diasporas in the New World." *Diaspora: A Journal of Transnational Studies* 1, no. 3 (1991): 261–84.

Sharpe, Christina. *In the Wake: On Blackness and Being*. Durham, NC: Duke University Press, 2016.

Sheller, Mimi. *Consuming the Caribbean: From Arawaks to Zombies*. London: Routledge, 2003.

———. "Creolization in Discourses of Global Culture." In *Uprootings/Regroundings: Questions of Home and Migration*, edited by Sarah Ahmed, Claudia Castañeda, Anne-Marie Fortier, and Mimi Sheller, 273–94. Oxford, UK: Berg, 2003.

Smith, Mark M. *How Race is Made: Slavery, Segregation, and the Senses*. Chapel Hill: University of North Carolina Press, 2006.

Stalin, Joseph. "The Nation." In *Nationalism*, edited by John Hutchinson and Anthony D Smith, 18–21. Oxford: Oxford University Press, 1994.

Stanyek, Jason. "Transmission of an Interculture: Pan-African Jazz and Intercultural Improvisation." In *The Other Side of Nowhere: Jazz, Improvisation, and Communities in Dialogue*, edited by Daniel Fischlin and Ajay Heble, 87–130. Middleton, CT: Wesleyan University Press, 2004.

Sterne, Jonathan. *The Audible Past: Cultural Origins of Sound Reproduction*. Durham, NC: Duke University Press, 2003.

Stoever, Jennifer Lynn. *The Sonic Color Line: Race and the Cultural Politics of Listening*. New York: New York University Press, 2016.

Stoler, Ann Laura. *Duress: Imperial Durabilities in Our Times*. Durham, NC: Duke University Press, 2017.

Stora, Benjamin, René Bénélus, Jacques Dumont, Serge Mam Lam Fouck, Louis-Georges Placide, and Michelle Zancarini Fournel. *Commission d'information et de recherche historique sur les événements de décembre 1959 en Martinique, de juin 1962 en Guadeloupe*

Bibliography / 223

et en Guyane, et de mai 1967 en Guadeloupe: Rapport à Madame la ministre des Outre-mer. Paris: Ministère des Outre-mer, 2016.

Stovall, Tyler. "Race and the Making of the Nation: Blacks in Modern France." In *Diasporic Africa: A Reader,* edited by Michael A. Gomez, 200–218. New York: New York University Press, 2006.

Taylor, Timothy D. *Global Pop: World Music, World Markets.* New York: Routledge, 1997.

Thomas, Deborah A. *Modern Blackness: Nationalism, Globalization, and the Politics of Culture in Jamaica.* Durham, NC: Duke University Press, 2004.

Thomas, Nicholas. "Cold Fusion." *American Anthropologist* 98, no. 1 (1996): 9–16.

Thomson, Patricia. "Field." In *Pierre Bourdieu: Key Concepts,* edited by Michael Grenfell, 65–80. Stocksfield, UK: Acumen, 2008.

Trouillot, Michel-Rolph. "Culture on the Edges: Caribbean Creolization in Historical Context." In *From the Margins: Historical Anthropology and Its Futures,* edited by Brian Keith Axel, 189–210. Durham, NC: Duke University Press, 2002.

Tsing, Anna Lowenhaupt. *Friction: An Ethnography of Global Connection.* Princeton, NJ: Princeton University Press, 2004.

Turino, Thomas. *Music as Social Life: The Politics of Participation.* Chicago: University of Chicago Press, 2008.

———. *Nationalists, Cosmopolitans, and Popular Music in Zimbabwe.* Chicago: University of Chicago Press, 2000.

UPLG. *Pour une collectivité nouvelle associée de Guadeloupe: Projet de l'UPLG.* Pointe-à-Pitre, Guadeloupe: n.p., 1992.

"L'UPLG S'explique." *Ja Ka Ta,* June 1980.

Ury, Alex, and Françoise Ury. *Musiques et musiciens de la Guadeloupe: Le chant de Karukera.* N.p.: n.p., 1991.

Vanony Frisch, Nicole. "L'origine des esclaves en Guadeloupe." In *Les musiques guadeloupéennes dans le champ culturel afro-américain, au sein des musiques du monde,* 47–54. Paris: Éditions Caribéennes, 1988.

Vergès, Françoise. *Le ventre des femmes: Capitalisme, racialisation, féminisme.* Paris: Albin Michel, 2017.

Wendt, Albert. *Nuanua: Pacific Writing in English since 1980.* Honolulu: University of Hawai'i Press, 1995.

Wilder, Gary. *Freedom Time: Négritude, Decolonization, and the Future of the World.* Durham, NC: Duke University Press, 2015.

———. *The French Imperial Nation-State: Negritude and Colonial Humanism between the Two World Wars.* Chicago: University of Chicago Press, 2005.

———. "Race, Reason, Impasse: Césaire, Fanon, and the Legacy of Emancipation." *Radical History Review* 90 (2004): 31–61.

William, Jean-Claude. "Aimé Césaire: Les contrariétés de la conscience nationale." In *1946–1996: Cinquante ans de départementalisation Outre-mer,* edited by Fred Constant and Justin Daniel, 315–34. Paris: L'Harmattan, 1997.

Wilson, Olly. "The Heterogeneous Sound Ideal in African-American Music." In *New Perspectives on Music: Essays in Honor of Eileen Southern,* edited by Josephine Wright and Samuel A. Floyd, 327–38. Warren, MI: Harmonie Park Press, 1992.

Zébus, Marie-Françoise, and François Causeret. "La canne à sucre résiste en Guadeloupe." *Agreste cahiers* 3 (2007): 1–11.

INDEX

Abenon, Lucien, 35
abjection. *See* race: racial abjection
abolition: of 1794, 38; of 1848, 3, 45
Abraham, Harold, 91
abyss (*gouffre*), 26, 29, 117, 126–28, 136, 137, 138, 139, 140, 204n48
accommodation, 5, 11, 29, 44, 94, 101, 105, 109, 113
"Adieu foulards, adieu madras," 53
Admiral T, 152
aesthetics, 2, 29, 34, 53, 60, 63, 75, 82, 87, 90, 91, 102, 117, 138, 145, 153, 156; black musical aesthetics, 79, 121, 128, 130, 131, 132, 135, 139. *See also* homing: transnational aesthetics
Agawu, Kofi, 78–79
agency, 10, 33, 39, 119, 132
Agenda 21 for Culture, 172, 210n80
Aigle, Kristen, 71, 84
Akadémiduka, 23, 152
Akiyo, 7, 18, 151
Algeria, 67, 69, 97–98; Front de libération nationale (FLN), 68
alienation, 4, 13, 45, 49–50, 79, 99, 130, 166
Alliance révolutionnaire caraïbe (ARC), 5, 114
Amselle, Jean-Loup, 123
"An domi déwò," 197n5
Anduse, Roland, 72, 75, 76
Anselin, Alain, 98
anticolonialism, 4, 7, 27, 48, 70, 74, 77, 103, 108, 113
Antile, Emilien, 104

Appadurai, Arjun, 130
Aristide, Julie, 153, 158
assemblage. *See* Ochoa Gautier: acoustic assemblage
assimilation, 11, 15, 27, 33, 44, 45, 46–50, 52, 53, 55, 56, 64–65, 67, 71–73, 75, 76, 77, 79, 81, 84, 86, 90, 100, 104, 122, 123, 130, 139, 150, 161, 166, 168
Association générale des étudiants guadeloupéens (AGEG), 31, 66–69, 80, 91, 99, 104, 110, 161, 163; *Rapport culturel*, 38, 45, 71–76. *See also* new culture
atonality. *See under* tonality
Attali, Jacques, 59
aurality: anticolonial aurality, 27, 63, 70, 75, 77, 78–83, 131; colonial aurality, 32, 33, 35, 39, 40, 44, 45, 87; contested and contesting aurality, 5, 9, 49, 82, 94, 139, 175; creolized aurality, 6, 7, 9, 11, 43, 44, 113, 116, 117, 146; definition, 8–9; diasporic auralities, 29, 117, 128; (post) colonial aurality, 29, 100; postnational aurality, 141, 146, 151, 162
autonomy, 4, 57, 114

Baie-Mahault, 1, 59
Baillif, 19
bamboula, 37, 38, 188n15
Baraka, Amiri, 120
Barclay, 111–12
Bébel-Gislert, Dany, 45, 73, 130
bèlè: Guadeloupe, 15, 165; Martinique, 44, 75, 85
Bèlè Nou, 85

226 / Index

Beriss, David, 100
Bernos, Marc, 116, 145–46
Bérose, Dominic, 145
Bhabha, Homi, 109, 146
bigidi, 22, 30, 176
biguine, 11, 18, 45, 46, 47, 52–54, 71, 74, 75,
    76, 77, 79, 91, 104, 105, 113, 116, 138,
    139, 154, 155, 160, 196n83, 199n41
black Atlantic, 29, 108, 134
Blou, Léna. *See* Lénablou
Boisdur, Esnard, 16
bomba, 75, 118
Bonilla, Yarimar, 3, 55, 147–48, 150,
    206n10
Bordeaux, 67, 69, 72
Bordin, Alza, 79
boula, 16, 17, 44, 60, 62, 77, 81, 86, 92,
    131, 157
boulagyèl, 15, 112
boularyen, 16, 20, 22
Bourdieu, Pierre, 123
Boym, Svetlana, 161, 166
Braflan-Trobo, Patricia, 23
break, 11. *See also* rupture
Briscante, La, 65
BUMIDOM (Bureau pour le développe-
    ment des migrations dans les départe-
    ments d'Outre-mer), 4, 56, 65–66,
    90–91, 97–98, 100, 106, 198n19
Burton, Richard D. E., 3, 185n28, 195n44

Cachemire-Thole, Jacqueline, 23
cadence-lypso, 75, 90, 91, 92
calenda, 37, 38, 44, 188n15; Labat's
    description, 41–42
calypso, 155
Camarade Jean. *See* Théodore, Louis
camp patriotique, 69, 77, 114
Canne à sucre, La (cabaret), 110
Canonge, Mario, 140
capitalism, 63, 74, 207n17
Caracas, Frédéric, 91
carême, 186n58
Caribbeanness. *See* Glissant, Édouard:
    Antilleanness (*antillanité*)
carnival: groups (*gwoup a pò*), 6–7, 107,
    152, 184n19; music (*mizik a mas*), 19;
    parade (*déboulé*), 6, 152
Carnot, 51, 101
Cassagnac, Granier de. *See under* European
    chroniclers

Castry, Jean-Fred, 83
Céleste, Chérubin (Father Céleste), 96
Célini, 102
Cérol, Marie-Josée (Ama Mazama), 35
Césaire, Aimé, 3, 5, 57, 66, 74, 98, 120,
    123, 125; on departmentalization,
    55–56
Chabin (singer), 104
chacha, 20, 92, 107
Chamoiseau, Patrick, 124, 150–51
chanté nwèl, 19
Chatterjee, Partha, 48–49
China, 68
Chivallon, Christine, 122
Chomereau-Lamotte, Charlie, 153, 156
citizenship, 5, 7, 55, 93, 99, 148, 168; cul-
    tural, 90, 91, 92, 93, 98; differentiated, 5.
    See also under Creole postnationalism
classical music, 52
Clifford, James, 9, 122
Coco, Dominik, 20, 161; "Mwen sé gwad-
    loupéyen," 1–2
Coco, Gilbert, 107–8
Code Noir, 35, 38
Cold War, 68, 69
Comaroff, Jean and John, 83
commission Stora, 193n27, 193n29
communist party. *See* Parti communiste
    (PC)
communist songs, 77
constrained poetics. *See* forced poetics
    (*poétiques forcées*)
continuance, 30, 93, 109, 113, 146, 162
conviviality, 10–11, 33, 37, 41, 173
Cosaque, Erick, 18, 90–92, 110, 157; "A koz
    don biyé san fwan", 90; X7 Nouvelle
    Dimension, 91–92
cosmopolitanism, 106; Creole cosmopoli-
    tanism, 29, 116, 161; diasporic cosmo-
    politanism, 29, 108, 116, 129–32, 135,
    139; as ethics, 129; and nationalism,
    92–93, 109, 116; vernacular cosmopoli-
    tanism, 108–9
Cotellon, Félix, 25, 30, 68, 77, 84, 162–65,
    167, 171–72, 209n60
counterpoetics. *See* forced poetics (*poétiques
    forcées*)
creoleness (*créolité*), 117, 119, 120, 159,
    169–70, 208n38; creoleness in Gua-
    deloupe, 11, 124–25, 145; *Éloge de la
    créolité*, 9, 115, 123–24, 145; rejection

of, 115–16, 139; vernacular creoleness, 124–25, 139–40
Creole postnationalism, 29, 148–51, 158–59, 162, 166–70, 173; aesthetics, 155–58; citizenship, 30, 146, 150, 168
creolization, 9–11, 14, 44, 51, 89, 93, 115, 117, 119, 126, 176; and cosmopolitanism, 109; definition, 10–11, 123, 149–50; discrepant creolization, 27, 29, 94, 101, 113; and early rapid synthesis, 10, 126; in French scholarship, 122–23; in Glissant's poetics of Relation, 126–27, 151; intellectual history, 9–10; in metropolitan spaces, 93–94, 101; moments, 94; in music scholarship, 121–22; nationalist rejection of, 11, 29, 74, 76, 80; of quadrille, 44; and race, 121; theoretical and vernacular usage, 9. *See also under* diaspora; Hesse, Barnor
Crichlow, Michaeline: fleeing and homing, 5, 11, 27, 28, 29, 41, 44, 83, 87, 89, 93–94, 101, 113, 117, 126, 139, 176; with Patricia Northover, 49, 125–26, 130, 149; post-Creole imagination, 10. *See also* diaspora: Crichlow on
Cuban revolution, 68, 69
cultural intimacy. *See* Herzfeld, Michael
Curtius, Anny, 99, 100
Cyrille, Dominique, 25, 35–36, 44, 113, 164

Dahomay, Christian, 15, 83, 102, 103, 107
Dahomay, Marie-Line, 23, 166
Damas, Léon Gontran, 53–54
dancehall, 18, 152, 153
dances, of slaves, 34; as catharsis, 39, 43; as entertainment, 38–39. See also *calenda*
dansè (dancers), 19
Debré, Michel, 97–98
Debs, Henri, 102, 110, 199n42
décalage, 29, 44
Décimus, Pierre-Edouard, 112
decolonization, 3, 4, 7, 45, 54, 69, 71, 87, 123, 150
de Gaulle, Charles, 69
département d'Outre-mer (DOM): interdependence, 151; Overseas Department dependency, 64, 192n87
departmentalization, 3, 53–56; disenchantment with, 64–66; as ruse, 55, 170. *See also* Césaire, Aimé; Overseas Department

Derrida, Jacques, 93, 127, 175
Deshayes, Fred, 5, 16, 18–19, 153–62, 165; critique of Gérard Lockel, 154; on difference, 159–60; "Lavi fofilé," 154
Deshayes, Maxence, 153, 158
desire (colonial), 27, 33, 37, 38, 54
détour (detour, diversion, or circumvention), 11, 14, 40, 44, 46, 56, 87, 93, 99, 114, 146, 149, 163, 168–69, 170, 172–74; in ethnography, 25; in Glissant's poetics of Relation, 13, 161–62, 173; Trouillot on, 13, 43
détournement, 11, 13–14, 33, 54, 84
diaspora, 29, 117, 119, 126, 130–31; as community of style, 135; creolization of, 29, 125–26, 136–38, 140; Crichlow on, 136; diasporic authenticity, 121; diasporic intimacy, 132, 134; diasporic networks, 53; diasporic nostalgia, 133; diasporic refusal, 29, 129–33; diasporic resonance, 139; in French scholarship, 122–23; Jewish diaspora, 137; in music studies, 121; practice of diaspora, 117
diasporicity, 117, 119
diglossia. *See* language use
disco, 112
disenchantment, 29, 139, 146, 147, 150. *See also under* departmentalization
dissonance, 162
diversalité (diversality), 124
diversion. See *détour*
diversity, 127, 163, 172. *See also* France: cultural diversity
Dixon Gottschild, Brenda, 121
Dolor (singer), 104, 199n41
Dorville, Serge, 145
double consciousness, 50, 168
doudou, 53, 77
doudouisme, 65, 82
DuBois, W.E.B., 50
duress. *See under* Stoler, Ann Laura
Du Tertre, Jean-Baptiste. *See under* European chroniclers

education, 47–48
1802 (revolution and repression), 24
Ellis, Nadia: horizons of possibility, 101; territories of the soul, 137–38
Eluther, Ena, 120
empire: imperial formations, 3; imperial nation-state, 150; Negri and Hardt, 149,

empire (*cont.*)
150, 173. *See also* entanglements: imperial; France: as imperial nation-state
empty signifier, 25, 163, 172
engagés, 34
entanglements: audible, 7, 11, 27, 30, 33, 51, 146; of colonialism and republicanism, 45; of culture and politics in ICH, 170–72; diasporic, 88, 138; of hospitality and hostility, 93; imperial, 4, 6, 27, 33, 43, 64, 65, 85; (post)colonial, 14, 85, 113, 118, 148–49, 167–68
epistemological privilege, 51
epistemology: drumming as epistemology, 43, 54; (post)colonial epistemology, 8, 14, 78, 176, 195n56, 204n46. See also *gwoka modènn*: as epistemological project
Epstein, Dena, 38
Erlmann, Veit, 135
European chroniclers, 36–42; Cassagnac, 37, 38; Du Tertre, 36, 37; Labat, 37, 38, 40, 41–42; Léonard, 42; Longin, 38; Rochefort, 36, 37, 39
exemptions and exceptions, colonial politics of, 4
Exxos, 153

Fallope, Josette, 46
Fanm Ki Ka, 20, 22
Fanon, Frantz, v, 12, 26, 45, 50, 68, 123, 129, 143, 146
Farrugia, Laurent, 124
Fédération mondiale de la jeunesse démocratique, 67
Feijoada (restaurant), 110
Feld, Steven, 132, 135
Félix-Prudent, Lambert, 120
Festival Gwoka (FGK), 18, 31, 84, 117, 143, 152, 158, 163–64, 165, 167, 176
fest-noz, 171
field, 7, 8–9
fieldwork (*enquêtes de terrain*), 72
fleeing and homing. See Crichlow, Michaeline
Floyd, Samuel, 121
forced poetics (*poétiques forcées*), 28, 51, 64, 65, 78, 85–88, 89
Foubap, 20
Fournier, Laurent-Sébastien, 170–71
France, 2, 3, 27, 28, 34, 97–98, 100, 114, 115, 122, 129; cultural diversity, 30,

124, 146, 171; Fifth Republic, 97; as imperial nation-state, 7, 8, 46, 54–56, 123, 139, 170, 175; Third Republic, 45–53.
See also jazz: Antillean jazz in France
France-Antilles, 69
Francophilia, 49, 89
Front Antillo-Guyanais pour l'autonomie (FAGA), 68
Front de libération nationale (FLN). *See under* Algeria
fugitivity, 176

Gabaly, Joslen, 31, 133
Galta, 85
Gama, Raymond, 150
garawoun (Belize), 118
Garret, Kenny, 116
Gilroy, Paul, 10, 84, 120, 122, 126, 134, 195n56
Glissant, Édouard, 26, 50–51, 57, 68, 78, 84, 115, 119, 120, 123, 161, 166; Antilleanness (*antillanité*), 50, 99; camouflage, 46; *chaos-monde*, 127; *Le discours antillais* (*Caribbean Discourse*), 123–24; dominant versus determining culture, 13, 87, 190n57; *langue et langage*, 51, 87, 191n66; *lieu commun*, 195n56; on music, 127; poetics of Relation, 26, 33, 106, 117, 123–24, 126, 138, 151, 204n46. *See also* abyss (*gouffre*); creolization; *détour* (detour, diversion, or circumvention); forced poetics (*poétiques forcées*); mimetic drive (*pulsion mimétique*); opacity; *retour* (reversion); trace
gouffre. See abyss (*gouffre*)
Grosse Montagne. *See* 1975 (general strike)
Groupe de la libération armée (GLA), 95, 107, 114, 197n16
Groupe d'organisation nationale de la Guadeloupe (GONG), 68–71, 76, 153, 193n29; GONG resigners (*démissionnaires du GONG*), 70–71, 95
Guadeloupe: history, 3, 34–36, 47, 64–71, 94–101, 113–14, 147–48; political status, 3–5
Gueyle, Abdoulaye, 122
Gwakasoné. *See* Oumaou, Robert
gwoka: ballet, 32, 187n2; basic rhythms, 16, 24, 25, 80–81, 84, 181–82; codes, 22; as commodity, 112; contemporary forms, 6;

definition, 2, 14–16, 160; drum, 17; gender, 22–23; in Guadeloupe's musical landscape, 17–18, 152–53; history of, 5, 47, 51, 75–76, 83, 101–2, 109–10, 118; instrumentation, 16; as lifestyle, 15; as national symbol, 18, 71, 75, 80, 85, 86, 166; as overdetermined, 6, 162; in Paris, 94, 99–100, 106, 110, 153; performance structure, 21; as performative anticolonial practice, 84; and politics, 5, 82, 90, 141; as *potomitan* (central pillar) of Guadeloupean music, 153; and recording industry, 110; scales, 25; as soul of the people, 92, 166; and spirituality, 2; traditional, 6, 77–78

gwoka modènn, 16, 60–64, 76–83, 85–88, 102, 128, 129, 139, 154, 163, 195n50; as discipline, 82–83; as epistemological project, 62–63, 81, 85–88; gwoka scale, 61–62, 76, 79–80, 131; and jazz, 60, 80, 82, 115, 130–32; musical notation, 81–82; *Traité de gro ka modèn*, 61, 81–82. *See also* Lockel, Gérard; tonality: atonal-modality

Hall, Stuart, 121, 122, 126, 150, 204n44
Halley, Michel, 107
Hannerz, Ulf, 9
harmony. *See* tonality
Hartman, Saidiya, 39
Hayat, Yves, 111, 112
hegemony, 163, 170, 171
Herskovits, Melville, 119, 201n14
Herzfeld, Michael, 33; cultural intimacy, 70. *See also* poetics: social poetics
Hesse, Barnor, 33; creolization of the political, 33, 47, 54–55, 173
Hill, Edwin C., 36, 53; hearing double, 37, 117; *ratés*, 37, 43, 175
hold, 5, 7, 175, 184n15
homing: 14, 29, 30, 41, 44, 49, 56, 83–84, 87, 98, 100, 108–9, 110, 112, 125, 146; transnational aesthetics, 94, 131–32, 139. *See also under* Crichlow, Michaeline
Horizon (musical group), 60, 85
hospitality, 92–93, 113
Hutchinson, John, cultural nationalism as moral regeneration, 72, 74

identity, 196n82; Guadeloupean, 144–45, 158–60

imaginary, 6, 28, 29, 93, 94, 101, 144
imperialism, 6, 31, 72, 73, 74, 75, 79, 132, 136; American, 136
indentured workers, 3, 33, 75
independence, 3, 56, 57, 63, 68, 69, 72, 114, 147, 150, 151, 173
Indestwas Ka, 20, 31
intangible cultural heritage of humanity (ICH), 23, 30, 56, 86, 143, 148, 162, 163; Convention for the Safeguarding of ICH (ICHC), 163, 164, 167, 169; critique against, 165–66; and interregional cooperation, 169; and regional nationalism, 170–71; and separatist demands, 171–72. *See also* Lyannaj pou gwoka
invagination, 175

Jabot, Alex, 116
Jabrun, 101–2, 107
Jacobinism. *See* republicanism
Ja Ka Ta, 31, 73
Jalème, Jacky, 23, 165, 167–68
Jalet, Marc, 116
jazz, 18, 76, 169; Antillean jazz in France, 140–41; as Creole music, 122, 127; within Guadeloupe's musical landscape, 116. *See also under gwoka modènn*; Lockel, Gérard
jazz ka, 16, 115, 136, 139, 152
Jean, Alain, 14–15, 116, 140
jing ping, 18
Juraver, Georges, 145
Juraver, Yvan, 131
Juste, Didier, 153

Kafé, 85, 110
Kamodjaka, 23, 152
Kannida, 16, 152; "Kréyol," 133
Karibana, 91
Kassav', 92, 112, 156
kaz a blan, 198n33
Khaznadar, Chérif, 164
Kiavué, Klod, 29, 115, 133–36, 139, 166, 175
Kimbol, 116
klé, 17
Kolektif pou gwoka, 166, 209n64
Konket, Guy, 29, 94, 101–9, 113, 157; "Baimbridge chaud," 102, 106; "Bamileké," 108; "Ban klé a Titine," 102; "Faya faya," 104; first creolization moment, 104–5; "Jo

230 / Index

Konket, Guy (*cont.*)
    mayé dé grenndé-la," 102, 198n35; "Ky-
    embé rèd," 106; "La Gwadloup malad,"
    102, 106, 107; "Lapli ka tonbé," 102, 103;
    "La tè touné," 108; and musical universal-
    ism, 104–6; second creolization moment,
    106–9; "YouYou," 108, 205n68; "Zèzèl w
    kalé?," 106. *See also under* Murray, David,
    and the Gwo Ka Masters
konpa, 18, 75, 76, 90, 91, 92, 152, 155, 160
Koséika, 22
koud tanbou, 18, 51, 52, 65, 100, 191n68
Kriyolio, 116

Labat, Jean-Baptiste. *See under* European
    chroniclers
labor, 40
labor activism, 45, 48–49; labor strikes and
    repression, 66, 96. *See also* May 1967
    (Mé 67); 1975 (general strike)
La Briscante, 65
La Canne à sucre (cabaret), 110
lack. See *manque* (lack)
Laclau, Ernesto, 172
Ladrezeau, François, 136, 152
Lafontaine, Marie-Céline, 52; Creole con-
    tinuum of Guadeloupean music, 108
"La Gwadloup sé tan nou, la Gwadloup sé
    pa ta yo," 7
Lamentin, 70
language use, 12, 36, 49–50, 51, 52; Creole,
    11, 12, 13, 15, 28, 48, 63, 65, 70–71, 75,
    79, 85, 135, 137, 152; diglossia, 50, 65;
    French, 49, 158
Largey, Michael, 131
Larochelle, Joël, 153, 158
Laumuno, Marie-Héléna, 23, 164, 166–68
Laviso, Christian, 60–62, 116
lawonn, 20
Légitimus, Hégésippe, 70
Lénablou, 5, 7, 20, 23, 30, 31, 117, 120,
    146, 176
Léonard. *See under* European chroniclers
léwòz (*swaré léwòz*), 15, 19–23, 51, 52, 65,
    70, 71, 77, 85, 99, 102, 110, 137, 151,
    165, 186n59
léwòz o komandman, 44
Lionnet, Françoise, 93, 109
Lirvat, Al, 52
listening: colonial, 36–39, 40, 78; con-
    tested, 3, 11; diasporic, 132; imperial,

12; and power, 8–9; regimes, 26, 37,
    188n17
Liyannaj kont pwofitasyon (LKP), 5, 7, 32,
    106, 147–48, 157
Lockel, Gérard, 26, 27, 53, 89, 102, 103,
    104, 112, 134, 153, 157, 161, 175;
    biography, 61, 76; concert-debates, 84;
    foyer de resistance culturelle, 59; "Fò zot
    save," 86, 105, 196n83; and jazz, 76,
    115; "Lévé pèp," 105; "Lindépendans,"
    86, 155, 166; listening to, 59; theory of
    three cultures, 31, 46, 77, 104, 139.
    See also tonality: atonal-modality
lokans, 24–25
Lomax, Alan, 81
Longin. *See under* European chroniclers
Losio, Daniel, 110–11
Loyson, Robert, 104, 155, 157, 197n13,
    199n44
Lucas, Jean-Michel, 172
Lurel, Victorin, 124
Lyannaj pou gwoka, 30, 143, 146, 147,
    148, 164–65, 166–70, 173

Magic Malik, 140–41
Magnat, Marcel, 110–11, 112
makè, 16, 20, 86, 92
Man Adeline, 65, 193n10
Mangin, Timothy, 134
manque (lack), 28, 87, 90, 187n64
Man Soso (Solange Athénaïse Bac), 101
Maoism, 70, 72, 73
Marley, Bob, 111
maroon (*nèg mawon*), 31, 32, 41, 74–75,
    83, 144, 175
marronnage, 31, 41, 43, 67, 84; *grand*, 40,
    175; *petit*, 13, 38, 109
Martin, Denis Constant, 121
Marxism, 67, 68, 72–73
maskò, 25–26, 170
Maultsby, Portia, 121
May 1967 (Mé 67), 24, 31, 69, 153
Memel, Alfred, 116
métissage, 53, 89, 115, 123, 126–27, 159,
    161, 200n3; *métisse*, 53
migration, 24, 52, 65, 68, 90, 94, 99, 101,
    122, 157. *See also* BUMIDOM (Bureau
    pour le développement des migrations
    dans les départements d'Outre-mer)
mimetic drive (*pulsion mimétique*), 44, 50,
    56, 124, 161

minor transnationalism, 28, 93–94, 108, 170

Mitterrand, François: and liberalization of radio, 155; *politique des régions*, 113–14, 171

mizik rasyn (Haiti), 137

modernity, 49, 55, 83–84; as a condition of conscription, 83, 87, 101; cosmopolitan modernism, 84; European modernity as "super norm," 84; modernist reformism, 6, 63, 74, 83; taming of modernity, 84, 89, 102, 150

Monza, Wozan, 20, 143–47, 165, 168–70; "Nasyon," 144–45

Moreno, Jairo, 8, 185n26

Mounien, Rosan, 76, 89–90, 92, 103

Mouvement populaire pour une Guadeloupe indépendante (MPGI), 95

Mouvement pour l'unification des Forces de libération nationale guadeloupéennes (MUFLNG), 95

Mouvement rural de jeunesse chrétienne (MRJC), 96

Munro, Martin, 39, 43, 54

Murray, David, and the Gwo Ka Masters, 29, 109, 116, 133–36, 139; blues aesthetics, 133–34; *Creole*, 133; *The Devil Tried to Kill Me*, 133, 135; and Guy Konket, 106, 133, 135; *Gwotet*, 115, 133, 135; language and languageness, 134; "On jou matin," recording with Gérard Lockel, 29, 135; *Yonn-dé*, 133, 135

mutual-aid societies, 42

Nankin, Joël, 107

nationalism, 48, 117, 126, 161, 194n35; anticolonial, 7, 48–49, 63, 70; Antillean, 46, 48, 51; Creole nationalism, 9, 125; cultural nationalism, 7, 54, 72–76, 87, 125, 168 (*see also* Hutchinson, John, cultural nationalism as moral regeneration); Guadeloupean nationalism, 49, 53, 87, 99, 125, 129, 152, 162, 163. *See also under* cosmopolitanism

nèg mawon (maroon slave). *See* maroon (*nèg mawon*)

Négoce, 135–36

négriste, 47, 49

Négrit, Frédéric, 15

négritude, 48, 53, 74, 77, 84, 125, 130, 160; and French language, 54; and rhythm, 54

neocolonialism, 10, 28, 57, 64, 66, 94, 97, 101, 148, 149, 157

neoliberalism, 4, 11, 85, 147, 149, 209n70

network, 6; versus field, 8

new culture, 28, 63, 71–76, 83

Nicolas, Franck, 83, 115, 136, 139, 140, 145

1975 (general strike), 96

Non-Aligned Movement, 67, 68

nostalgia, 156; reflective, 161; restorative, 28, 161, 164

Ochoa Gautier, Ana María, 8–9, 82; acoustic assemblages, 8, 16, 44

octroi de mer, 4–5

Olaniyan, Tejumola, 84

Ong, Aihwa, 90

opacity, v, 11, 29, 41, 62–63, 71, 82, 126, 128, 134, 161, 167; and ethnographic research, 23–26, 78; in Glissant's poetics of Relation, 12, 117, 127, 160; and sound, 12–13, 36–37, 78, 80, 132, 135. See also *maskò*

Oumaou, Robert, 107; Gwakasoné, 85, 109

Overseas Department, 4, 5, 33, 64, 162, 171; as anomalies, 3; definition, 3; as protected markets, 64. *See also* departmentalization

Palmié, Stephan, 9–10, 121, 125

Paris, 28, 69, 90–92, 133. *See also under* gwoka

Parti communiste (PC), 67; français (PCF), 55, 57, 67; guadeloupéen (PCG), 67, 74; martiniquais (PCM), 67

Parti des travailleurs guadeloupéens (PTG), 95

Parti populaire martiniquais (PPM), 57, 67

patrimonialization, 162–63, 170, 208n52

Phipps, Jean-Pierre, 60–61

plantation, 31, 33, 34–45

poetics, 32; of belonging, 6; social poetics, 33

political economy, music and: for gwoka, 109–11; on the plantation, 40

politics (black radical), 128–29

Pollock, Sheldon, 109

(post)colonialism, 7; colonial versus postcolonial, 4; (post)coloniality, 6, 11, 30, 117, 176, 209n70; (post)colonial ontology, 8, 14, 29, 175–76; (post)

232 / Index

(post)colonialism (*cont.*)
 colonial republic, 93; (post)colonial
 subject, 7, 28; (post)colonial worlding,
 14; spelling, 5
postnationalism, 138, 147–49, 163,
 209n70; France as postnational state,
 56. *See also* Creole postnationalism
Poullet, Hector, 124
Poumaroux, Gérard, 116, 145
power, 8, 10, 11, 33, 37, 39–40, 49, 84, 90,
 93, 101, 125–26, 134, 188n17; positive
 power, 44, 46, 83, 163
Price, Richard, 10, 125
Privat, Gregory, 116
problem-space, 7, 45, 57, 63, 64, 73, 87,
 163, 184n21
Puri, Shalini, 4, 6, 148, 209n70

quadrille, 11, 18, 33, 40, 44, 45, 51, 71, 74,
 75, 101, 104, 105, 109, 113, 139, 151,
 165

Rabanne, Paco, 110–13
race: and class, 74–75, 129–30; in France,
 122–23, 140, 203n30; and Guadeloupean identity, 130; racial abjection,
 33, 37, 39; racial authenticity, 125;
 racial formation, 132; racial imagination, 122; racialization, 98–101; racial
 project, 120; racism, 100, 113, 132,
 134. *See also* socio-racial categories of
 Guadeloupe
Radano, Ronald, 40, 79, 139
radio broadcasting: colonial radio, 47; FM
 radio, 154–55
Radio Caraïbes International (RCI), 18
Radyo Inité, 155
Radyo Tanbou, 14, 155
reconnaissance, 56, 168–69
Reed, Ishmael, 136
Régent, Frédéric, 35
Reinette, Luc, 155
répondè, 20
representation (political and aesthetic),
 6–7
Règpri (CMDT, Centre des musiques et
 danses traditionnelles et populaires de
 la Guadeloupe), 25, 143, 147, 162, 164,
 165, 171; ethnomusicology symposi-
 ums, 143, 146, 164, 169

rèpriz (structuring element in gwoka), 21–
 22, 24, 25
republican colonialism, 27, 33, 45
republicanism: ideology, 3, 73, 100, 122,
 123, 162, 163; Jacobinism, 5, 46; republican habitus, 47; republican universalism, 5, 100, 124, 125, 172
Réseau France Outre-mer (RFO), 14,
 186n52
resilience, 30
resistance, 5, 9, 10, 31, 32, 33, 44, 94, 101,
 105, 119, 128, 130, 175; against colonialism and imperialism, 6, 7, 31, 75, 78,
 84, 132; against slavery, 6, 43
retention (African), 34, 42, 119, 121, 132–
 33, 201n7, 202n22. *See also* trace
retour (reversion), 28, 54, 63, 74, 76, 84,
 118, 123, 133, 161
rhizome, 123, 138
rhythms (seven rhythms of gwoka): affect,
 32, 81; *granjanbèl*, 81; *kaladja*, 2, 133;
 léwòz, 77, 107; *léwòz indestwas*, 22;
 menndé, 145, 156; *padjanbèl*, 81; *toumblak*, 77, 107; *woulé*, 32. *See also* gwoka:
 basic rhythms
Rico Toto, 153
Rochefort, César de. *See under* European
 chroniclers
Rospart, Bébé, Sòlbòkò, 19
rue piétonne, 18, 151, 152
Rupaire, Sonny, 1
rupture, 3, 11, 13, 83, 128, 151, 173,
 194n35, 196n75

SACEM (Société des auteurs, compositeurs
 et éditeurs de musique), 111
Sadikalay, Philippe, 153, 158
Sainte-Anne, 163
Sainte Rose, 70–71
Sainton, Jean-Pierre, 20
Sakitaw, 152
Sanders, Pharoah, 135
santiman, 16, 76, 79, 92, 134
Schwarz-Bart, Jacques, 29, 136–38, 140;
 Abyss, 137; and affective identity, 137;
 Hazzan, 137; *Jazz Racine Haiti*, 138; *Soné
 ka la*, 139
Schwarz-Bart, Simone and André, 132,
 137; *Un plat de porc aux bananes vertes*,
 132–33

Index / 233

Scott, David, 46, 83, 119–20
Senghor, Léopold, 54
Serin, Jacky, 99–100
7Son@to, 20
Shih, Shu-mei, 93
Simènn Kontra, 85
Sista Kee, 136
slavery, 6, 24, 29, 31–32, 37–40, 74, 75, 78, 113, 117, 119, 133; ethnic origins of enslaved Africans, 34, 35, 41; Middle Passage, 43; nations, 42; slave trade, 34–36. *See also* abolition
soboun (Bénin), 118
soca, 18, 155
socialism, 48
socio-racial categories of Guadeloupe, during early colonial period, 35–36, 44; black, 158; black bourgeoisie, 46, 48, 49; *blan péyi*, 158; *métro*, 66, 69; *mulâtre*, 11, 46, 47, 48, 49, 51, 190n51; *nèg*, 74, 75, 83, 129, 144; *petits blancs*, 33, 187n3; white plantocracy (*béké*), 4, 46, 49
Soft, 16, 29, 153–62, 170; "Change My World," 155; "Frenchi," 155; "Gouté Gwadloup," 19, 154; "Jean Fouyé," 155; *Konfyans*, 157; "Krim kont la Gwadloup," 156; "Léritaj," 161; "Révolution," 157
solidarity networks, 41, 42
Solitude (the mulâtresse), 6, 31, 184n18
Solvet, Patrick, 164
son (Cuban musical style), 75
sovereignty, 3, 5, 7, 30, 93, 148, 151; partial, 49, 173–74
Soviet Union, 68
Stalin, 72, 194n35
Star Jee, 153
Stoler, Ann Laura, 3, 4; colonial presence and colonial present, 4; duress, 4, 33
Stora, Benjamin. *See* commission Stora
subaltern subjects, 175
subjection, 33. *See also* subjugation
subjectivity: black, 41, 120; (post)colonial subjectivity, 73, 77, 84, 87, 90, 94, 117, 119, 126, 127, 148, 159, 160; and reversion drive, 28, 50, 84, 133; self-, 50, 63, 127
subjugation, 39–40, 151
sugar industry, 95
swaré léwòz. See léwòz (swaré léwòz)

Taj Mahal (singer), 136
takout, 25
Takouta, 25, 107
Tamas, Jean, 145
tam tam, 191n76
tanbouyè, 19
Taylor, Timothy, 135
Théodore, Louis, 67, 70, 76
theory (role of), 27
Tirolien, Guy, 53
tonality, 77; atonality, 76; atonal-modality, 24, 61–62, 79, 131; as colonial weapon, 78–79; harmony, 2, 134
Torin, Raymonde, 23. *See also* Kamodjaka
trace, 24, 34, 43, 49, 117, 118, 126, 204n44; Derrida on, 127; in poetics of Relation, 26, 29, 127, 136; sonic, 11, 131, 132, 133, 134, 137, 139
transnationalism, 6. *See also* minor transnationalism
Trente Glorieuses, 56, 66, 94–101
Troupé, Georges, 83
Troupé, Sonny, 107, 116, 153
Tsing, Anna, 162
Tumblack (musical group), 29, 94, 109–13; "Caraïba," 111, 112; "Chunga Funk," 111, 112
Turino, Thomas, 6, 47, 63, 83. *See also* modernity: modernist reformism

UNESCO. *See* intangible cultural heritage of humanity (ICH)
Union des paysans pauvres de la Guadeloupe (UPG), 71, 95, 96
Union des travailleurs agricoles (UTA), 71, 73, 76, 95, 96
Union des travailleurs issus de l'emigration guadeloupéenne (UTEG), 91
Union générale des travailleurs guadeloupéens (UGTG), 24, 71, 73, 76, 95, 96, 147
Union internationale des étudiants (UIE), 67
Union populaire pour la libération de la Guadeloupe (UPLG), 73, 76, 95, 107, 114, 147, 162, 163
unions, 6, 48

Valentino, Paul, 55
Vamur, Olivier, 82, 85

Vanony-Frisch, Nicole, 35
Vélo (musician), 103
Vergès, Françoise, 171
vernacular universalism, 106
Voukoum, 7

Wacquant, Loïc, 123
wakes, 14–15, 37, 75, 92, 102

Weekes, Travis, 169
Wilder, Gary, 3, 46, 123
William, Jean-Claude, 56
work songs (*chan travay*), 15, 37, 40, 61

zoban, 17
zouk, 17, 85, 90, 100, 112, 113, 156, 160